THE 1950s

THE 1950s

Edith Horsley

DOMUS BOOKS
A Bison Book

1950 1951 1952 1953 1954

PAGE 6   **PAGE 30**   **PAGE 62**   **PAGE 76**   **PAGE 98**

Edith M. Horsley
USA/Quality Books
Copyright © 1978 Bison Books Limited
All rights reserved

ISBN 0-89196-015-5

Printed in Hong Kong
Produced by Bison Books Limited
4 Cromwell Place, London, England
Published by Quality Books Inc.

973
H

1955
PAGE 122

1956
PAGE 148

1957
PAGE 178

1958
PAGE 202

1959
PAGE 234

Prologue

The Earth is now a familiar sight, spinning in space, thanks to sophisticated advances in modern photography – its geography appears at a glance. To understand its history demands something of the same treatment. The camera of the historian needs a 'fish-eye' lens that brings an overall view into a single focus, raising historic events to renewed life by its very distortion. Traditional narrative, fitting events into the development of a political or social theory is too static. The monks of the Middle Ages, recording a gobbet of fact for each year as they scratched away at the annals of the Anglo-Saxon Chronicle in the cloistered peace of the scriptorium, were maybe wiser than they knew. The sequence formed its own pattern, touched chords of interlocking memories: the death of a king, the rape by Norsemen of a neighboring religious house, the appointment of a new abbot – the drama, the terror, the intrigue were all implicit in half a dozen words for those who had lived through the events.

Today the matter is not so simple. But, to select events from the plethora of a decade of this century, and to treat them in their sequence in time, while at the same moment glancing back to the more distant past in which their beginnings are hidden, as well as forward to the future events they foreshadow, may convey with greater urgency the living impress of time past on our time present.

The horn of plenty poured its fruits on the Western world in the 1950s. Like a volcano World War II had brought death and destruction; but it left behind such enrichment of the soil that a new civilization rose out of it in tropic opulence. In gathering its strength for the war effort America had become the focus of world productive energy, a powerhouse of scientific and technical innovation, drawing in specialists from Britain and all the rest of the world, including the defeated enemy. In the early postwar years, this power had been directed to the essential task of restoration, the supply of neglected necessities, but in the 1950s the emphasis was on production for the very zest of production, for pleasure, for luxury.

A hundred, a thousand times more American citizens were engulfed by it than had ever been touched by previous booms. Before the war Hollywood movies had created for the masses unattainable dream palaces. Its heroes and heroines moved in vast halls with crystal chandeliers, where uniformed servants hovered. In the dining room they sat at tables of tremendous length until, in the classic moment, they moved their places together at one small corner as romance bloomed. The bedroom had silk sheets and cavernous wardrobes filled with Paris creations the heroine would need to be sewn into.

The new dream was different, and, best of all, attainable, a detached house in the suburbs, or even further afield, with a double garage, in the new white-walled American style which threw overboard the old traditions of grandeur inherited from Europe; no gardeners and house servants, but gadgets to wash and cook and clean and cut the lawns. Automobiles brought the social life of the country club within easy reach, just as it enabled the man of the house to commute to his work, which got cleaner and cleaner. Blue-collar workers were turning white in their myriads as automation emptied the factory floor and filled up the offices, and the old-time clerk became a new-style young executive. The same automobile, or maybe an aircraft, acted like a magic wand to bring vacations in parts of America that had once been like a foreign land. Often the travelers liked what they saw so much, they upped sticks and settled in the new sunshine areas in California and Florida, and the places between. If their work would not let them, then they got there in the end when they retired. By the end of the decade new towns, specially designed to cater for and cushion the later years, sprang up fully equipped. Working or retired, they also saved for the great trips, out into the new sunspots of the Pacific, or eastward to England and Europe, or – greatly daring to out-Jones the Joneses – into the once-secret places of storybook travelers, which were now conveniently available to them through packaged tours.

For everyday entertainment, they still turned up, from old habit, at the movies once or twice a week, maybe as part of a shopping trip which was now automatically made by car to the nearest supermarket, where the brands, and the range of incoming goods from the rest of the world, and the packaging, made them seem like Aladdin's cave in contrast to the old-type store. In the corner of every sitting room, however, was a small but ever-expanding eye fixed on an opening world. Television sprang like Athene from the head of Jove, fully formed, in that its techniques were easily adapted for films and its means of support – advertising revenue in America and licence fees in Britain – was at hand. The pundits who looked forward to an education boom, however, were disappointed. It was not the opera and the ballet which got them out of the tip-up cinema seats and glued to the living-room chairs, but the boxing and the wrestling, the baseball and the football. America even had such weird eccentricities as the Roller Derby. Muscular young women on roller skates circled a track – once shuffled over by marathon dancers in an earlier sadistic pre-war craze – and ended in mauling mêlées of waving legs in their fight for position in the race.

The new patterns of life were not set all at once. As in fashion – that infallible indicator of the pulse of the time – there was an initial hint of uncertainty. The waist had once been a marker of sacred significance in the rulings of Paris, and in the opening of the 1950s the 'wandering waistline' spread alarm among the fashion writers. What was beyond doubt was that fullness was the thing. Materials were running off the looms at unprecedented rates as new machines took over, and the mass market could now afford the yards of stuff that went into widening skirts and petticoats in layers – at least in America – and it was now America that was beginning to set the fashion. The rule of the Parisian couture houses, revived so successfully immediately after the war with Dior's 'New Look,' was undermined by the newer 'American Look.' It was young, and it did not filter down to the public from the favored millionaire few, those socialites who would have long moved on to wearing something quite different by the time the ordinary woman could afford to buy it. It was instantaneous. The American garment trade might skip its seam finishes, but it was equipped for lightning change, and aware of an enormous new youthful market. Static between 1930 and 1940 at some thirty million, the number of children in school increased by a million in the 1940s, and in the first half of the 1950s surged up by eight million.

The young had everything in their favor. Dr Spock, who had begun writing in the mid-1940s, had canalized an already growing trend. The phenomenon of the 'teenager' had truly arrived in the 1950s as the embodiment of the new system of free upbringing. Juniors of both sexes were like the precocious Renaissance offspring of Italian ducal houses in being exposed early to an increasingly varied world. Toys and books for children formed a highly exploitable market; and increased pocket money from increased parental incomes began to make the early teenage market an attractive proposition, but the bonanza came with the later teen years.

When the young worked, they were ready to tackle a modern push-button job at once. Apprenticeships had long been old hat, but in the new postwar world 'a worker was a worker was a worker.' The new vast organizations which proliferated across the country and set up bases abroad as independent empires within the state looked at their employees without regard to age or responsibilities. The older workers spent on the new-style homes and furniture and the other solid goods, the teenagers – often living at home with few expenses – went to town on the more ephemeral side of life.

The girls went for the clothes and the cosmetics. The mustard manufacturers used to say that it was what the customers left on their plates that made their fortunes. It was the part-used lipsticks, the tubes of this, the pots of that, which cluttered millions of dressing-table drawers that left the tills tinkling for the purveyors of the face and soon – the body – beautiful.

It was incredible that a generation earlier, make-up had been limited to lip salve and a little powder, sometimes sold in discreet little books about two inches by three of *papier poudré* – the sheets being torn out and smoothed over an offending shiny nose at discreet moments. Then in the run-up to World War II, Hollywood had taken over with 'pancake' make-up applications designed for the film camera and which was later adopted by fans of the great stars. The changes were rung rather on how it was arranged than what it was: the fashionable jump from the Clara Bow little pursed mouth to the full-spread warmth of Joan Crawford's smile. Now new dyes and processes brought new subtleties of color, new consistencies of texture not merely in cosmetics themselves, but in the preparations used before they were applied or after removing them. The magic promise of beauty was offered in language anxiously tailored for maximum appeal by skilled copywriters. When Elizabeth Arden, in 1958, presented a new foundation called 'Veiled Radiance' it was described as, 'More liquid than a cream, more creamy than a liquid, it veils all faults yet reveals the inner radiance.' Beginning with a stylization, which was later seized on as a barrier against uncertainties, the 1950s moved on to a new natural look which required a blended use of the best ingredients and the expenditure of a great deal of time.

Equality of the sexes, encouraged by the wide use of women in the services and industry during the war, had unexpected side effects. Cosmetics for males were still out of the question, but deodorants and after-shave with a tang of spiced aroma were becoming acceptable even in England. Fashion, too, after decade upon decade of standardized drabness, began to invade the masculine world, where new clothes had always been bought as mere replacements for what had been worn out. The impetus came in Britain with the abolition of clothes rationing in 1949. Needing, and for the first time able, to replace his clothes, the young British male turned to brighter ties, shoes and socks, and to suits with a mildly draped cut and long lapels. The inspiration was a traditional one – the Edwardian era – and even in the stronghold of Scottish conservatism, Edinburgh, overcoats with velvet collars caused a sensation in 1951. By 1953, even Savile Row literally came to life when its representative body, the Men's Fashion Coun-

Above left: Inchon was quickly evacuated after the North Koreans invaded South Korea in June 1950. Below left: Three members of an American tank crew help an old refugee get away from the front line. Above: A child flees from his bombed-out town near Seoul. Left: The flight of refugees from the Seoul area to the south involved hundreds of thousands of people, and their jamming of the roads made the defense of the Pusan perimeter more difficult for UN troops.

9

Left: Johnny Ray, popular singer of the early 1950s, lets his hair down and cries.
Right: One of Johnny Ray's ecstatic fans.
Below: Johnny Ray visits a boys' club in Britain.
Bottom: An impromptu performance by Johnny Ray in London.

cil, gave its first presentation with live models in 1953. Liveliness was the keynote to almost too great an extent, for with the crumbling of class barriers as wages and salaries (the one paid by the week and the other by the month) began to converge in amount, the new fashions were excessively exaggerated at the bottom of the scale and 'Teddy Boys' emerged. Milling in groups at street corners they came to be something that staid and solid citizens skirted with disapproval, and sometimes with justified nervousness.

Such associations threatened a setback, but the spirit of change was in the air and would not be stifled. Even the more conservative risked a fancy waistcoat – that warmth-giving fortification of the ribcage before the departure of braces and the coming of central heating – and right at the top of the social scale the Duke of Edinburgh flabbergasted the press by his independent venture into a Norfolk jacket and full-cut plus-fours in 1951.

Clothes, cosmetics and toiletries used up a great deal of excess youthful spending power, but something else was needed to form the basis of a new teenage culture. The something was provided by popular music – which could not be classified as 'Pop.' At the turn of the decade between the 1940s and the 1950s the talk was of the inroads of records on the sales of sheet music, regarded as deleterious and somehow surprising. The rage in 1951 was for the tunes of the Rodgers and Hammerstein musical *The King and I*, which like so many decorous things carried the seeds of revolution in it. There was the hint of the adventurous in the setting and in the suggestion of attraction between the much-married King of Siam and the governess of his multitudinous children. There was also the song 'Hello, Young Lovers,' with its gentle patronage, telling the new generation that its elders knew everything and that youth was not the innovator it thought it was.

The response of youth was a very soft remonstrance. 'Too Young' topped the hit parade in both America and Britain – 'they tell us we're too young to really be in love' they sang tremulously, but the reaction of the adult world was stern. One critic wrote in condemnation of the very title as 'vaguely suggesting the encouragement of juvenile delinquency.' The implication that youth was not merely wet behind the ears but on a steady downward path seemed justified by its favorite performer of 1951 – Johnny 'Cry' Ray. The nickname of this American singer was very literally earned, for the love-songs he sang called forth his tears by the bucket on stage. The watery display revolted an older audience, but the teenagers loved it. Here was the agonized emotion of pent-up youth expressed as they themselves expressed it in the tear-soaked pillows of teenage frustration: he was on their side. Moreover his performances were something in which they could participate.

The response to concert performers, even of a popular kind, was in those days standard. The audience clapped, with greater or lesser enthusiasm, at the end of an item. On rare occasions, at the end of the whole event, cheers might be heard. Now, and especially in the case of the young female participants, the paying customers jumped up and down in the stress of emotion at any appropriate moment, clapped and shouted, but above all gave vent to a sound of ecstasy which was unique. It was half way between a moan and a scream, excruciatingly high-pitched, and rising and falling in a punctuated way. Such a sound one might imagine coming from the lips of Irish banshees, for it was a veritable 'keening.' It was heard in the theater by the critics, by passers-by when the young hordes besieged the stage-door to catch a glimpse of their hero or wrench off his buttons as he made his exit and it hit the respectable Englishman like a blow in the solar plexus when Johnny Ray came to London. That he could, by the mere power of his name fill a major theater in the capital, was in itself the mark of a new era.

In Britain the prosperity of the 1950s came at first on rather halting feet. Clothes rationing might have ended, but food rationing, with the wearisome business of points and coupons flourished still. While the American housewife was processing ever more gargantuan quantities of food in a kitchen crammed with automatic equipment and graduating to the status of a 'homemaker,' her counterpart in Britain was gazing askance at the mean sliver of bacon on the breakfast plate which threatened at times to disappear during 1950. At the beginning of the previous year the ration had been one ounce a week; in the following twelve months it had risen by cautious stages to five ounces; and during the next twelve it would be reduced, again by stages, to three.

The Welfare State legislation of the Attlee

Below: Marines ashore at Inchon after the September counteroffensive caught the North Koreans in a vise.
Bottom: Marines in their landing craft prepare to come ashore at Inchon.
Right: Further landing craft come ashore once the Inchon beachhead had been secured.
Center right: British forces in Korea on their way to the front after disembarking at Pusan.
Bottom right: US forces in Inchon after the seizure of the port.

Labour government which had swept out Churchill in 1945 had largely been the result of consensus – a general determination that no one should suffer hunger, lack of medical care, poor educational opportunity, through no fault of his own in the postwar world. But, perpetual self-sacrifice is a hard diet.

World War II was supposedly the greatest victory over the greatest evil that the world had ever known. People in Britain began to think that something in the way of 'spoils' ought to be coming to the country which had stood alone, and paid so high a price for doing so. Yet in January 1950 it was Germany – the conquered enemy – which was announcing the forthcoming abolition of food rationing, whereas Dr Edith Summerskill, the Parliamentary Secretary to the British Minister of Health, was predicting ever direr penalties for the illegal importation across the Irish Sea of 'canned and dried fruit, table jellies, chocolate and sugar confectionery.' If they had been smuggling heroin they could hardly have been denounced in harsher terms by that redoubtable lady politician who was also renowned for her attacks on boxing, and such speeches punched the first holes in the dike of Labour's power.

In the general election of February 1950 an overall Labour majority of 142 was reduced to five. It was a stalemate decision for both sides, but only for the moment. The Labour government was disintegrating in the sphere of health. The Chancellor of the Exchequer, Sir Stafford Cripps, resigned with a diseased spine; the Foreign Minister, Ernest Bevin, retired with a heart condition and his successor, Herbert Morrison, was not only little acquainted with foreign affairs but himself struggling with the after-effects of a thrombosis a few years earlier; and the Prime Minister himself was hospitalized with a duodenal ulcer. On top of this, the new Health Minister, Hugh Gaitskell, introduced charges for false teeth and spectacles into the new 'free' Health Service, and the fiery young men on the left – Aneurin Bevan and Harold Wilson – handed in their resignations.

Idealism had surrendered to the realities of rising costs. Running like a counterpoint to the innocence and good intentions of the 1940s, which overlapped into the 1950s, was an awakening to a new realism and awareness of complexities. This shows in the films of the time. Ealing Studios, the stronghold of comedy, had been known from their beginnings in the early 1930s as being on the side of the good and the right. Under Sir Michael Balcon, as head of production from 1938, they had been devoted to the presentation of a 'people's war,' and in 1945 Balcon recast the mold for a people's peace. The studios would produce 'films with an outdoor background of the British scene, screen adaptations of our literary classics, films reflecting the postwar aspirations, not of governments or parties, but of individuals.'

Outstanding in 1950 was *The Blue Lamp* – the lamp outside British police stations – which showed a devoted policeman shot down in the course of a cinema hold-up. The killer was hunted down with the cooperation of outraged citizens and an equally outraged underworld.

Comically enough the film was so popular that the dead 'Bobby' had to be resurrected and the actor – Jack Warner – embarked on a television series *Dixon of Dock Green*. It was revived time and time again in further series until, in the 1970s, every rule in the police book had to be broken to explain why he was still in service. The world of crime around him was allowed to get a little dirtier, though remaining nostalgically non-violent, but the program was now deliberately kept to the time slot when children in the younger age-groups would be watching. The rot had set in the previous year with *Kind Hearts and Coronets* – in which Alec Guinness played all the various male and female members of a ducal house which needed to be eliminated before the hero-villain could assume his coronet. Dennis Price, as the would-be nobleman, was even allowed to be seen carrying on a relationship with a mistress after his marriage with undisguised relish. The black comedies of a later period were being curiously foreshadowed.

Far left: USAF airman during an assignation with a Korean girl.
Below left: British forces in Korea move up to the front.
Bottom left: Wave after wave of assault craft hit the beaches at Inchon in September 1950.
Right: A street in Inchon after its capture.
Below: Argyll and Sutherland Highlanders in Korea.
Bottom: Marines climb a sea wall at Wolmi-do during the Inchon invasion.

In America the emphasis at the beginning of the 1950s was on real, rather than fictional crime, and here it was taking on new dimensions. Brink's Inc of Boston, so stalwart in impregnability that they were known as 'the bankers' bank,' were robbed in January 1950 of a record $2,775,395 (£1,110,158). The blow was the greater in that the meticulously planned crime was the work of small-time operators caught up in the new technological and expansionist era of crime in the 1950s.

In March a special Senate Committee was set up to investigate organized crime in interstate commerce. At its head was Estes Kefauver, a Democrat from Tennessee, and the Senator struck gold. The public hearings in New York were televised to an audience estimated at thirty million. Housewives set up their ironing boards in front of their sets, in order not to miss a minute of the hearings, and the six hundred witnesses lived up to expectations. Nor was the report, which appeared in 1951, unequal to its task. Its findings revealed that since the days of prohibition new types of gangs had appeared which had an 'infinitely greater' capacity for evil. Their revenue was drawn, not from predatory forms of crime such as robbery and burglary, but from gambling, the sale and distribution of narcotics, prostitution, various forms of business and labor racketeering, and black market practices.

This put Brink's in the shade. The Committee declared itself convinced that an 'underworld government' existed which enforced its own laws and carried out its own executions, so that it would 'if not curbed' become the basis for a subversive movement which could 'wreck the very foundations of this country.' Just as in every good gangster film ever made, there were two major crime syndicates, with a network of operators covering the whole country. The triumvirate of Frank Costello, Joe Adonis and Meyer Lansky ruled over the one operating between Miami and New York, and the 'Capone syndicate,' run by a committee consisting of Tony Accardo, the Fischetti brothers and Jake Guzik, worked between Miami and Chicago. Disagreements between the two groupings were said to be ironed out by Charles 'Lucky' Luciano from his exile in Italy, where deportation had marooned him in 1946. Acting as an 'adhesive' between the two groups at all levels was the Mafia, responsible for such 'a ruthless enforcement of its edicts and its own law of vengeance' that it was responsible for hundreds of murders throughout the country.

It was grand stuff. 'The most shocking revelation,' went on the report, 'of the testimony before us is the extent of official corruption and connivance in facilitating and promoting organized crime. The Committee has found evidence of corruption and connivance at all levels of government – Federal, State and local.' Millions upon millions of dollars in tax revenue was being magicked away with the aid of expert accountants and lawyers for investment in legitimate areas of business which would then come under the same corrupt aegis.

There was a delicious innocence in the concept that forces of such alleged power could be arraigned before the television eye of the Special Senate Committee. The front runner for the premiership of the underworld government about to take over was Frank Costello, the Mafia 'boss of bosses,' who was stage-managed to be the star of the hearings.

He was practically a real-life incarnation of a Humphrey Bogart role. An Italian immigrant, whose real name was Francesco Castiglia, he had been born in 1891, and had arrived in America with his parents in 1896. Crime had been his easiest way out of poverty, but Frank was marked out from the ruck by his ability to use his head. He gave up carrying a gun, for example, when he worked out that hard metal in the holster meant hard sentencing from a judge whether he had used the weapon or not. So far from being a new type of gangster, Costello was an overlag from the glorious days of bootlegging. He had been one of the 'legitimate' practitioners in that he had had a well-run fleet bringing in the stuff (often imported from Britain) past the coastguards, rather than specializing in hoisting liquor from his rivals.

At the time of the Kefauver hearings his trade was in casinos, the numbers racket (lotteries) and off-track betting, then still illegal in the States. A dark, stocky, broad-shouldered man, a bit sensitive about his age – which he understated to the Committee – he was beautifully groomed, with manicured hands, a tan maintained by sunray lamps, and a line in discreet suits. His home was a seven-room penthouse on the eighteenth floor of a block in a fashionable area of New York – 115 Central Park West – where logs burned in the fireplace and the cosy glow from antique lamps fell upon gold hangings with scalloped valances. He smoked 'English Ovals,' drank in moderation, and met his colleagues for dinner at the Waldorf Grill.

The surface of respectability was superb. His lawyer would have been well-advised to show it. Instead, he objected to his client being televised while under questioning, and – not to be out-maneuvered – the companies focused their lenses on Costello's hands, eloquent in their restless, nervous movements as only an Italian's could be. Yet the load of guilt on his mind was relative. If Costello had not been so anxious to dissociate himself from the drug traffic, which he had never touched, he could have pleaded the 5th Amendment to the United States Constitution, which provides that no person 'shall be compelled in any criminal case to be a witness against himself.' He need then have answered no questions at all. His income came from gambling, and just as the State had put him out of bootlegging by legalizing liquor – and

taxing it – so there were going to be state lotteries and off-track betting shops. In a sense his crimes were largely technicalities, for he had no liking for thuggery, much of his time being occupied in peacemaking between rival interests. As the man on the spot, he fitted the role better than Luciano, and his skill in diplomacy was one of the chief reasons he had remained so long at the top.

The Kefauver hearings were not breaking new ground either when they revealed his influence over Tammany Hall, the New York Democratic political organization. This had happened in 1943, when the wonder had been equally divided between his influence in such matters as the appointment of judges and the uprightness of his candidates. Now, however, the spotlight was brighter via television, and his powers wilted under the blaze of the cameras. This did not mean that future choices would be more democratic, only that the choosing would be one step further removed from sight. A man who depends for his power on the strength of his personality, as Costello did, has to be in touch with people, and he was popular. As Raymond Chandler's detective, Philip Marlowe, says in *The Big Sleep* 'I always got along with bootleggers myself.' It was not so much the outraged American, as Senator Kefauver thought, who watched the hearings, just the fascinated one.

On 4 April 1952 Costello was at long last found guilty – of contempt of Congress for refusing to answer questions on how much he was worth. These were meant to get him for perjury if he put the figure too low, or tax evasion if he put it high. The 'Prime Minister of the Underworld' – a title that had some significance in its civilized ring – was sentenced to eighteen months and fined $5000 (£2000). Bureaucracy then extended its claws and the next few years were a round of court appearances and prison sentences – the grand old faithful 'tax evasion' getting him a sentence of five years in 1954.

By now, however, the biggest worry for Costello was not the Government but the aspirants to his tottering throne. Robbed of political influence, and worn down by courts and jails, he would have welcomed a quieter life, but his prestige was still so great that he would have overshadowed any other 'boss of bosses.' The obvious way out of the impasse was assassination. In May 1957 he was back in New York, in an interval from jail while he waited the result of an appeal. Returning from dinner with friends, he found a six-foot shadow in the hall of his apartment block. A bullet, fired at point-blank range, carved a groove round the back of his head, from one ear to the other. A couple of hours later he walked out of hospital with a bandaged head, and in a classic phrase the rasping voice – which owed its quality to an old operation on the vocal chords for a tumor – told detectives: 'I don't know who could have done it. I don't have an enemy in the world.' Maintaining the same stance before a grand jury cost him thirty days in the Toombs, the establishment catering for the drunks and gutter criminals of New York, while his would-be assassin, Vincent 'the Chin' Gigante, went free. 'Thanks Frank,' he said, as they shook hands after the trial.

Meanwhile the man behind Gigante – Vito Genovese – momentarily shifted his attention to eliminating a rival contender to the throne. On 25 October 1957 Albert Anastasia went out for a shave. His henchmen deposited him in the barber's chair and, the place being well-populated, thought it safe to depart for a little relaxation. A whoosh of bullets hurled their boss out of the chair at such velocity that his dead body crashed into the facing mirror.

Costello was now alone in the front line. Taking the bull by the horns, he contacted Genovese, indicating that he was as anxious to retire as his rival was to take over, and Genovese saw the advantages of a legitimately formal accession to power. He arranged a conference in the house of a Mafia leader in a quiet residential locale in upper New York state. It was too quiet. The sudden concentration of black limousines struck a policeman on the beat as unlikely to be an undertakers' convention, and all the invitees – forty-eight gangsters – were carted off to jail.

Within a short time both leaders were enjoying the hospitality of Atlanta penitentiary. By courtesy of the prison authorities, a meeting between the two men was arranged. Most of the inmates of this particular prison were Costello supporters, and the Warden was at his wit's end to know how he could otherwise prevent Genovese himself from being rubbed out. The meeting provided him with a convenient loop-hole. A photograph was taken of the moment of transfer of power, and Genovese began the rule which he continued for many years from behind bars. Costello died in his bed in 1973 at the age of eighty-two, after a peaceful retirement. In its way the event was as significant as Georgy Malenkov's being allowed to walk out of the Kremlin when Nikita Khrushchev took over. But here, liquor and gambling now being respectable, the world of crime concentrated on matters which are less easy to make respectable and harmless – in himself, Genovese was a poor exchange for Costello.

Senator Kefauver, having published a book, led the running to oppose Dwight Eisenhower in the 1952 presidential elections, but lost out to Adlai Stevenson. National feeling was not with him. The American public had not enjoyed anything so much as those hearings for years, but they knew, with the common sense of the people as opposed to the high-flying thought processes of their politicians, that subversion of the state does not arise from catering for the ordinary man's liking for a glass of liquor and a bet.

The investigation of the Senate Committee led to legal action against a number of public officials in New York and New Jersey, and the New York police hit the drug traffic a bit harder, but the actual ripples were uncommonly small. The report had claimed that criminals had 'deliberately planted' doubts in the mind of the public as to the existence of organized crime operating on big business lines. After the amount of films on the subject, such doubts would have been hard to raise, even in the 1930s, and in the postwar world all businesses were that much bigger because communications were that much easier. Maybe the hearings helped to check a further increase, maybe things just went underground. However, when some local authorities – in the words of the report – 'insisted, orally and in writing, that there was no organized crime in their jurisdictions,' and subsequent evidence was said to have 'proved them pathetically in error,' maybe their error was not always as great as all that. The number of hard prosecutions did not live up to the claim of the report. Certainly Costello, the man who backed off 'hurt' when refused membership of the top country clubs, was no subverter of governments.

Below: Korean refugees after having been told that they must be moved on. Bottom: British forces in Korea relax after disembarking in Pusan. Right: Defense Secretary George C Marshall is congratulated by his deputy Robert Lovett after Marshall's return from Korea.

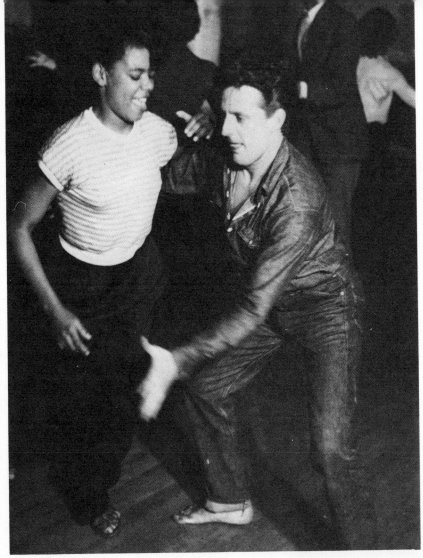

level was registered and laboratory examination confirmed the presence of fission isotopes.

President Harry S Truman brooded on the information. It was something his advisers had not expected to happen before 1952 at the earliest. On 23 September 1949 he made the public announcement that the Russians were known to have detonated an atom bomb. The US nuclear monopoly was over. Joseph Stalin could smile his wily Georgian smile, and lean a more attentive ear when little Kim Il Sung, the ebullient North Korean leader, paid him a visit. At a high-spirited dinner at Stalin's *dacha*, he was full of his plan to re-unite the two halves of his country, split between Russian and American troops when the Japanese had been evicted at the end of the war.

All the omens were good. Secretary of State Dean Acheson had made a statement in January 1950 to the National Press Club in Washington indicating that both Taiwan and Korea were beyond the American defense perimeter. After the withdrawal of American troops during 1949 the South Koreans had been left with American advisers, but their weapons were strictly World War II vintage, whereas the North Koreans had had stiff Russian drilling with supplies of the latest Russian weapons, including an improved design of the famous T-34 tank, to spearhead their advance under an umbrella of Russian aircraft. Kim Il Sung thought he could even count on a joyous uprising among the South Koreans to meet their liberators from across the border, for in the recent elections the

corrupt Synghman Rhee, almost apologetically supported in the exercise of his semi-dictatorship by the Americans, had managed to win only 45 of the 210 seats in the national assembly. Besides, it would all be over before the Americans knew what was happening.

Stalin was not quite so sure about the absence of American intervention, but, smarting a little still from the failure of the Berlin blockade of the previous year, he was inclined to take a chance, so long as his direct involvement could not be proved. He consulted with Peking – as yet very much a junior partner – and Mao had no reservations. In early May the North Korean troops began moving into position. In early June John Foster Dulles, the Republican pundit whom Truman had adopted into his Democratic administration to demonstrate American unity on foreign issues, dropped in on Synghman Rhee. Dulles was on his way to make a peace treaty with Japan which, after having been physically and intellectually converted to complete disarmament, was now to be lured back into armor on America's side. Synghman Rhee needed reassurance about the forthcoming rehabilitation of his old enemy. Across the northern border of Korea, Kim Il Sung hastened on his preparations.

It was the time of the monsoon. On Sunday 25 June 1950, rain fell in a continuous curtain on the 38th parallel as the South Korean guards waited for dawn. Flashes of light seemed to presage a storm, and they waited to judge its nearness by the interval before the thunder. The 'thunder' came in devastating blasts as shell holes opened at their feet. The North Korean army was on the move.

The South Koreans resisted strongly. Synghman Rhee was not popular, but Communism on the North Korean pattern had even less allure. Back in Japan General Douglas MacArthur was confident: he could handle the whole thing 'with one arm tied behind my back.' Then, resistance from the South broke. The training had not been thorough, the weapons were far from good enough, and fanatic spurts of courage were not sufficient to dent the Russian tanks. As dusk fell on 25 June, the invaders had opened the way to the southern capital, Seoul. A weary tide of refugees flowed before them, and the city fell on 28 June: the 'concertina war' was on.

The precision of the North Korean advance was matched on the side of the Western world by the textbook moves of their reaction. Trygve Lie, the Norwegian Secretary-General of the United Nations, assumed at once that this was World War III. Truman was convinced it inevitably would be if the challenge of the Korean move was allowed to pass as Hitler's once had been. On 25 June – the same day as the invasion began – an American resolution was passed through the United Nations Security Council, calling for a ceasefire and withdrawal of the North Koreans to the 38th parallel. It was ignored.

A second resolution followed two days later, calling on members of the United Nations to

Right: Princess Anne is christened in the presence of Queen Mary, Princess Elizabeth and Queen Elizabeth. King George and the Duke of Edinburgh stand behind.
Below: From DA to crew cut as 18-year olds are conscripted into Britain's National Service.
Below right: Princess Elizabeth holds Princess Anne as the two pose for the cameras with Prince Philip after the baby's christening in October 1950.

assist the Republic of Korea in repelling the attack. The same day Truman announced that he was sending American air and naval forces. He called it the suppression of a 'bandit raid' – it was a reporter who redefined the phrase as a 'police action' – and Truman thus sidestepped the necessity for enlisting the constitutional authority of Congress to make a declaration of war. On 30 June, the day after the fall of the South Korean capital, American ground forces entered the conflict.

General MacArthur, sent by Truman to reconnoiter Korea on a flying visit, had advocated their introduction, and by 7 July was appointed Supreme Commander. Like an old war horse he had snuffed the breezes from the mountains of Korea – the landscape has been compared with Scotland – where the characteristic mingled odor of rotting garbage and sewage-turned fertilizer was now being reinforced by an overlay of putrefying corpses.

The only readily available American troops were his own occupation forces in Japan, where MacArthur had almost become a replacement Emperor. Very many were draftees who had never heard a gun fired in anger, and never expected to. Their weapons were the same as those which had won America World War II, and their transport had spent more time bucketing round the tourist paradise of postwar Japan than on its way to training exercises. Set down in the smelly morass of Korea in the period of a monsoon, mentally and technically unprepared, they not surprisingly downed weapons and 'headed for home' when the bullets

flew, sometimes leaving their wounded in enemy hands, or sat down to await collection for a prisoner-of-war camp, innocently imagining it meant merely the exchange of one barracks for another. Their sense of being 'picked on' was emphasized by the fact that the United Nations was more eager to pass resolutions to 'assist' than to send any large quantity of troops to do the assisting. Throughout the conflict America supplied five times the men despatched by other countries altogether.

However a United Nations force did come into existence as a result of the resolution, which had been passed with uncluttered speed only because the Russian delegate to the Security Council had earlier withdrawn from it in a huff. The Soviet Union had objected to the presence at the table of the Chinese Nationalist representative, rather than one representing Mao's Communist regime. It was not a tactical error that the Russians would repeat.

In Britain during 1950 a number of assorted topics were occupying the public mind. The gossip columnists were more than usually concerned with matters royal – the enthronement of Prince Rainier in Monaco, the marriage of the Shah of Persia to the glamorous Soraya Esfandiary-Bakhtiari. and, most absorbing of all, the progress of the pregnancy of the Queen and the birth of Princess Anne in August. In technology and science, there was the welcome news of the first television transmitter outside London going up at Sutton Coldfield; the *cognoscenti* among motorists were discussing the world's first gas turbine car; women were about to be presented by ICI scientists with their invention of Terylene (to be known in the United States as Dacron) and government experts had settled on a site for a new research establishment, a former bomber field of World War II, at Aldermaston in Berkshire. Taxpayers filling up

Extreme top left: The largest and smallest TV sets in 1950, from a 1-inch to a 21-inch screen.
Far left: UN representative Jacob Malik and Soviet Foreign Minister Andrei Vishinsky.
Extreme bottom left: Alida Valli and Joseph Cotten on the set of The Third Man.
Left: Superman about to take flight.
Below: Orson Welles on The Third Man *set. Welles played the role of the racketeer Harry Lime.*
Bottom center: Harold Wilson and Sir Stafford Cripps leave 10 Downing Street after a meeting with Prime Minister Attlee.
Bottom: Valli and Welles in The Third Man.

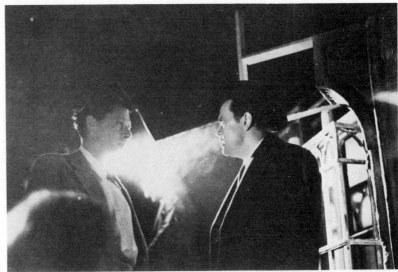

their forms learned without surprise that repayment of their 'postwar credits,' the part of the penal taxation exacted during the conflict which had been earmarked for return when the bombs stopped dropping, was now to be made 'to the estate of deceased persons only.' Ardent Roman Catholics were looking forward to a trip to Rome, where the Pope was to proclaim to a crowd of seven hundred thousand gathered in the mystery of candlelight about St Peter's Square, that stumbling block to reunion of the churches, the new dogma of the bodily assumption to heaven of the Virgin Mary. Lovers of literature were dipping into the *Journal* of André Gide, an openly homosexual Nobel laureate who was still something of a novelty, or relaxing with Nevil Shute's *A Town Like Alice*. Bernard Shaw was not far from the fall out of an apple tree that led to his death, and the break of a link that went back almost to the beginning of Victoria's reign, and the *Strand Magazine* – in which Sherlock Holmes had made his debut – was to cease publication, for in modern times even the circulation of over a hundred thousand which it still retained was not enough to keep it afloat. The breezes over the lawns of Wimbledon startled a decorous audience with glimpses of the frilly panties of 'Gorgeous Gussy' Moran, and students in Scotland were plotting the first outrage of nationalism, the theft of the Coronation Stone or 'Stone of Destiny.' Captured by Edward I from the Scots, who had crowned their own monarchs on it from the ninth century, it reposed under the seat of the Coronation Chair, made in special semi-commode form to accommodate it, in Westminster Abbey. Some months later it was recovered, embarrassingly split in two as was rumored, but restored to unity by the wonders of modern adhesives.

Yet, despite such preoccupations, the response to the American call for action in Korea, delivered via the United Nations, was immediate and sustained. The Conservative Party is usually thought of as the war party, but it was Labour – under the idealistic concept of the League of Nations having found its true reincarnation in the United Nations – which hastened to participate. As Churchill wryly commented, 'the Old Man' (by which he meant the Deity) had been good to him in bringing the crisis up while Labour was still in office, since if he had urged sending troops he would inevitably have been dubbed warmonger once again.

Some action had already been taken in the remaining outposts of the British Empire as the fitful rumblings of Communist aggression had made themselves felt in the Far East. The garrison in Hong Kong had been stepped up and the 1st Argyll and Sutherland Highlanders and the 1st Middlesex infantry battalions were now selected from the troops there for service in Korea. It is symptomatic of the run-down of the forces at this period that, to bring battalion strength up to six hundred men each, they had to be reinforced: the King's Shropshire Light Infantry, the Leicesters and the South Staffordshires, joined the Middlesex, and the King's Own Scottish Borderers linked with the Argylls.

When the troops arrived at the chief Korean

Left: Lucille Ball, star of the very popular TV show I Love Lucy.
Below left: London's 'Teddy Boys' in their Edwardian gear.
Right: Girls of the New York Chiefs Roller Derby team. Roller Derby was a craze in the early 1950s which involved jockeying for position while on roller skates around a banked oval.
Below: Pedal pushers, boleros, bare midriffs and strapless suntops were popular beachwear in 1950.

port of Pusan, they were addressed by Malcolm MacDonald, Commissioner-General for South-East Asia, speaking from the deck of HMS *Ceylon*, as she lay alongside the dock. 'This is an historic expedition,' he said. 'You will be fighting as if on the soil of France or on the beaches of Britain. The Korean War is part of a Russian attempt to conquer the world and make slaves of us all.' It was difficult for his bemused listeners to equate a threat to Britain with the thousands of miles which lay between them and home. The places they would be fighting for had names they had never heard of, and which all sounded alike, not even lending themselves very often to the kind of adaptation that had once made Ypres into Wipers. It was not going to be very uplifting for morale to give one's life for Hill 235, and new names came in – Heartbreak Ridge, High Hell, Iron Triangle, or names making a link with the known – Little Gibraltar, the Utah Line, the Punchbowl. For the Americans (and the world's pressmen) were going to feel the same need to put color into a war which was eventually to become 'part of the wallpaper' as far as newspaper readers and television viewers were concerned.

As the ships transporting the British contingent had chugged their way from Hong Kong, the men had been fortified by the officers with lectures on Communism. These addresses tended to be somewhat short, and to end rather abruptly when question-time came, for Marxist theory was not the British Army's strongpoint. In the United Kingdom National Servicemen were called up at eighteen, and not allowed out to Korea (much to the disgust of many a likely lad) until they were nineteen, and had had a little training in the rudiments of delivering rather than receiving bullets. (Reginald Streeter, a plumber's mate from Guildford, had reached the maturity of nineteen and a half, with only three months left to serve, when he became the first British soldier of that small expeditionary force to be killed.)

They had not had far to go to reach the front. It had moved down to meet them. The United Nations forces had been penned into the limits of a perimeter running in a half-circle forty-five miles from Pusan. The retreat before the North Korean forces of sixty thousand men and their hundred Russian tanks had been so rapid that contact had been lost with the enemy over great distances until the stand to defend the foothold of the port. Once dislodged from this the United Nations would need to mount a massive invasion operation before hostilities could be renewed. If the North Koreans could now sweep them from the peninsula, they knew it would be problematical whether the Americans would return.

In this situation the North Koreans concentrated every man, every gun, to break through the defense perimeter before the Americans could rush reinforcements in. Typical of the mettle of the men engaged in fending off the onslaught was Sergeant William Jecelin of the US 35th Infantry Regiment, who was awarded a posthumous Congressional Medal of Honor. Ammunition ran out in the position his men were holding, and surrender would have been

no disgrace after the battering they had endured, but Jecelin knew there was one way of getting fresh supplies. Going out under full enemy fire, he grabbed grenades and weapons from the piled bodies of the dead attackers, and returned to fight again. By the time the final order for withdrawal came, he had been so badly wounded as to be paralysed from the waist down. His men would need to carry him. He would not let them jeopardize their slim chance of escape. With a loaded carbine, he remained behind 'to take some of them with me' – and he did.

By such means the Pusan perimeter had been rendered safe by 15 September, where there were men to do it, and where men failed – from very lack of numbers – Mustang fighters and napalm (a form of jellied petrol) held the line with a thousand degrees centigrade of liquid fire. The North Korean thrust was spent, and the time had come to strike back, if the weary troops could brace themselves in the day's

Below: Seretse Khama with a District Commissioner in Bechuanaland. Khama made headlines in 1950 because of his marriage to a white Englishwoman. He was a chief of the Bamangwato tribe.
Below left: Listening to a jukebox in a roadside cafe.

1951

Over on the West Coast, however, pivoting between Los Angeles and San Francisco on the shoulder of the young and the 'young middle-aged' was a new instrument, the guitar. The French-Canadian Jean-Louis 'Jack' Kerouac had published his first book *The Town and the City* in 1950. In part it was a reaction against a sophistication that could not be afforded by the 'new poor' at the bottom of the pile, who did not fit into the ever-more rigid conventional rules governing those in the mainstream of the consumer society. In part it was the discovery of a new freedom in the sunny climate which obviated the need for heated housing and anything much in the way of clothing. They wore khaki surplus trousers (not yet jeans), sandals instead of smart shoes, and – for the women – cheap leotards with the romance of balletic associations, and beads rather than jewels. They went in for the expression of real feelings in real songs, which in the event became as commercial as anything else. In 1951 'Kisses Sweeter than Wine,' written by Paul Campbell of The Weavers in conjunction with Huddie Leadbetter – more popularly known as 'Lead-belly' – was to start the movement off with sales of a million records. They also went in for blues, beards, intellectual paperbacks instead of 'proper books,' and added the zest of wickedness without which few movements can draw the young, by smoking pot and enthusing about sex as a natural urge to be satisfied the way it took you.

Such earthiness and the real-life menace of war in Korea was too much for some, and scanning the skies for Unidentified Flying Objects, alias UFOs or 'flying saucers,' was a growing craze. From the first sightings way back in 1947, it developed during the 1950s with a publishing trade of its own. The real

Above: Joe Louis hits the canvas prior to being knocked out by Rocky Marciano in 1951. Marciano remained undefeated heavyweight champion and the mantle of boxing honors passed to the Brockton Blockbuster.
Top right: Lady Summerskill at a lunch honoring her new book **The Ignoble Art.**
Center right: The vital statistics on Marciano and Louis when they weighed in for the big fight.
Right: Frank Costello arrives in a Federal Court to testify with his attorney. He plead the Fifth Amendment and refused to give anything to the investigators except his name.

respite before the planned break-out on 16 September. It looked like being a yard-by-yard grinding battle to regain ground that had been lost like the run off a spool.

The situation was all the darker for the richness of the tapestry that blotted it out for Americans at home. For them 1950 was the year of a high in sophistication, a peak in a wave that was already cresting. On the big screen were Judy Holliday, naivety incarnate amidst the lush trappings of the settings of *Born Yesterday*. On a metaphorically even bigger screen was Bette Davis as the ageing Broadway star Margo Channing in *All About Eve*. She delivered with unforgettable panache the line, 'Fasten your seatbelts, it's gonna be a rough evening.' Batting heavy-lashed lids over pop-eyes, she focused venomously on her treacherous protégée. Making a stunning debut beside a suave George Sanders, her breasts like siren bubbles atop the sculptured drapes of a dress in the fashion of an inverted trumpet, Marilyn Monroe was more hauntingly displayed as the sex-symbol of a new era than if it had been made of glass. As Cecil Beaton put it, 'she walks like an undulating basilisk,' but he saw her at the same time as 'an urchin pretending to be grown up.' It was to be part of the cult that the new goddess did not really know what she was doing: it was too early to admit that she knew, accepted it, and reveled in it. There were too many paying customers among the respectable – men and women alike – for that to be risked. In publicity her appearances on girlie calendars in the nude was attributed to desperate need for cash, a choice between bread and photographs that were only photographs, never a sale of the body itself. From the titillated eye to the titillated ear, the 'Harry Lime' theme, picked up from the 'cold war' film *The Third Man*, made the zither the musical instrument of the moment.

Bottom left: Ezzard Charles lands a left to Joe Louis' mouth. Charles upset the longtime heavyweight champion in 1950 and took the title.
Bottom: Paul Robeson, controversial actor and singer, was hounded because of his left-wing affiliations in the early 1950s.
Below: Roller Derby queen grinds her skates.

MARCIANO		LOUIS
27	AGE	37
	HEIGHT	
5 ft. 11 in.		6 ft. 2 in.
	WEIGHT	
184 lbs.		210 lbs.
	NECK	
16¾ in.		17 in.
	REACH	
67 in.		76 in.
	CHEST NORMAL	
39 in.		42 in.
	CHEST EXPANDED	
42 in.		45 in.
	FOREARM	
12 in.		12¼ in.
	BICEPS	
14 in.		15¼ in.
	WRIST	
7½ in.		8 in.
	FIST	
11½ in.		11¾ in.
	WAIST	
32 in.		36 in.
	THIGH	
22 in.		22¾ in.
	CALF	
14¾ in.		14¼ in.
	ANKLE	
10 in.		10 in.

devotees spoke of interviews with the crews of the ships from outer space, but somehow never brought a live specimen before the waiting television cameras. Present, but ignored as if they were invisible visitors from outer space were the colored members of the population, whose service in World War II had begun to give them a slight toehold on official existence. They began to move on new tracks, and it became a matter of news when a member of the President's Committee on Fair Employment Practices was refused a meal on a train because all the tables were partly occupied by white passengers. They also began to seek higher education, and where black universities were thin on the ground growing numbers of them sought admission to the white. For one Negro at the University of Oklahoma it turned out a pretty lonely venture, since he was required to sit apart from whites in the lecture room, library and cafeteria.

Ousting all these pre-occupations, however, was the Red Menace; although nothing could have been greyer than the original focus of the trouble. Klaus Emil Julius Fuchs had been born in Germany in 1911. Anti-Nazi, and so, in the youthful climate of the time pro-Communist, he fled to England. In 1940 Britain was less concerned with Communists than that the Germans she had interned should be cleared of the crime of liking Hitler, and, after vetting, Fuchs was released in 1942 for unspecified scientific work at Birmingham University.

Fuchs found himself engaged on the atom bomb project. He believed that the Allies were deliberately letting Russia and Germany fight to a mutual death, and ignoring the vociferous cries of the Soviets for a 'second front' – an idea which had never occurred to Russia when the Battle of Britain had been fought. Fuchs was filled with 'complete confidence in Russian policy.' The result was automatic: from 1942 until 1949 he passed on information to the Russians on the bomb, including material which had become available to him in visits to America.

In the postwar period, with Fuchs now head of the Theoretical Physics Department at Harwell, he found disillusion set in. He no longer approved of Russian policy. Once his 'conscience' had demanded that he betray his adopted country, now it demanded that he cease to betray it. He decided to leave Harwell, but 'I was confronted with the fact that there was evidence that I had given away information in New York.' Failure to continue to 'deliver' to his Soviet masters, to whom he was bound by 'a token payment' of £100 ($250), possibly hastened his downfall by a deliberate leakage from the Communist side. This, and the fact that only his own full statement to the authorities made possible the prosecution which led to his fourteen-year sentence from the formidable Lord Goddard, were in themselves suggestive of the depth and unassailability of Communist penetration. It led to the kind of unease which prompted the *Evening Standard* to accuse John Strachey (Secretary of War and a former Minister of Food) of being an avowed Communist. In fact as a convert from former

leftist leanings, he was mentally further removed from Communism than many of his colleagues.

Fuchs had been formally charged on the day preceding the weekend on which America celebrates Lincoln's birthday. As part of the innocuous rejoicings, a ladies' club in Wheeling, West Virginia, had invited a guest speaker. As far as his fellow senators were concerned, Senator Joseph McCarthy was low man on the totem pole, but he had the con-man tricks of the huckster in the street market. While he spoke he believed himself in the goods he was selling, and could pick out a telling point with infallible instinct. For his audience, no man who spoke his mind with such blunt coarseness so loudly could be all wrong. In Wheeling his audience had sons, brothers, husbands in line for Korea if the fighting went on long enough, and he was on a safe pitch in what was to be a speaking tour against the Reds.

As early as 1947 Truman had created a federal loyalty program to weed out Communist sympathizers. It worked in the sense that it got rid of a lot of people who happened to know a Communist or to have attended a Communist meeting. Their careers in public service were now finished, while their chances of employment in the private sector were also wiped out. As to posing a real danger to the state, most of them came into the same category as Dr Hewlett Johnson, the 'Red Dean' of Canterbury, who had in 1948 been refused a visa to visit the United States. Not much more dangerous were the eleven leaders of the American Communist Party, convicted in 1949 of advocating the violent overthrow of the United States government, whom not even the Soviet Union took very seriously.

None of these moves was enough to satisfy the growing frustration which had been brought to a head by the Korean conflict. People resent the flies in the ointment of their prosperity more than the hardships of wartime, and treachery from within had come to be the only explanation for the aggressive success of Communism in China, and the troublespots elsewhere – Korea and Vietnam, not to speak of the Philippines. Nothing else could be at the bottom of the defeat of the United States, the world's greatest power, on both the military and technological fronts. The explosion by Russia of an atom bomb had been an affront as well as a threat, and with the accusations against Fuchs, the answer as plain.

If only they knew who they were, there were people in top places who had betrayed America on the political-cum-military front as well. Nixon, and Kennedy, too, had not been backward in fairly generalized lambasting on this theme in their public speeches, and in Wheeling, McCarthy spoke pretty well word for word on their lines. Where he differed was in a gesture of impromptu theatricality. He held up a piece of paper, and claimed to have 'here in my hand' a list of two hundred and five people who were known to the Secretary of State as members of the Communist Party, but who were 'still working and shaping the policy of the State Department.'

Left: Frank Costello after
he had been told that the
government would not
deport him back to Italy.
Bottom left: The four men
held in Detroit in connection
with the half-million dollar
Brinks robbery.
Below: Some of the million
dollar loot left behind by the
Brinks robbers after the
sensational Boston holdup.

Presumably it had been a good lunch, but his claim gradually seeped up to the State Department through the media. They wished to investigate the list – which was not forthcoming – the figure two hundred and five had been of people whose dismissal had been suggested when some four years earlier wartime employees were being screened for transfer on a permanent basis to the State Department. Time had reduced them to a quarter that figure who were on the actual payroll. McCarthy's actual speech existed only in a reporter's notes – the technician who cleaned the tape on which it had been recorded for local radio use must have cursed the moment he threw away a fortune – and when the senator later inserted it in the Congressional record, he made it read: 'I have in my hand fifty-seven cases of individuals who would appear to be either card-carrying members or certainly loyal to the Communist Party, but who nevertheless are still helping to shape our foreign policy.' There was a difference.

The difference was not great enough to prevent his staggering into the Senate on 20 February with a briefcase stuffed out with photostatic copies of a little over a hundred obsolete State Department dossiers, and holding the floor in full flow until almost midnight with a sleight-of-hand display of his suspect goods. McCarthyism had lift off. The contamination spread. The 'Hollywood Ten,' the group of writers and directors who had refused to testify before the Un-American Activities Committee in 1947 as to whether they were, or had ever been, Com-

munists, were finally sentenced to fines and imprisonment. Paul Robeson had his passport canceled because, said the State Department, he had made speeches in foreign countries which did not reflect 'a prevalent American view.'

The hunt was also on for the accomplices of Fuchs in America. His evidence led to the courier, Harry Gold, who acted as go-between on behalf of machinist David Greenglass, a worker in the atom center at Los Alamos. Greenglass had provided sketches of the so-called 'lens' which served as the vital triggering mechanism used to detonate the bomb, and Gold had conveyed them to his sister, Ethel Rosenberg and her husband.

These 'grubby scraps of paper,' as Eisenhower was to call them, led to sentences of fifteen years for Greenglass, thirty for Gold, and – for the Rosenbergs – death. These two alone had failed to confess. Although the sentence came in March 1951, it was June 1953 before it was carried out. Some of those at the mass meetings and pickets crowding the intervening years believed the Rosenbergs, despite all the evidence, were innocent. The greater number were either genuine or 'rent-a-crowd' sympathizers or protesters against capital punishment in general. A few protested in chivalry against the execution of a woman, although the broadening attitude to the activities a woman might undertake – though not yet Women's Lib – affected this angle. Eisenhower, whose unpleasant duty it was finally to 'pull the plug out' on the Rosenbergs, had as few illusions in

this as in most else. Writing to his son John, then serving in Korea, he pointed out that 'in this instance it is the woman who is the strong and recalcitrant character, the man is the weak one.' To commute her sentence, he considered, would merely encourage the Communists to recruit more women for espionage!

In the general routing out of spies that went on in 1950, a certain Emil Goldfus escaped remark. He had slipped into America in 1948, using a passport which established him as a Lithuanian, Andrew Kayotis, supposedly returning home to his new country after a visit to the land of his birth. The real Kayotis had died abroad in 1947, and quickly 'died' again when his impersonator turned up in New York in 1950 with the new assumed name of Goldfus. The real Emil was also dead having breathed his last when little more than a year old.

Goldfus was elderly, slightly stooping, and claimed to be a semi-retired photographer with belated ambitions as an artist. As a kindly father-figure, he became well-liked among the leftish brew of intellectuals and artists frequenting the building where he rented a studio. Intellectually gifted, good with his hands, and with a mathematical and scientific bent, as well as a knack with the classical guitar, he was an interesting addition to their circle. What matter if he kept a little degree of reserve about his affairs? They were not of the conforming bland body of American society that demanded everything should be in the open, no secret places in the mind any more than in the new open-plan houses. The secret of Goldfus would have astonished them: he was a KGB colonel, the so-called Rudolph Abel (for Rudolf Abel was yet another of his assumed names).

In 1952 Reino Hayhanen, a Russian posing as a Finn – 'Eugene Maki' – was sent to join Abel in New York, as an assistant. No spy comedy could have chosen anyone more unsuitable. He spoke appalling English, was incompetent at every trick of espionage from coding messages upwards, and in his personal life was a raging drunk who quarrelled endlessly with his wife. The KGB decided it was time for him to have a 'vacation' in Moscow: Hayhanen decided it was time to defect. On his information FBI special agents called at seven in the morning on 21 June 1957 at the Hotel Latham. Abel, naked and still half asleep opened the door. His assembled belongings were submitted to a thorough search, and among the foot powder (for his athlete's foot), thirty-three white hankies that he kept in rotation for his sinus trouble, aspirin (for his headaches), shaving cream and deodorant, and sundry rather shabby clothes, they found incriminating items. Notable were a 'one-time cipher pad' and a pencil with an eraser at the end. When the eraser was removed, eighteen microfilms were discovered in the cavity.

When it came to the trial the members of the court were sitting on the edge of their seats as these films were produced after a suspense-filled recess for lunch. Some turned out to be schedules for Abel's radio listening sessions. Others were letters from his wife and daughter – the former writing about a newly-acquired dog

and a television set, and the latter about her forthcoming marriage. In the final letter, written four months after the wedding, the girl claimed that the intervening time had seemed like 'eternity' it had been so dull, and declared her preference for her father's company. It was odd, but, unless the letters were in some code which has yet to be cracked, there was nothing in them concerning defense or atom secrets. Heyhanen was the better bet for televised courtroom drama, with his stumbling English, and his tales of a white thumb-tack stuck into a sign in Central Park to tell his contacts of his safe arrival in America, and of ingenious 'drops' for the passing on of secret messages.

Yet the fundamental mystery remains. What did Abel send back to Moscow in his nine years of undetected activity? There was no discoverable link with the Fuchs-Gold affair. The 'British' spy Gordon Lonsdale claimed that he had met Abel in 1943, when the latter had infiltrated the Abwehr – German Army Intelligence – at officer rank. The fact that he was a 'colonel' in the KGB makes one presume that what he did was important; yet for a high-class agent he was very careless with incriminating evidence, and from the way the Russians behaved it almost seemed as though they wanted him betrayed by sending him a helper as inept as Heyhanen. In lieu of other explanations, it seemed possible that he was on a kind of retire-

Extreme top left: FBI agents escort Julius Rosenberg into the Federal Building in Manhattan. Rosenberg was charged and convicted of handing over atomic secrets to the Russians.
Extreme bottom left: Julius and Ethel Rosenberg on their way to prison. They were executed for espionage.
Above left: Marilyn Monroe reached her pinnacle as a film star in the early 1950s.
Above: Humphrey Bogart and Katharine Hepburn during the filming of The African Queen.
Center bottom: The Dalai Lama of Tibet, who was forced into exile when his country was overrun by the Chinese Communists in 1951.

ment mission, collecting day-to-day background on life in the United States. However, if this was the case then when Khrushchev made his celebrated visit to America in September 1959, his lack of 'briefing' was still incredible.

Eisenhower's invitation to him to stay at Camp David was suspected of being an insult. 'I couldn't for the life of me find out what this Camp David was,' Khrushchev wrote in his memoirs. The Soviet Ministry of Foreign Affairs did not know, the Soviet Embassy in Washington itself could not say for certain, and he had to make special inquiries and 'get someone to research the problem.' At length he discovered that he was being highly honored by such an invitation, and confessed to being ashamed – not of the suspicion, but of 'how ignorant we were in some respects.' Maybe Abel was part of a plan to remedy such ignorance, but never got as far as a 'run-down' on Camp David, and when it came time for his retirement perhaps the KGB decided to get one last bit of mileage out of him by betraying him. While the American authorities were devoting their energies to him and Heyhanen, maybe something more important was going on elsewhere in America. Maybe.

Heyhanen disappeared into 'protection,' though there were rumors that he died in an 'accident' despite the care of a grateful American government. Abel ended up in Atlanta peni-

Left: Viscountess Boyle sports a new hat in 1951. Bottom left: English soldiers guard the Suez Canal in 1951. Britain was soon to lose control of this vital waterway after King Farouk of Egypt was overthrown. Right: Egyptian workers are searched before being allowed into Buller Camp along the Suez Canal. Below: Ousted General Douglas MacArthur throws out the first ball in a game played in New York between the Giants and the Philadelphia Phillies. Giant manager Leo Durocher is on the left. When the General left the Polo Grounds a fan shouted, 'Hey Mac, how's Harry Truman?' The fans roared with laughter and the MacArthur bubble burst.

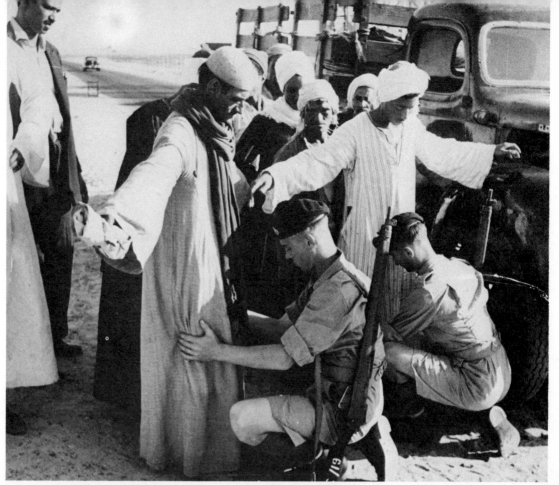

tentiary with Mafia stool-pigeon Joseph Valachi and Frank Costello's successor, Vito Genovese, though there is no record of their fraternizing. Then in 1962 prisoner No 80016-A was smuggled out of his cell and whisked to a plane. At the Gleinicker Bridge in Berlin (ironically named the 'Bridge of Unity'), he walked from one side, and Gary Powers, the American 'spy pilot,' walked from the other. An exchange of agents had been effected. The Russians claimed his innocence and unimportance, then later held him up as a model espionage agent for Soviet youth to admire and copy. It would be nice to think it was just a rare example of Russian humor.

Despite the absence of precise evidence that Abel had stolen any particular secret material, the United States government continued to believe that he had spent his nine years in the country as 'resident agent' in charge of the entire Soviet espionage network in North America. Confirmation of the breadth of Abel's operations surfaced in 1961, at the Old Bailey hearing of the Portland Naval Secrets Case. He had attached $5000 (£2000) to a couple of photos by an elastic band – presumably to aid in identification when a payment was made to the man and woman shown – and although these were at the time unidentified, they had turned out to be the so-called 'Peter' and 'Helen Kroger,' accomplices of Gordon Lonsdale.

Top left: The lights of the Festival of Britain in 1951.
Left: Special Police query a Malay native during the insurgency of the Communists in the early 1950s.
Above: Some of the buildings constructed for the Festival of Britain.
Right: Prime Minister Clement Attlee lost the 1951 election after the Labour Party held office for six years.

Far left: Klaus Fuchs, one of Britain's atomic spies who sold secrets to the Russians.
Left: MacArthur's car arrives at Honolulu on his way back to the US after he was relieved of command. Leis festooned his path.
Below left: MacArthur salutes a color guard in Lower Manhattan during his triumphal return to New York on 20 April 1951. More confetti was strewn across his path than in any ticker tape parade before or since.
Below: General MacArthur and President Synghman Rhee of Korea in Tokyo prior to the general's sacking by Harry Truman.

On the Korean front there was not much humor going that September of 1950, as the troops nerved themselves for the counter-attack. The moment of strike had been delayed. The reason was one which lifted the hearts of all America as much as the men at the front. Greatly daring, MacArthur had shown all his old skill against much seasoned advice. At dawn on 15 September he had successfully made a magnificent sweep of the Korean peninsula and landed the US 10th Army Corps and 1st Marine Division at Inchon, on the west coast.

The landing was the largest since the massive amphibious operations of the Pacific against the Japanese. The whole area had been softened up by two days of pounding from the sea by the United Nations force of two hundred and sixty warships, of which nearly two hundred were American. MacArthur himself was present on the flagship and waded masterfully ashore as the complete success of the operation was guaranteed by weighty air support. By 29 September the 'smoking ruin' of Seoul, some twenty miles inland from Inchon, was recaptured. Thirty thousand of its people had been killed as a by-product of the battle; another twenty thousand had been executed for political reasons by the Communists before they left; and another twenty thousand had been deported to the North Korean concentration camps. At a formal ceremony General MacArthur returned the remains of the city to the belligerent septuagenarian, Synghman Rhee, and received in return the Korean Order of Military Merit. He spoke of his 'fervent hope that from the travail of the past there may emerge a new and hopeful dawn for the people of Korea.'

At that moment it looked as if it might. Truman congratulated his general on a 'brilliant maneuver,' and a British-sponsored resolution in the United Nations Assembly on 7 October authorized the taking of 'all appropriate steps' to stabilize conditions *throughout* Korea. The next day American and Commonwealth troops crossed the 38th parallel. Millions of leaflets had twice been dropped on the North Koreans calling for their surrender, and prisoners of war were being taken in tens of thousands everywhere. On 19 October the North Korean capital, Pyongyang, fell without resistance, and by 26 October the Yalu River was reached. Such had been the rapidity of the United Nations advance that confusion was rife, and a party of Scottish soldiers – being white and not obviously

American – were hopefully hailed by a group of North Koreans as Russian allies.

By this stage the Russian allies were not greatly in evidence. Stalin withdrew all Russian advisers with the North Korean forces as soon as any danger of their being taken prisoner by the United Nations arose. 'We don't want there to be evidence for accusing us of taking part in this business,' he angrily snapped, when Khrushchev appealed for more support for Comrade Kim Il Sung. After the fall of Seoul, however, the Chinese Foreign Minister and Premier, Chou En-lai, proclaimed that 'The Chinese People will not supinely tolerate seeing their neighbors being savagely invaded by the imperialists.'

Even so, the Chinese were careful not to declare war. It was 'volunteers' who crossed from Manchuria into Korea about a fortnight later, and who were reported in action on the Yalu by the end of October. From MacArthur's Headquarters came the message that the presence of these troops was to be considered a mere 'face-saving operation' and that there was 'no cause for alarm.' The Chinese had reason to be alarmed, if MacArthur had not. On the other side of the Yalu lay the industry and mineral wealth of Manchuria, a thought not absent from American spokesmen's minds when they lamented the 'loss' of the area to Communism in the wartime agreements. Even the Yalu itself supplied electrical power to factories in Manchuria as well as on the Korean

Above: Doris Day was one of the most popular recording artists throughout the 1950s.

Above left: A two-piece
bathing suit in 1951. This
style soon gave way to the
bikini later in the decade.
Above: Strapless evening
gowns were in high fashion
in 1951.

side. Having the Americans poised on its far shore was rather like having a Chinese expedition landing in Mexico and advancing on Texas and its oil wells.

It is the slowness of the Chinese response that is remarkable, rather than their ultimate action. However, China had had other preoccupations. The return of Tibet to the 'Motherland's big family' had been listed as a primary task for the People's Liberation Army as early as the beginning of 1950, for the prodigal child was reluctant to come home. Rumors of a Chinese invasion in the summer were followed in October by official Chinese confirmation that her troops had crossed the border. In such remote mountain terrain, with winter also on the march, it was not easy to complete the conquest, and in November the Chinese were still three hundred miles from the capital at Lhasa. Tibet appealed to the United Nations, but the General Assembly postponed action indefinitely on 24 November 1950. The Indian government, on tenterhooks and concerned for the safety of its own borders, gave an assurance that it was believed a settlement was possible which would protect the autonomy of Tibet. It was a somewhat fortuitous belief. On 21 December 1950, at the break of dawn, the little cavalcade of the Dalai Lama, with his high officials and an escort of six hundred soldiers, fled from the great Potala Palace. Later, he returned, only to find he had got it right the first time. In 1958 he

Above left: A roundup of Communists in the guerrilla war in Malaya.
Below left: coffin carries the body of Sir Henry Gurney, who was killed by terrorists. Gurney was the High Commissioner of the Federation of Malaya.
Above: Barbed wire is strung around a 'strategic hamlet' in Malaya, one of the devices used to break the Communist insurgency.
Left: Head-hunting Dyak on patrol in a search for Communist guerrillas.

again went into exile. Shangri La was no more.

The delay in the Chinese response in Korea encouraged a reckless irresponsibility in MacArthur, but over in the White House a more realistic Truman was pacing the floor of the Oval Office in nervous tension as to whether the general would precipitate a crisis by using non-Korean troops too near the Russian or Chinese borders. On 15 October, unable to stand it any longer, he flew to Wake Island for Dutch-uncle talks – seven thousand miles to MacArthur's two thousand as a concession to the general's inability to be away long from his Tokyo headquarters.

MacArthur, bent on making the little President come out of the aircraft to meet him on equal terms, dallied on the way. Seeing nothing but empty tarmac, Truman sat tight. At last MacArthur could spin it out no longer and loungingly appeared, further signifying his disrespect, as Truman later angrily noted down, by having 'his shirt unbuttoned, and wearing a greasy ham and eggs cap that evidently had been in use for twenty years.'

The general said blandly of the Chinese: 'We are no longer fearful of their intervention.' He estimated that the Chinese had some three hundred thousand men in Manchuria, of whom about a third were actually on the Yalu River, which was an accurate assessment. He went on to claim that 'only fifty-sixty thousand could be gotten across,' since they had no air force, and if an attempt were made to reach Pyongyang, there would be 'the greatest slaughter.' This was where he began to go wrong, for with winter coming, the Chinese would not need to do anything but walk across the Yalu before very long, and 'the greatest slaughter' was not only going to be on the side he was referring to. Yet, he actually had the answer, for he then added (after commenting on the Russian lack of available ground troops) that 'the only possibility would be Russian air support of Chinese ground troops.'

Truman accepted the more soothing part of assessment, and the days passed with no increase of alarm. One Chinese prisoner was taken on 26 October, something over a dozen a few days later, and by 5 November MacArthur had given the United Nations notification of Chinese Communist participation. On the strength of this he demanded permission to bomb the Yalu River bridges, and to pursue raiding planes into their 'privileged sanctuary' in Manchuria. Already, in contempt of his instructions, he was using American troops in the advance border area. They would be replaced with South Koreans when the Americans went off to eat their 'Christmas dinner at home.' He had no misgivings in allowing the two halves of his army to be split by the central mountains of Korea (rendering concerted action impossible), for by the 7 November all the Communist forces had broken off action. It was all over.

On 25 November the United Nations troops woke to a day of intense cold, and with it came the demons of the frost: a quarter of a million Chinese 'volunteers,' hard-hitting and mobile, came down the narrow valleys on the southern

ide of the Yalu. The first Russian MIGs had also appeared in November, but in this terrain the ground soldier had less need of air support, and was also less vulnerable to strafing by the enemy. 'We face an entirely new war,' said an aggrieved MacArthur, and a retreat began in blinding snowstorms. The frost reached 45° at its worst, and hot drinks, grabbed at by crippled hands, froze before they could be drunk. Rearguard duties fell to the new British brigade, just arrived in Korea, the 29th, for which even veterans from Dunkirk had had to be recalled to bring it up to strength.

Scarcely had the year turned than, on 4 January, Seoul was once more in Communist hands. The Chinese were not well-armed, but in such numbers troops who had only grenades in their pockets made impact, and the very unexpectedness of their appearance had immense psychological punch. Despite their missionary contacts, the Americans had never understood the Chinese, and suddenly their fear of all the more sinister aspects of the 'legend' which surrounded them erupted – the 'tongs,' the inscrutability and cruelty, the 'yellow peril.' They were seized by a kind of horror at the swarms of little figures who now flung themselves upon them in the blind fanaticism of an attack by giant insects. Kill one and five took his place. They gained such a reputation for being impossible to defeat that only the hardiest of old campaigners could resist the temptation to believe it. Corporal 'Evil-eye' Everleigh, an Australian who had fought in New Guinea against the Japanese and had

Top left: Houses of Parliament lit up for the Festival of Britain.
Extreme left: The Gloucestershire Regiment returns from Korea after enduring a four-day stand on the banks of the Imjin River in 1951.
Center left: Cadets ready to go to Korea as reinforcements pause for a snack at Waterloo Station.
Above: A fashionable evening gown in 1952.
Left: An engine is named after the Gloucestershire Regiment upon their return from Korea.

47

already won the Australian Military Medal during the earlier fighting in Korea, was one who broke the legend. 'If them flamin' Chinks are invincible,' he said, in famous phrase, 'then my bum's a frying pan,' and went on to prove his point.

By 15 January 1951 the offensive was halted, and on 21 January Lieutenant General Matthew Bunker Ridgway was himself on the attack. By March Seoul was once more in United Nations hands with the 38th parallel again in sight. Truman was not going to let it be crossed this time. The police action had become an east-west confrontation in which neutral countries could see themselves being indirectly involved. The world climate of opinion was changing – no one anywhere in the world was beyond reach of the atom bomb.

Already, at a press conference on 30 November 1950, Truman had been closely questioned on the possible American use of the bomb. Was it 'under active consideration'? The President replied that it always had been, as 'one of our weapons,' and in an impromptu added: 'Selection of the objectives or targets was for the military authorities to decide.' Like wildfire the impression spread that MacArthur's finger was on the button.

In Britain the Prime Minister, Clement Attlee, who had already seen his majority clipped to negligible size in the general election of February 1950 was faced with revolt by about a hundred of his remaining faithful if he supported Truman's stance. This he could see would topple his government at once. Nor through its links with the Commonwealth, Britain could not afford to ignore the depth of feeling evident in India and the Arab countries, and although her share of the financial cost and military casualties in Korea might seem small in comparison with that borne by America, it was large in proportion. She also had commitments of her own in the fight against Communist guerrillas in Malaya. There were

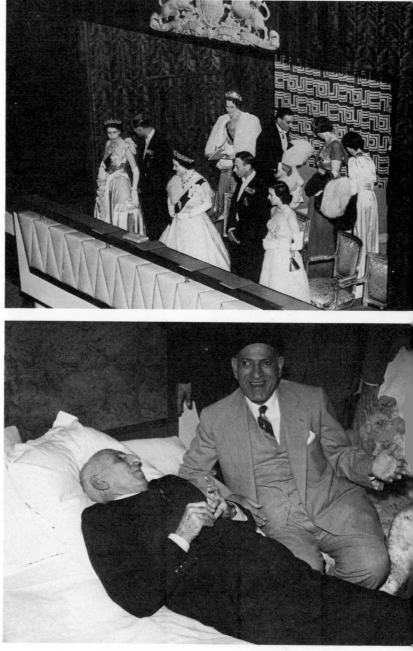

implications of another character, too. At first American stockpiling had enhanced prosperity, but as it continued it turned the terms of trade against Britain – postwar inflation was to be a potent factor in the general election of 1951.

The American resolution before the United Nations, condemning China as an aggressor, was passed with less than united enthusiasm in February 1951. On the other side Russia was concerned, but, in his colloquies with Chou En-lai, Stalin allowed himself to be convinced that the combination of North Korean troops and Chinese 'volunteers' would be able to surround and finish off the United Nations force. Mao Tse-tung's 'brightest star,' General P'eng Te-huai, was to be in command.

In the following months Mao's dream came true. The United Nations forces were annihilated many times, but only on paper in the battle reports P'eng sent back to Peking: in the field they remained obstinately active. Even China could not afford to go on losing at the rate of something approaching a quarter of a million men, especially while inflicting only a fraction of that number in casualties on the enemy. The

realization was bitter. Bitterest of all, perhaps, for Mao himself. At one point in the fighting south of the 38th parallel the Americans had carried out a routine air raid on a Chinese command post. A Chinese general lay dead in the ruins when the planes passed – a son of Mao Tse-tung.

On 24 March 1951 MacArthur authorized the re-crossing of the 38th parallel. In an equal mood of insubordination he made a personal offer 'to confer in the field with the Commander-in-Chief of the enemy forces' which he combined with a declared plan to reduce China to 'military collapse.' Not surprisingly, the only thing which inevitably collapsed was Truman's hope for a peace initiative. Already toying with the idea of dismissing MacArthur, the President was even now compelled to hold his hand by the need to get the appropriations through Congress for NATO and the Marshall Plan. On 5 April, however, Joseph W Martin, Republican leader in the House of Representatives, read in the House extracts from a letter written to him by the general, with the defiant closing sentence: 'There is no substitute for victory.'

On 11 April the Supreme Allied Commander in Japan, the Commander-in-Chief, United Nations Command, and the Commanding General of the US Army in the Far East, was relieved of his posts – General of the Army Douglas MacArthur had been relegated to history. At first it seemed as if it might not be so. The Japanese Emperor came in person to say farewell, and a million Japanese lined the streets as he drove away. In the United States itself, the headlines roared and telegrams arrived at the White House in stacks. Senator Joseph McCarthy accused Truman of having made the fatal decision while drunk, and Senator William Jenner talked boldly of impeaching the President. The livelier elements of the general populace burned the leader of their nation in effigy, or joined the seven and a half million spectators who lined the route of MacArthur's triumphal drive from the New York Battery to the Civic Hall under a snow of ticker tape.

The general was invited to address a joint session of Congress as the climax of his return, but within days enthusiasm was cooling. The Chiefs of Staff, whose support MacArthur had claimed, revealed their opposition before the Senate Inquiry. As General Omar Bradley commented, MacArthur's strategy 'would involve us in the wrong war, at the wrong place, at the wrong time, and with the wrong enemy.' Two million words of evidence were spilled, and it was decided that no formal report of the inquiry's views would be presented. Only the voice of Australia's Prime Minister, Robert Menzies, reminded the world that, not so many years ago, the southern continent had not been alone in saying in the midst of World War II: 'Thank God for MacArthur.'

At this date it is possible to look back and see that, within his own terms of reference, MacArthur was right. It was the last time that America would have an overwhelming preponderance of atomic warheads, and to have used them might have maintained American world hegemony. Exactly what MacArthur would have done, given his head, was revealed in interviews given by him after his dismissal, but held back from publication until his death. Up to half a hundred atom bombs would have hit military targets in Manchuria, and half a million Chinese Nationalists from Formosa would have been toughened by a couple of divisions of US Marines for a pincer landing on either side of the Korea/China border. A deterrent belt of radioactive cobalt would have been laid along the Yalu, once the fighting was over, in order to prevent the Chinese coming back across the river at any future date.

As it was, the spilling of blood began again as the first green of spring tinged the rice fields. On a hundred-mile front the North Koreans and their Chinese allies began an all-out offensive in April to break open the way to Seoul, and the United Nations began a strategic withdrawal. The most exposed position of all, on the direct approach to Seoul, across the Imjin River, was allotted to a mainly British force.

It was the Gloucesters who caught the brunt of the attack. They saw the moonlit water below their position break into ripples as the first of the enemy began to ford the river, and they turned it again and again to blood and silver as they fought back against the lemming-like Chinese invasion of the southern shore. Eventually the numbers were too great, and the Gloucesters found themselves surrounded. For three days and three nights the 1st Battalion of the Gloucester Regiment, under the command of Lieutenant-Colonel J P Carne, held on. They were outnumbered beyond counting, food and water ran out, and ammunition was nearly gone. Longed-for supplies coming in by air on parachutes fell short, and no helicopter could land, even to extricate their wounded. But they saved the left flank of the United Nations corps in the vital sector and held up the enemy advance, so that the line could be reformed and held. At last, their purpose achieved, they were broken up into three sections to find their way back to the United Nations lines. Of the six hundred and twenty-two of the 'Glorious Gloucesters' who had gone into action, forty-six officers and men returned. Even the Chinese had held their fire as the survivors finally left their positions, in tribute to their courage, but as they made their way across country, others had been shot as they ran into other enemy forces, some being gunned down by American tanks in error before they could be recognized. Carne was among the few who found their way into the long-drawn horror of the prisoner-of-war camps.

Of the sixty-thousand Chinese taking part in the attack, ten thousand were killed and wounded. The strike for Seoul was off. It was following this operation that, for the first time

in any war, a Commonwealth Division – comprising British, Australian, Canadian, Indian and New Zealand troops – was formed under a unified command. There had been an inevitable tendency for separate contingents to be used as stopgaps in desperate situations, rather than to regard them as part of the overall force, especially since – and it was a tribute to their quality – they were regarded as 'professionals.'

Meanwhile the scale of the fighting and the potential risks were alarming even the Kremlin. In June, speaking on the United Nations radio from New York, Jacob Malik – the Soviet representative – made a speech which opened the way for negotiation. Significantly the proposal was for 'mutual withdrawal of forces from the 38th parallel': China was no longer demanding as part of the settlement a United Nations seat, recognition of its title to Formosa, and withdrawal of the United Nations from Korea. Truman hastened to meet the offer and soon the peace negotiations were under way at the 'Peace Village' of Panmunjom.

Left: The new Prime Minister Winston Churchill greets Russian Ambassador Andrei Gromyko at 10 Downing Street.
Bottom left: Crowds wait in Piccadilly Circus for the 1951 election results.
Right: Anthony Eden waves to the crowd outside Downing Street after his first Cabinet meeting as British Foreign Secretary.
Below: Alec Guinness stars as Hamlet at the New Theater, London in 1951.
Bottom Center: A lady of the night waits for a 'date' in London's Leicester Square.
Bottom right: Ballot box is taken by bus to be counted.

In England as the casualty figures were still coming in from the Imjin, the Festival of Britain was dedicated by George VI in a service at St Paul's Cathedral. The original suggestion had been that the ceremony should be performed on Tower Hill, with the monarch alighting from the royal barge, but the King had not been a naval man for nothing. He knew that the royal barge took in water and had no intention of wearing his Wellingtons (rubber boots) for the occasion – if no worse befell – nor did he care to start a frolicking festival on a spot where so many heads had once rolled bloodily down.

'Fun, fantasy and color' had been the goal of the festival architect, Gerald Barry. On the South Bank of the Thames, just across from the Houses of Parliament, a three hundred foot 'Skylon' went up (rather like a Churchillian cigar lit up with colored lights from the inside). Alongside was the great span of the Dome of Discovery, illustrative of the new architectural techniques coming into use, just as the new concert hall which was to be the one permanent feature of the exhibition site broke with all prewar tradition. The fact that nothing, even the Festival Hall, was finished on time, rather added than detracted from the carefree public enjoyment. It was pleasant to have a project that was not a matter of wartime or any other desperate urgency. Adding to their pleasure was the river, which up until now had been regarded as an industrial sewer, visible only in limited stretches and which still at low tide, sent questionable aromas across the tea tables of the House of Commons terrace. However active interest in the care and conservation of the English heritage had begun again and it prompted a program for cleaning up the Thames, so that fish would be swimming once again in those reaches. In the meantime the crowds enjoyed taking the steamer trip on its waters. There, in Battersea Park, were pleasure gardens and a funfair which outraged the local residents but re-opened in many succeeding summers until more sophisticated amusements took the public away again.

When the Festival ended in September, with Gracie Fields there to sing in the final concert, there were other changes on the way. It was in that same month that the King, ill with cancer, had an operation to remove a lung. Later, in October, came the long-expected general election. Peace talks, with the Communists 'fighting to negotiate' dragged on in Korea, and a few recondite speakers brought up the refusal of the government to join the European Coal and Steel Community (the embryo Common Market) in April 1951. But the issue – the campaign scandal – was the war that never happened. Persia nationalized her oil when Labour's dividend controls prevented her getting the increase in royalties to which she felt entitled. The great refineries ground to a halt, but what could only be termed as 'comic opera' was on.

The ageing Iranian Prime Minister, enemy of the Shah and with the temperament of a prima donna, claimed to have been waylaid by two men disguised as women, and sought sanctuary in the Majlis or Parliament, where he collapsed and had to be carried out. Always appearing in public in tears and pyjamas, he was yet a wily bird, and when the Shah sent the commander of his guard to arrest him for treason, he had already been forewarned. Thus it was the Shah who had to rush to escape in an aircraft, but only to turn the tables a few days later and succeed in landing the old man in the dock. He did not do it alone. Richard Helms, who has been called 'the closest thing to a master spy that America can claim,' is said to have helped to overthrow the leftish Iranian Prime Minister. Certainly it was America who eventually benefited when the oil started flowing again, and the pattern was begun of America stepping in where Europe stepped out, in hotspots all over the world.

Herbert Morrison, the Labour Foreign Minister, had been in favor of sending in the troops, but American support had been lacking and the 'pre-Suez war' never came off. Few people knew of this off-stage plan, however, and so in the election it was Churchill who was challenged as wanting war on the Persians. 'Whose finger do you want on the trigger,' demanded the *Daily*

Far left: Marlon Brando and Vivien Leigh star in A Streetcar Named Desire. Bottom left: Marshal Tito of Yugoslavia inspects HMS Liverpool, *Britain's Mediterranean flagship.* Bottom center: Vera Lynn, a popular British singer of the war and postwar years. Left: A drive-in film theater in Hollywood. Drive-ins were multiplying all across the US in the early 1950s. Below: R A Butler with a young debutante soon after Butler joined Churchill's 1951 Cabinet. Far left: British motorcycle driver wins race in Paris.

Mirror, 'Attlee's or Churchill's?' In case anyone had missed the point it had a large pistol on the front-page on polling day captioned 'Whose finger? Today YOUR finger is on the trigger.' The accompanying letterpress enlarged the smear to such as extent that Churchill sued for libel, and got an out of court settlement, an apology, costs, and payment to his favorite charity. It was an interesting case, if only in the contrast it made between the American and British approach to libel: in similar circumstances Truman would not have stood a chance!

This was Britain's first television election, though only one in ten households as yet had a set: it was used to show what was going on, rather than to serve as a weapon in itself. The Conservatives were slightly in the minority as far as votes cast, but again the Labour vote was concentrated where they were already safe, and Churchill returned to power with a majority of eighteen seats in the House of Commons. It was enough to govern without the need to look over one's shoulder all the time.

The Tory slogan had been 'set the people free,' which led to the first casualty of the bureaucratic wartime structure – the abolition of the little folding identity card. These cards which everyone had to carry by law during the war, had to be produced on demand. Each bore a number which, for convenience sake, was converted to the one used by the members of the population as participants in the new health service. A shackle once forged never quite drops off. Abolition of food rationing was more difficult. Churchill was concerned and demanded that the Minister of Food should lay out for him on a tin dish modeled amounts of meat, sugar and other rationed items, so that he could see for himself what the people were eating. He smiled with satisfaction when it was produced. 'Not a bad meal,' he commented. The Minister ventured to correct him – these were

the rations for a week. Food rationing did not actually end until 1954. Housing was another preoccupation. The Conservatives had promised three hundred thousand houses a year, and a younger member of the Cabinet (as politics uses the term) was made Minister of the newly renamed Ministry of Housing and Local Government to get it done – Harold Macmillan.

Altogether it was a more hopeful Christmas that year than had been known for a long time. In the cinema that season Alec Guinness had enchanted in *The Lavender Hill Mob*, even if the indestructible garments which he wore in his *Man in a White Suit* had raised a query as to what might happen to the textile industry with all these new inventions in the pipeline, and the filmed version of Rattigan's *The Browning Version* had reached the acme of perfection in Michael Redgrave's portrayal of a schoolmaster who fails both in his calling and in satisfying his voraciously sexual wife. The Guinness magic had failed in the theater, for his *Hamlet* had never fully recovered its impetus after a disaster with the lighting, but there had been reassurance in the dual luxury of Vivien Leigh and Laurence Olivier playing in Shaw's *Caesar and Cleopatra* and Shakespeare's *Antony and Cleopatra*, and confirmation of a world restored to something like stability when N C Hunter's comedy *Waters of the Moon* had a cast of two theatrical dames, Edith Evans and Sybil Thorndike, while the younger feminine

role went to Wendy Hiller, herself even then inevitably heading towards the DBE which became hers in the 1970s. The world of opera had been set buzzing by Igor Stravinsky's *The Rake's Progress* and Menotti's *The Consul*, and though Benjamin Britten's *Billy Budd* had found many Britons puzzled rather than moved, there was a universal pride that an Englishman was writing operas which were not only staged but accorded international respect. On a more popular plane another link with the past had snapped with the death of Ivor Novello. In middle-brow literature the new aspirations to intellectualism were being satisfied by C P Snow, with books such as *The Masters*, which conveyed a sense of inside knowledge of Oxbridge and its ramifications and had good snob value. In architecture the general public tried to come to grips with Basil Spence's design for the new Coventry Cathedral, and felt that the retention of the old tower of the ancient cathedral, the ruins of which were left standing adjacent to the new building, was the sop intended to make them swallow the rest. In art the endeavor was to be more modern, provided the impact was diluted: the ordinary visitor to the art galleries had closed his eyes to the blurred horrors of Francis Bacon's works, but had managed to survive a passage of Victor Pasmore's 'Waterfall,' painted on tiles outside the Regatta Restaurant at the Festival of Britain, without loss of appetite.

Interests had been widening too, in 1951, for it was not only archaeologists who watched with interest the reports of the progress of Agatha Christie's husband – Professor Mallowan – in excavating Nimrud out in Iraq. The bug was catching. Finds on sites that had been bombed flat by the Germans had been a reminder that it had not all stopped with the discovery of Tutankhamen's tomb, and that the ordinary man or woman who knew how to use his eyes could find something of interest. It was worthwhile for the Council for British Archaeology to issue a poster telling people where to take their discoveries. Interests had not widened, however, as far as entente with Europe was concerned. At the tail-end of the year, on 11 December 1951, Paul-Henri Spaak, President of the Consultative Assembly, told how he and his colleagues had thought that political change in England would give them an opportunity for more intimate collaboration. 'Almost in anguish,' he said, 'we waited for what the representatives of the Conservative government were going to tell us.' What then had been the reply of Churchill, that Great European? 'We will never go along with you: not along this road nor in this direction.' Among those who gritted their teeth was Edward Heath who, on entering the Commons in 1950, had made his maiden speech on the necessity of cooperation with Europe. Even the Americans expressed their disappointment.

For Americans at this moment the times were out of joint. It wanted Europe to look after itself, and did not see any way that could be done without Britain being part of that Europe. The edginess, the ideas slightly askew with uncertainty showed in the films of 1951. In the new Bogart film *The African Queen*, for which the actor collected his only *Oscar*, he abandoned the line, 'I don't risk my neck for anybody,' in favor of putting greater emphasis on chivalry and patriotism. Vivien Leigh, no longer Scarlett O'Hara, was cast into the emotional steam laundry of Tennessee Williams' *A Streetcar Named Desire*. When it came to Hitchcock the sour note – and the high one – of *Strangers on a Train* was when a cigarette was stubbed out in a fried egg.

The nagging ulcer of the time was Korea. During the peace talks both sides were carrying out 'limited offensives' to gain additional bargaining counters. The limits were pretty high, an estimated ten thousand shells were showered on the Commonwealth Division on 4 November 1951, some six thousand of them on the King's Own Scottish Borderers. The desperate ferocity of the fighting could be judged by the fact that the guns of the valiant Scots had to be cooled with precious beer.

An outstanding hero of the engagement to the west of Unchon was Private 'Big Bill' Speakman, twenty-four years old and six and a half feet high. Slow to anger, he finally lost his temper with the three Chinese divisions trying to retake the positions they had lost a month earlier. Stuffing hand grenades into his pockets and every other available place, including the front of his shirt, he charged alone at the ridge the enemy were holding and delivered his cargo to good effect. It must have been a startling and demoralizing sight for Mao's warriors. Speakman was now joined by half a dozen other men, and together they made about fifteen such charges, so that, by this and other efforts of the Borderers, a whole Chinese division of about six thousand was left dead on the field. Speakman was subsequently twice wounded, once the enemy recovered enough from their surprise to shoot straight. The incident gained him the VC.

American casualties during the talks about peace at Panmunjom were heavier than they had been during the period of unlimited warfare, and back in the States an almost anarchic situation had arisen on the home front. John Foster Dulles, originally an ardent supporter of Truman's intervention in Korea, was among many who had rapidly changed position within a few months of the Chinese entry into the conflict. In contravention of the facts, he now maintained that he had counseled against the use of ground troops. Public expenditure had rocketed to $85,000,000,000 (£34,000,000,000) a year, and the average American was paying the highest taxes in the nation's history, with the additional prospect as the casualties mounted of paying for the war with either his own or his children's blood. Even the bedrock steel industry, essential to the country in war and peace had disintegrated. The Wage Stabilization Board, desperate to contain the inflation that

had been triggered off by the war, had decreed that there should be a wage increase of $17\frac{1}{2}$ cents per hour, with the cost being absorbed by the employers. In spite of record profits, the employers did not see it that way, and the work-force was not prepared to back down either. On 8 April 1952 Truman ordered the industry under government control, was accused by the press of attempting dictatorship, and was found by the Supreme Court – by six votes to three – to have made an illegal seizure. The industry was returned to private control, and ninety per cent of it promptly closed down. Apart from the six hundred and fifty thousand workers in the industry itself, a million others were also thrown out of work, and military production was reduced by twenty to thirty per cent for 1952, with three to six months needed to restore it to normal levels. Robert Lovett the Secretary of Defense bemoaned the 'calamity,' and said its effects were 'much worse than any bombing raids that anybody ever launched.' Some seventeen million tons of steel were lost. In the end, of course, both employers and employed got their money, but the situation did not quite get back to normal. The jolt had been just that much too great, and the Democratic supremacy of twenty years fell apart under the impact of a foreign war that had been started without the approval of Congress and a home situation precipitated the same way.

The stage was set for a real up-and-downer in that presidential election of 1952. All America was agog before its television sets for the first major political event to hit the nation's screens, and it was a contest that had the kind of personal edge which makes big money in a prize-fight. Though the viewers did not know it, Truman had twice offered the Democratic ticket to Eisenhower before the election in 1948. He had been willing to stand down himself, all to no avail, and now saw the man to whom he had offered this unbelievable opportunity accept it from the other party. The little haberdasher was considerably put out, the more so as it took some doing even to find out some remote link which would enable Eisenhower to qualify as a member of the GOP.

As his running mate, Eisenhower chose Richard Nixon, whose 'political philosophy generally coincided with my own.' Nixon was the coming young man at this juncture. He had been the joint sponsor of the McCarran–Nixon Internal Security Act of 1950, which had compelled all Communist-front organizations to register with the Attorney-General; excluded Communists from employment in defense plants; rendered it illegal to conspire to perform any act which would 'substantially contribute' to establish a dictatorship; debarred from entering America anyone ever affiliated with a totalitarian organization, or with organizations looking to the revolutionary overthrow of government; authorized deportation for aliens involved in suspect organizations; withheld passports from Communists; decreed that subversives should be interned in the event of war, and established a Subversive Activities Control Board. It had been vetoed by Truman, and passed by Congress over his head by

Above: Black immigrants to Britain arrive at Southampton.
Right: West Indian immigrants arrive at London's Heathrow airport. Black immigration to Britain increased dramatically in the 1950s.
Far right: Black mother in Britain attends funeral procession of King George VI in 1952.

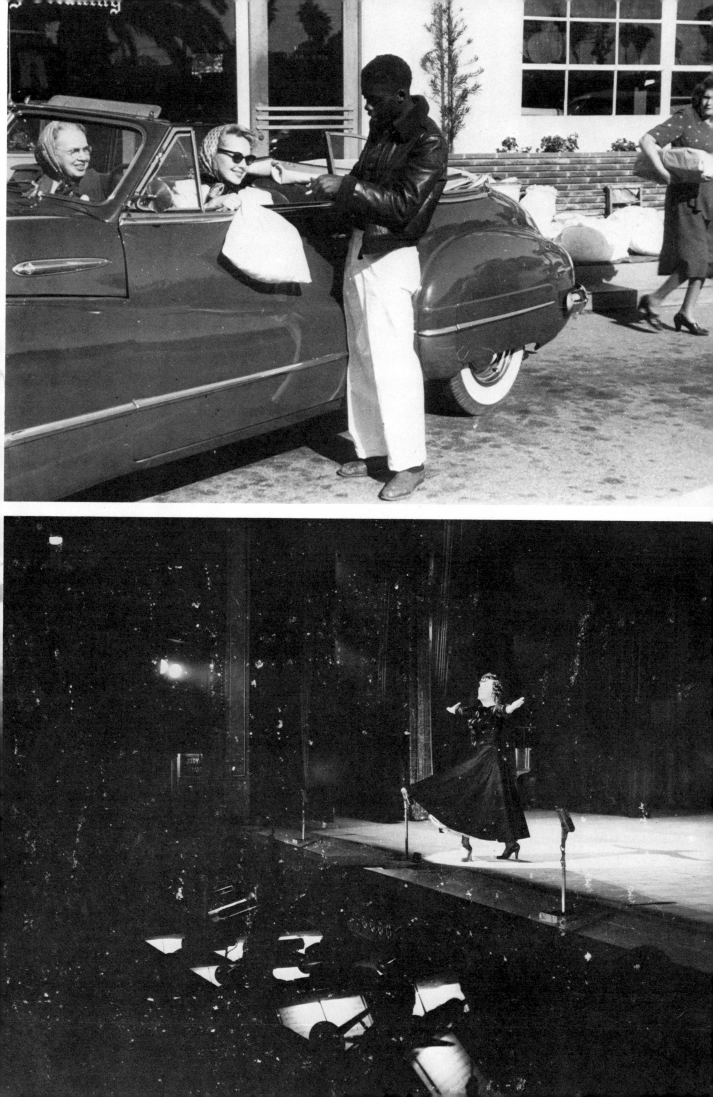

1952

To the Western world Korea was by now merely irksome. There was so much else afoot, so much else coming into the foreground to mark new directions. For Britain the landmark came typically with traditional ceremony. In February George VI died. The departure of this personally courageous man, respected for his fight against the handicap of a stammer and the pain of his long final illness, affected the British deeply. Through the war years he had visited blacked-out factories and bombed cities, decorated heroes and grieved with the bereaved. Now, as the lines of people waited in biting cold to pay a last tribute of respect at the lying-in-state in Westminster Hall, they said not only good-bye to him but to an era. The splendor of the setting, the richness of the royal purple and the watching guards, and the mystery of the veiled faces of the royal women as they passed

like shadows, were felt to be not only an end, but a preliminary to a new and potentially exciting reign.

There had, after all, never been an accession so exotically set as that of the young Queen. Thousands of miles from the decorous drawing-rooms of Buckingham Palace, she had heard the news in Kenya at Treetops. In this fantastic game look-out, built on pillars against which elephants tried the strength of their shoulders, and sited in a jungle clearing where the narrowed eyes of the great cats glinted in the darkness when night fell, Elizabeth II had succeeded to her throne. When she returned to London, she brought the sunlight of that remembered setting with her, and lit the greyness of London in winter with the freshness of her youth. She held the hope of her people of a new Elizabethan age.

Even the more material aspects of British life

Above: Senator Estes Kefauver helps push a supporter through New Hampshire snows during the primary election in which he sought nomination for President on the Democratic ticket.
Top right: Senator Kefauver had already made his name nationally through the investigation of organized crime when he announced his candidacy in January 1952.
Bottom right: Governor Adlai Stevenson of Illinois was Kefauver's principal opponent in the race for the Democratic nomination, which Stevenson won in the summer.

were beginning to improve. Visitors from the States at the beginning of the 1950s found people, in contrast to the prodigality they had left behind, as having absolutely nothing. They were, as one of them bluntly put it in his astonishment, 'dirt poor.' The new houses were going up – Macmillan, against all prognostications, was fulfilling the target figure of three hundred thousand – and they were being built with garages as a matter of course. In the older streets of smaller houses, built before automobiles were thought of, cars were parked outside house after house. Inside radios and televisions were becoming a common luxury, and in the kitchens, although food mixers were still felt to be a bit exotic, washing machines and refrigerators, and new-style ranges of cabinets were becoming standard. Utility furniture, produced in wartime to simple standards – and rediscovered in the 1970s for its stripped elegance of line – was being thrown out, and replaced by newer and lusher styles, and new fabrics were appearing for furnishings. Only one man in three now belonged to the same social class as his father had done, and in the upper ranks of the professions the upward movement was even more marked, for less than half the topnotch doctors, lawyers and university professors had parents who had reached the same heights.

National pride was boosted when on 2 May 1952 Britain opened the world's first jetliner passenger service by DeHavilland Comet between London and Johannesburg. In the atomic field something of the resentment felt against Britain's exclusion from America's bomb secrets by the Macmahon Act was purged when she detonated her own bomb on 3 October off northwest Australia aboard a navy ship. There had also been at the close of the previous year the reassuring recognition of Britain's primacy in early atom research when Sir John Cockcroft and Ernest Walton, both pupils of Lord Rutherford, had been awarded a Nobel Prize for their work in first splitting the atom by high-tension electric bombardment at the Cavendish laboratory in 1932.

At long last, in May 1952, peace had been signed between West Germany, the United States, Britain and France, and the Allied High Commission had been abolished. The way was open for normalization of relations with the old enemy, though there were still awkward reminders of the past, such as the publication of the diary of Anne Frank, and the rather ham-fisted revival by Germany of the old national anthem, made acceptable by the omission of the bit that everyone remembered only too well, the opening line: 'Deutschland, Deutschland über alles, über alles in der Welt.' Instead, only the third verse, beginning 'Unity, law and freedom for thee German Fatherland,' was legalized.

In the realm of popular song – still not really pop – there was also a German note this year. Vera Lynn, the 'Forces Sweetheart' of World War II recorded 'Auf wiedersehn sweetheart' with an appropriate backing of vocal soldiers, sailors and airmen, and became one of the first British artists to top the charts on both sides of the

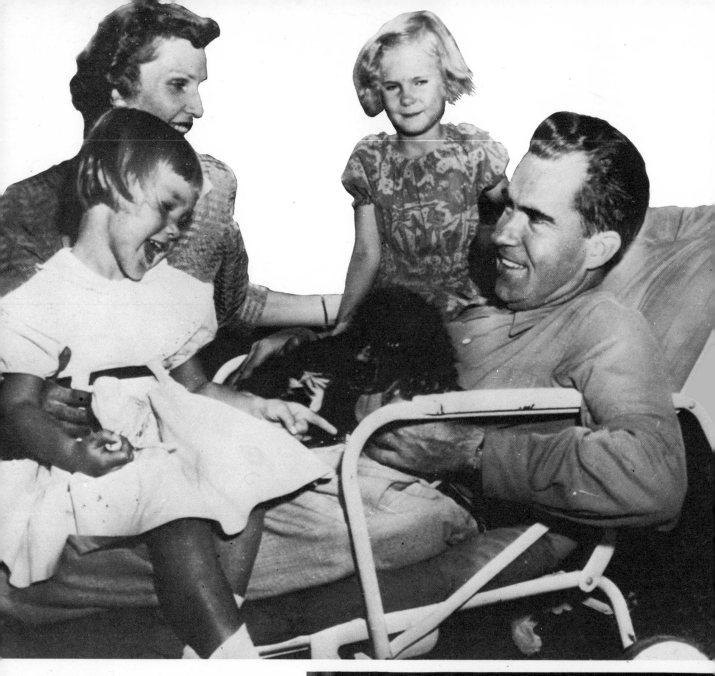

Atlantic. The most applauded male singers of the period tended to be simply good and loud, and it was partly the immense variation in tone he achieved which made the impact of Elvis Presley so great when he appeared. Al Martino, whose 'Here in my heart' echoed through every Woolworth record section in the land in 1952, was credited by one critic with 'a bellow to fill the Albert Hall.' Frankie Laine was not short on lung power either, and in the early 1950s he was the lone cowboy singer image, from 'Cry of the wild goose' in 1950 through his interpretation of 'High noon' (sung in the actual film by Tex Ritter), which led to his doing soundtracks for such movies as *Gunfight at the OK Corral*, and blasting the knobs off television sets with his rendering of the theme of the *Rawhide* series.

Pop was in this year merely an ambient spirit in search of a setting in which to materialize. It found it in a local Philadelphia program in 1952 called – of all 'square' names, to use the favorite word of the period – *Bandstand*, redolent of Victorian parks and seaside promenades. Songs were filmed in performance for the occasion, and as the actual record played the

Above: London's Caxton Hall after the wedding of Foreign Minister Anthony Eden to Clarissa Churchill, niece of the Prime Minister in August 1952.
Top left: Drainpipe trousers replaced Oxford bags even at Oxford in 1952.
Far left: A poster and telegram signifying the death of King George VI.
Left: King George's funeral cortege passes through Marble Arch in London.
Right: The lying-in-state of King George VI at Westminster Hall.
Far right: Citizens of King's Lynn in East Anglia note the passing of their King.

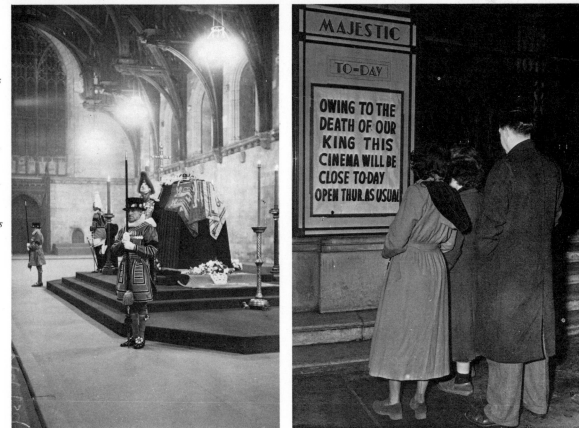

MAJESTIC

TO-DAY

OWING TO THE DEATH OF OUR KING THIS CINEMA WILL BE CLOSE TO-DAY OPEN THUR. AS USUAL

could be used once every six months,' but it was not that sort of frequency that the British had in mind as they flocked to the Post Offices to license their receivers. The number rose from one and a half million in 1952 to more than three million in 1953.

One of the pleasures of the new medium was the thrill of being able for the first time to see what it was really like under the sea. Jacques Cousteau, one of the inventors of the aqualung, which freed the underwater explorer from the limitations of vision and movement imposed by the old copper-top helmet and weighted boots of the traditional diver's suit, once more led the way. From 1951 in command of beautiful *Calypso*, he swam fishlike before the television cameras to guide the viewer over the great hulks of wrecks, through forests of seaweed and coral, and among clouds of tropical fish or the more sinister lumbering creatures of the lower depths of 'the silent world.' A world which, with the new recording apparatus, proved to be not so silent after all.

The 1950s saw great strides in the scientific exploration of the oceans. In 1951 a submarine mountain range was surveyed which ran from Wake Island to Hawaii, a thousand miles long and a hundred wide, and rising in its highest peaks to fourteen thousand feet. In the Atlantic work was beginning on the 'ridge,' through the center of which wells a constant rising of lava forcing the Americas fractionally away from Europe and Africa, and showing how over the

aeons the continents had been made. Even in the 1970s the record of the Soviet *Vityaz* in 1957 in plumbing the western Pacific's Mariana Trench to thirty-six thousand, one hundred and ninety-eight feet – some seven miles – had not been broken.

Yet the underwater feat which most captured the headlines in the 1950s was the patient search by a South African professor which had begun in 1938. In that year Professor J B L Smith, of Rhodes University, had heard that a fisherman had had an unusual catch in the waters north-west of Madagascar. He suspected what it might have been, but rapid decomposition in the blazing sun of the region left him no hope of proof. Never mind, what had happened once could happen again. He had leaflets printed showing what the creature he was so anxious to find looked like, and fourteen years passed. Then, in December 1952 a native fisherman hauled aboard his vessel a strange creature. Later he described it as 'a fish with arms.' It was the size of a small human-being, five feet long, weighed about a hundred pounds, and was a brilliant steel-blue.

Unfortunately he had not seen one of the professor's leaflets and his first thought was getting it to market. There it caught the eye of Captain Eric Hunt, and the professor's luck changed. Captain Hunt *had* seen a leaflet. He accordingly gave the specimen the requisite bath of formalin to preserve it, and in no time at all the professor was flying back in triumph to

Above: Chancellor of the Exchequer R A Butler and his wife leave their home in Smith Square prior to the presentation of the first peacetime Conservative Budget in March 1952.
Above right: Billy Graham, popular American evangelist, in London.
Above far right: Some of Graham's audience pray for redemption.
Right: Professor Millot examines a specimen of the coelacanth, a fish caught off Madagascar in 1952 which was thought to have been extinct for 50 million years.
Far right: Billy Graham preaches to a throng in Harringay Arena.

South Africa with his prize aboard a Dakota military transport provided by the government. His find was a prime specimen of Coelacanth, a creature deemed by scientists to have been extinct for at least fifty million years. As a bridging link between fish and amphibious reptiles, when life first took to the land, evolutionists believed it was a long remote human ancestor. To watching millions, it seemed as if Conan Doyle's *Lost World* had been discovered under the sea, and the Loch Ness monster took on a new lease of credibility.

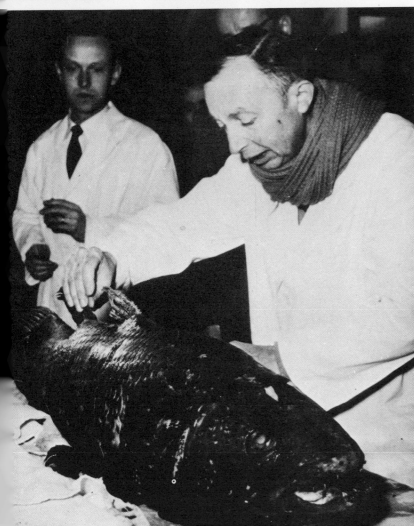

One talking-point in Britain in 1952 was the analysis of the census taken in 1951, the first since the war. Before the war the sight of a face of any 'color' – yellow, brown or black – had been enough to turn heads in surprise anywhere outside the area of the London colleges and embassies, or in the port districts. Now, for the first time, Britain had an identifiable colored population. It was small. Those who had been born outside the United Kingdom in all numbered only seventeen hundred thousand. Of these about half were from the Continent – mainly refugee Poles, Russians or Germans – or expatriate Americans – and some two-thirds of the remainder were from the Irish Republic. Only the remaining third of this second fraction came from the independent Commonwealth countries or the colonies. The greater mobility of the postwar world, the prosperity of the new Britain, and the appeals of undertakings short of labor, had begun to attract workers for the buses and the railways and the hospitals, and for industries where the pay and conditions no longer brought in eager applicants among the white population.

Mobility was also the key to a shift in America's color problem too. In the twenty years from 1940 the number of black workers migrating to war industries and those of the prosperous peace had increased from under three million to over seven. Moving from areas in the south where norms were fixed to places in the north where they were less rigid, was unsettling. More sophisticated blacks in the northern cities found, when confronted by the newcomers from the south, how far they themselves had in fact moved on, and it stimulated them to moving that bit further which would take them to full equality. Adding an edge was the sense of superiority that they could now feel, not only to fellow blacks but to some of the white newcomers to industrial life who were emerging from the hillbilly backwoods country.

Britain was not as yet worried by her colored immigrants. Indeed the popular press in 1952 was more concerned with the aftermath of one man's personal color problem in reverse. The youthful chief of the Bamangwato tribe, Seretse Khama, had studied law in Britain and while there married an English typist, Ruth Williams. His uncle, Tshekedi Khama, regent of Botswana during his nephew's minority, objected strongly to a white bride. The tribe objected too, until they realized that Tshekedi, an upright but somewhat harsh man, was likely to become their permanent ruler. The British government, one step behind events and subject to pressure from South Africa, permanently excluded Seretse from the chieftainship in 1952. This ensured festering discontent among the tribesmen for whom nothing that Seretse or the government could do would be recognized as disinheriting a true chief so long as he lived. Not until 1956 was Seretse allowed to return, and almost another decade passed before the government saved its face by allowing him to become first Prime Minister, then President of the newly independent republic, with a knighthood in the Order of the British Empire to set the seal on the reconciliation.

Above: Gene Kelly in Singin' in the Rain, *the most successful MGM musical of the 1950s.*
Far left: Milton Berle, famous American television comedian, as Cleopatra. 'Uncle Miltie' was the most popular television personality in the States in the early 1950s.
Left: Judy Garland has a standing ovation at New York's Palace Theater after she completed a 19-week stand in 1952. The audience sang 'Auld Lang Syne' to the famous singer.

America, too, had her colonial problems. An armed revolt in Puerto Rico had been quelled, but nationalism still seethed. In the winter of 1950 a couple of disgruntled Puerto Ricans took a trip to Washington. They were armed, though not apparently specifically on an assassination trip, when they learned that the President was 'camping out' in Blair House. The White House had become so rickety that Margaret Truman's piano had disappeared through the floor of the upstairs living-room, and re-building was now in progress. Blair House fronted the street in a much more vulnerable way than the official residence, and the sight of it, with only a couple of guards outside was too tempting to ignore. They tried to shoot their way in to where Truman and his wife were upstairs, dressing to go out and dedicate a statue to Sir John Dill, the British representative on the Combined Chiefs of Staff who had made such a hit with the Americans during the war.

Hearing sounds which she did not immediately identify as shots, Mrs Truman looked out of the window to see one of the secret servicemen crumple. 'Harry,' she cried, in the kind of astonishment that was still possible in the 1950s, 'someone's shooting our policemen.' Truman instinctively rushed to look, and only the dedicated shout of the other guard: 'Get back, get back!' prevented a preview of the tragedy in Dallas. As a result of this incident Puerto Rico became an 'associated free state' or 'common-wealth' of the United States, perhaps rather sooner than it otherwise would.

Not a colony still, but very much part of the American scene on the Pacific side, were the Philippines. Regarded as in the front line of

defense against Communist attack, they yet had within them a Communist movement – the Hukbalahap – waging a guerrilla war which there had been an all-out attempt to eradicate. Colonel Ed Lansdale, the original 'ugly' American, had been singularly effective in operating against the Communists, whose strength lay less in nationalism than in the need for land reform, and 1952 saw the capture of the head of Communist propaganda in the islands. It was the sort of item that fueled the fire of McCarthyism, for he was an American, a native of New York state, who had served in the American air force as a staff sergeant in the war, and had first landed at Leyte in action against the Japanese in 1945. It had been after his de-mobilization that he had returned to the island to organize the Communist guerrilla move-ment. Such successes had their embarrassments, but they were successes, and Britain, too, saw the tide turn for her in 1952 in her own private battle against Communism in Malaya.

The outbreak of attacks on planters which began in 1948 in Malaya and developed, as usual in such campaigns, into an onslaught of terror against the native peoples of the country, was never honored by the name of 'war.' Insurance claims do not get paid in a war; accordingly the hostilities became an 'emerg-ency,' and three-quarters of the total casualties were among the men of the greatly enlarged police force.

It seemed that a complete takeover by the Chinese Communists attempting the infiltration was almost inevitable. Hundreds of thousands of Chinese already in Malaya had fled the towns in the Japanese wartime invasion and settled

Above: Sugar Ray Robinson was as fast on his feet as a dancer when he opened at a Parisian night club as he was as a boxer.
Above right: A strapless creation by Jacques Fath in his 1952 Paris show.

precariously as illegal squatters in the country-side, and they had everything to gain by co-operation. That the Communists did not win was due to the courage of Malays, Chinese and British who worked together in an offensive which had a curiously personal nature. They knew their individual opponents on the other side, not only by name but by character, and often by having met them. A number were women. Lee Meng, the top Communist courier, was tracked down at the heart of her espionage network by Irene Lee, a Chinese policewoman whose husband had been killed by terrorists. (Irene Lee had the odd drawback of being too neatly svelte in her Chinese dress, so that the problem of where to conceal a gun for her pro-tection was considerable. It was only solved by providing her with one false bosom, and hiding a very small weapon where the other would have been.)

Other characters involved were equally strik-ing; there was Sir Gerald Templer himself who was in charge of operations, an elusive Chinese Communist, Osman China, noted for going into battle with a volume of Shakespeare under his arm, and the man to whom he ultimately sur-rendered, Special Branch officer David Storrier. With typical Chinese acumen, when Osman surrendered he brought with him enough of his fellow Communists to collect $80,000 (£32,000) in rewards to take with him into retirement.

The backbone was finally taken out of the Communist call to arms by settling some six hundred thousand Chinese squatters on land of their own in New Villages, protected against the terrorists. Their removal, with their bedding and cooking pots and wailing children was carried out by patient British soldiers who helped to carry everything to the waiting lorries, and encouraged the reluctant by pointing out that the first-comers at the new site would have the prime pick of the plots. Captured 'terrorists,' for the most part villagers who had been them-selves terrified into joining the Communists, were rehabilitated in camps where they were given language lessons and tuition in book-keeping, taught how to run a vegetable garden with a few poultry, or how to earn a living by making clothes, or repairing shoes and bicycles.

Precautions to keep them inside the camps were hardly needed, and their statements as to why they had surrendered and how they had been treated were broadcast or dropped as leaflets in the field. Comically enough, one of the chief complaints of the Communist rank and file was the shortage of women in the jungle and the unfair distribution of those there were. 'I surrendered when my commanding officer took away my girl friend,' struck a chord in many a breast. When reformed, the rehabilitees were settled in a safe area or might even be sent as members of the touring companies formed to put over the democratic message in dramatic form to the villagers. One successful piece, *New Life*, portrayed a peasant family in which the son was attracted to join the terrorists, but later came to see the error of his ways.

The nationalist element in the Communist appeal was finally eliminated in 1957 by the grant of independence to Malaya, and the emergency was finally declared to have come to an end in 1960. So great was the popular re-joicing that the victory parade took three hours to pass.

Above: Rocky Graziano staggers on the ropes of the Chicago Stadium after he was knocked out by Sugar Ray Robinson in the middleweight championship in April 1952.

1953

In northwest Europe 1953 was the year of natural, rather than man-made havoc. In the worst floods for half a millennium the chief sufferers were Holland, with nearly one thousand five hundred dead, and England, where the toll was three hundred and seven including seventeen Americans. A 'deep depression' in the Atlantic was so routine a phrase that no one took a great deal of notice until, as it moved to the northern end of the North Sea on the last day of January, the wind was screaming across Scotland at one hundred and thirteen miles per hour – the highest velocity ever recorded in Britain. Remorselessly the sea was driven down before it to the bottleneck of the English Channel. The water piled up, in combination with the high spring tides created by the united 'pull' of the Sun and the Moon at this time of year, to form a storm-tide of vast proportions.

That night it would have been better for the flat lands of East Anglia if there had been no sea defenses. The sea welled up behind them until, rising at the peak of the tide a good one-and-a-half feet above any anticipated level, the effect was like the burst of a dam. A great irresistible torrent coursed over the countryside with no time for warning to save the cattle, no time even to save human life. In Norfolk the tidal wave which swept through King's Lynn was seven feet high as the River Ouse, forced back up its course, rose to the record level of thirty-one feet. The concrete blocks of the sea walls were now dashed aside like a child's plastic bricks, and tremendous waves undermined the foundations of brick-built houses and carried more lightly-built bungalows bodily away. At a nearby air base American servicemen and their families were among the casualties. The swollen Thames itself, thrust back on London in full spate, tested the capital's defenses to the utmost. They held, but only just. The nightmare thought of an underground railway system under water, and district after district flooded 'next time' led to the construction of the barrage at Woolwich due for completion in 1978.

London and the whole of southeast England are tilting into the sea, just as the western Highlands of Scotland are rising, and the warning posters for Londoners on the subway walls at the time of the high tides reflect a long-term phenomenon. There is a pattern of climatic

Above: King Hussein of Jordan decorates a member of his famed Arab Legion.
Top right: Flood damage in Kent killed thousands of cattle unable to make it to high ground.
Center right: A boat searches for the stranded residents of Canvey Island after the English flood of 1953.
Bottom right: Floodwaters rise to ten feet during the 1953 flood in Sittingbourne, Kent.

change, and of emergence and submergence of the land masses in this part of the world, a subject fascinatingly explored by Alexander McKee in his *History under the Sea*. Not so long ago historians scoffed at the narratives of old inundations as wild impossible exaggerations. Yet the Saxons, ancestors of so many English and Americans, left the Continent of Europe some time after AD 400 in part because their population had grown, but also because much of their land had been lost to the sea. Now this mythical event was becoming clearer. In the fourteenth century, in England itself, there had been pleas for reduced taxation because the lands the tax was assessed on had disappeared. In the 1950s cosmic considerations became a matter of practical history and the future of the human race, instead of being confined to speculations about the fate of the dinosaurs.

Another new influence on the scene in 1953 was James Bond. Until his appearance this year, the popular hero had been the detective – not that he altogether disappeared. Agatha Christie's play featuring her little Belgian sleuth Hercule Poirot, *The Mousetrap*, took the London boards in 1952 and was still running at her death in 1976. But, change was in the air. Raymond Chandler felt it. In his last novel, *The Long Goodbye*, published in England – the country of his schoolboy years – in 1953, he was exploring in a new way the problems of the nature of friendship between men, and love between men and women. It was a way he did not seem able to work through. The trend of the times was in other directions.

Bond's creator, Ian Fleming, was the son of an army officer, owed his education to Eton, Sandhurst, and the universities of Munich and Geneva, and had worked for Reuters, and in merchant banking and stockbroking. In World War II he had been personal assistant to the British Director of Naval Intelligence. The new hero was not enlisted in war against the criminal who committed murder, the erosion of support for the death penalty in real-life legislation had taken some of the zest out of this chase anyway. He was committed to the 'cold war,' which he pursued in the hottest of forms: with the '00' in his Secret Service number 007 indicating that he was 'licensed to kill,' he was now a 'murderer' himself. Sleeping with a woman was no longer to be an insuperable bar to bringing about her death. The books in which Bond featured began to 'sell' from about 1956. Reflection was out, action was all. As Chandler himself wrote in a review of Fleming's *Diamonds are Forever*, 'I don't like James Bond's thinking. His thoughts are superfluous.' The smart, slick, and ruthless agent took over the scene. until the reaction of the 1960s with John Le Carré and his more naturalistically seedy spies.

On the film front 1953 was a happy blockbuster of a year. British films included *Genevieve*, in which those who did not care for vintage cars could concentrate on the exquisite Kay Kendall and the catchy theme tune, and *The Cruel Sea*, a realization of Monsarrat's novel of World War II convoys in which Jack Hawkins was as splendid a Royal Navy hero as ever kept

a stiff upper lip. It was a year in which an international flavor came as a relish for the general public and not only for the *cognoscenti*: the Anglo-Italian *Little World of Don Camillo*, Ingmar Bergman's *The Man with the Umbrella* from Sweden, and Jacques Tati's glorious romp *Monsieur Hulot's Holiday*. Hollywood was firing back against the menace of television on all cylinders. Victor Mature jutted agonized brows in 3-D Cinemascope in the Biblical epic *The Robe*; spines were chilled by science-fiction thrillers – *It Came from Outer Space* and *The Beast from Twenty Thousand Fathoms*; and the great outdoors came inside with Alan Kidd's super-western pic *Shane*, and Gary Cooper in *High Noon*, not to speak of the Cecil B De Mille's glorious spectacle *The Greatest Show on Earth*. America's vote for 'Star of Tomorrow' went unerringly to Marilyn Monroe.

Dancing, which had still effervesced in the energetic gyrations of the jitterbug in 1952, became a little less frenetic, the determination to find something new coming up with the Bunny Hop, also designed to make older competitors on the floor breathless as well as ridiculous to irreverent youngsters. Skirts had paused at eleven inches off the ground, with a lift to a couple of inches higher in London's fashion belt, but in Paris, desperate to keep the French inspirational lead, Dior swung them up to sixteen inches, though such daring was not widely accepted until the following year. During the whole of the year, designers were inclined to let science go to their heads, for the kind of construction that once required elaborate canvas stiffening, supplemented by whalebone and wire, had been made possible for the mass market by the new bonded backings (made like felt).

Songs tended to spill over from the film screen: the theme from *Moulin Rouge* and 'Wonderful Copenhagen' from Danny Kaye's *Hans Christian Andersen*. A rather special example of this was the melody from Charlie Chaplin's film *Limelight*, set to words as 'Eternally.' Chaplin's Communist sympathies and refusal to adopt American citizenship, made him Hollywood's most unloved famous movie-maker but by 1971 he belatedly received his only Oscar for the *Limelight* score. The happiest sensation of the year was the real-life comeback of Frank Sinatra. At the beginning of the decade the headlines had him 'SWOONING INTO OBSCURITY,' but in 1953 he not only topped the charts with the appropriately titled 'Young at Heart,' but carried off an acting Oscar for his performance in *From Here to Eternity*. Every man pondering whether to order a hairpiece walked a little taller. On the low note of the song scale, it was impossible to escape anywhere from the endless question, how much is 'That Doggie in the Window?' and the year's end was made saccharine with Tommie Connor's 'I Saw Mommy Kissing Santa Claus.'

A good antidote, the equivalent of a cold shower, could be found in the theater, listening to the verse convolutions of T S Eliot's *The Confidential Clerk*, the British audience uncertain whether it was correct to voice openly their relief that it sounded so remarkably like

DAILY SKETCH 2d

Townsend and Margaret meet again—dinner with the Wills's deep in the forest

WINDSOR WEEK-END

Prince

MARGARET 'AT PRE

Now they're te her cousin's

PRINCE

No annou 'at pre

CAR DRIVE

Daily Mail

NOW THEY MEET IN THE COU

Princess and Townsend spend week-end with Mrs Wills

NO STATEMENT YET ON HER FUTURE

AS YOU WERE AT MARGATE

POLICE DOGS ON GUARD AT THE LONELY RETREAT

They had 10-minute talk alone

CATAPULT HE JET IN SEA

Left: Archbishop Makarios on a visit to Cyprus during the British occupation of his island.
Bottom left: The Shah of Iran and Queen Soraya in London for a state dinner.
Right: General Sir John Glubb, Glubb Pasha, the commander of the Arab Legion, who was subsequently deposed by King Hussein of Jordan.
Below: Scene outside Holloway Prison in London when Ruth Ellis was executed. Her hanging aroused a movement against capital punishment in Britain.

Top left: Evacuation by tram was one technique of escaping the 1953 English floods.
Center left: Secretary of State John Foster Dulles with Harold Stassen are greeted by Selwyn Lloyd on their arrival in Britain in 1953.
Bottom left: The Shah of Iran is congratulated after the overthrow of his Prime Minister Mohammed Mossadeq.
Right: Prime Minister Winston Spencer Churchill was aging yet still defiant in 1954. He retired a year later.
Below: Queen Mary's coffin on the Mall in London is followed by the Dukes of Edinburgh, Windsor, Gloucester and Kent.

prose, and in America Robert Anderson gave a modern twist in *Tea and Sympathy* to the 'young Woodley' theme, by making the boarding school boy uncertain whether he might be a homosexual until the master's wife gave a practical demonstration that he was not.

In television 1953 was the year that Lime Grove took a shot in the arm from America. The shadow of a coming commercial channel loomed ever larger over the BBC, and it was decided that Ronnie Waldman, the Head of Light Entertainment, should take a look at what was being done in the States. His American counterparts, bemused by his title, wondered if their next visitor might be the BBC's Head of Heavy Entertainment, which would have been an apt name for much of the Corporation's existing output. When Waldman saw Eleanor Roosevelt on *What's My Line*, he felt rather as if he had seen Britain's dowager Queen Mary – who died that year – in the line-up of 'Bluebell Girls' in Paris, and then began to ask himself why Britain should not have the same acceptance of the importance of the medium. He decided there was no reason, and went ahead from there.

In one respect, however, American television men must have been green with envy of Britain. The head of BBC drama needed to commission new plays and adaptations of existing material to fill the small screen's voracious mouth, and Michael Barry had been given his own special budget for the purpose. It was all of £250 ($625). In a fit of recklessness, he blew the lot on Nigel Kneale, who turned out to be the world's number one shiver-maker. When the sci-fi serial, *The Quatermass Experiment,* was showing, the pubs and clubs without a set saw their takings plummet, and when his adaptation of Orwell's *1984* was shown in 1954 a quarter of the popu-

lation watched on the single channel in fascinated horror. Politicians and press tried to prevent a repeat – unsuccessfully – and when the fuzzy recorded version of the live performance was re-shown in 1977 it still gripped the audience with the same fascination. Strangely, though, it was as if *1984* were now itself in the past: what was to come true in the story had already done so, and, for the rest, the century had taken a new line.

Greatest of all entertainments of the year, however, was the Coronation of Elizabeth II in the first week of June. As a preliminary fanfare, the news came through on Coronation Eve that the world's highest mountain had been climbed by the expedition led by John Hunt. New Zealander Edmund Hillary and the Nepalese Tensing had reached the summit of Everest together on 29 May.

The Coronation itself had everything – religious ceremonial, traditional pageantry, and a family cast that was at once remotely glamorous and humanly loved. It was a once in a lifetime, rather than the 'once in six months' occasion that the Archbishop of Canterbury had allowed television, and the nation watched breathless. For the first time in history the sovereign's people were able to see the mystery of a crowning as if they were themselves in the Abbey; much better in fact than any of those privileged enough to be there, for they saw it from all angles as the drama moved from one place to another in the gorgeousness of the setting. There were other advantages, too, for they could eat while they watched, instead of having to smuggle a sandwich inside their coronets, as the peers were said to have been forced to do.

Some of the luckier people, with accommodation along the route, were able to have the best

Above: Sherpa Tensing, who was instrumental in the British ascent of Mount Everest.
Top left: Dylan Thomas, famous Welsh poet, just before his death in New York in 1953.
Left: Colonel Hunt (with flag) and Edmund Hillary arrive in London after their conquest of Mount Everest in 1953.
Right: Sir Winston and Lady Churchill on their way to Queen Elizabeth's Coronation in 1953.

of both worlds and watch the procession pass in all its color before turning to see the ceremony – still only in black-and-white – on the screen. A wonderful procession it was, too. The crowds lining the streets vociferously cheered in the new reign, despite the changeable 'Queen's weather,' which lifted to sunshine here and there, and allowed a shaft or two of natural glory to shine on the new monarch inside the Abbey itself. Fending off the rain with the welcome aid of the new plastics, with children peering round the damp blue serge columns of policemen's legs, the good-humored legions found their own favorites in the procession. Among the Commonwealth contingent the palm went to the magnificent, smiling six-foot Queen Salote of Tonga. Leaving the hood of her carriage down, she sat in the rain, like the people energetically returning her waves.

The celebrations were unending. In the more

Left: Queen Elizabeth's golden coach at Horse Guards Parade during the Coronation.
Top: The Archbishop of Canterbury about to place the Crown of St Edward on the head of HM the Queen.
Above: The crowned Queen on her throne surrounded by peers of the Realm.

matey areas of Cockney London street parties were held, with bunting criss-crossing from window to window. There were fireworks and bonfires, and the traditional review of the fleet at Spithead. Coronation mugs and every other possible kind of souvenir on which the royal portrait and arms could be crammed overflowed from the shops. It was a marvel that they could ever all disappear, and every household must surely have bought at least a cupboard-full and every overseas visitor a trunk-full.

In the general rejoicings not much attention was paid to the end of the discussions at Panmunjom, which came as an epilogue to the main coronation events in July. According to Arthur Larson, special assistant to Eisenhower, and the President's chief speech writer, Eisenhower revealed to him that the impasse in the negotiations had only been broken when he informed the North Koreans, Chinese and Russians 'through various secret channels' that unless progress were made previous limits on targets and weapons would be abandoned and that 'if we saw fit, we would use the atomic bomb.'

A more likely moment for the first breakthrough came on a Sunday evening in the first days of March 1953. Staying at his country home just outside Moscow, an old man did not call as usual for his late-night drink of tea. His temper was such that no one would venture in, and his old housekeeper was called on as the only one who could safely go and check if he were all right and nothing was amiss.

Above: Smog in London was a problem attacked by the government. This scene shows the Battersea Power Station belching out smoke as a steam locomotive passes by.
Top left: The Queen leads the procession through Westminster Abbey after her Coronation flanked by her Maids of Honor.
Right: Sir Winston Churchill leaves for Buckingham Palace to tender his resignation to the new Queen, a formality required of him as Prime Minister. She did not accept and Churchill remained in office.
Left: Dean Martin and Jerry Lewis were an extremely popular song and comedy team before they went their separate ways in the mid-1950s.

Above: Queen Elizabeth's Golden Coach used during her Coronation.
Above right: Guardsmen march to Westminster Abbey during the Coronation.
Right: The Coronation procession at Marble Arch.
Far right bottom: Guardsmen return to Buckingham Palace after the Coronation.

She reported that her master was sleeping soundly on the floor of his room, having apparently fallen from the sofa he used instead of a bed. It was a sleep from which they could not wake him. Dependent on no man's vote, and with the lives of millions at his whim, the most powerful man in the world had lost a little blood from the circuits of his brain – a cerebral haemorrhage had left Stalin paralyzed in his right arm and left leg, and silenced the deep rasp of his voice.

His nervous colleagues kept a round-the-clock vigil in pairs – Lavrenky Beria and Georgiy Malenkov, and Kaganovich and Kliment Voroshilov, and, on the unpopular night shift, the two considered as least likely to succeed to the power of the man they watched – Bulganin and Khrushchev. The macabre mingled with pathos as Stalin's young daughter, Svetlana, was sent for from school and comforted by a gruff, kindly Khrushchev. The watchers in the sick-room hardly knew which they dreaded most – the patient's recovery, or the in-fighting which would follow his death – with the exception of Beria, who was confident of snatching the abandoned crown.

For a while Stalin recovered consciousness

enough to shake by the hand, using the un-injured left one, the men to whom he had clung in these last hours before the final mindless, sightless struggle for breath, which turned his bold features to a bloated purple travesty racked by stertorous sound. A reign of terror was drawing to its close. Never again would Stalin come here, driving at speed from Moscow in dread of ambush on the way. Never again would the endless dinners be held at which every dish had to be 'tasted' by someone else before the host himself dare eat, and every bottle be proved innocent before he dare drink. No longer would the guests have to force them-selves to wakefulness because to fall asleep meant coming 'to a bad end' in punishment for their bad manners; or be made to dance the gopak or make themselves otherwise ridiculous to feed Stalin's humor; or to drink deep – per-haps to the number of degrees they erred in estimating the temperature in the dark Russian night outside – so that they might betray them-selves in their cups.

It was almost over. Beria, the secret service chief whom Stalin had seemed to trust, almost alone of those about him, openly mocked the helpless hulk of the old dictator. Then, suddenly, Stalin seemed to stir again. Beria was on his

Below: Dean Martin and Jerry Lewis feigning fear at the sight of a London crowd during their British tour in 1953.
Right: Josef Stalin, whose death in 1953 helped to end the Korean War and start a new era of Western relations with the USSR.
Bottom right: Lavrenti P Beria, Stalin's secret police chief, was purged and subsequently killed soon after Stalin's death.
Far right top: Maureen Connelly, known as Little Mo, was the American girl who captivated audiences while winning the 1953 Wimbledon tennis championship.

knees in a moment, kissing his master's hand. But the moment faded, and he drove away – when Stalin at last lay dead – with a triumphant smile. He did not smile for long. Khrushchev suspected, perhaps rightly, that Stalin had feared Beria, but had not known how to get rid of him. More likely, Stalin knew that the only way was through the legal joint action of the presidium. It was a method he dare not use because, unlike Khrushchev, he looked ahead and saw that, once used, it was a weapon that could be turned against himself.

Undeterred by such considerations, Khrushchev set about organizing the downfall of Beria and the rise of Khrushchev. The chubbily amiable Malenkov had become the front man of the new government, as both Premier and First Secretary of the party. Beria had settled for the behind-the-scenes controlling power as Minister of Internal Affairs, which post now included also the function of the former Minister of State Security, the two ministries having been merged. Khrushchev, within ten days of Stalin's death, had exercized sufficient pressure to have the post of first secretary taken from Malenkov, though he delayed until the autumn his own assumption of the post. At the same time he was busily canvassing the rest of the presidium on their attitude to Beria, and swinging the waverers into line. Finally he detached Malenkov from Beria by telling tales of steps Beria was

secretly taking to discredit Malenkov with the people. At last everyone was agreed that Beria must go: it was a question of how.

To avoid Beria having any suspicion of what was going on, the evening before the coup was devoted to a night out for the boys at the opera. All the conspirators, and Beria himself, went together in a smiling body to the Bolshoi Theater. The next day the trap was to be sprung in the only place where Beria would never expect an attack – at a governmental session in the Kremlin. Sure of the protection of his strong Chekist bodyguard which always kept watch outside the 'cabinet' room, and of the rule which ensured that all weapons were handed in by anyone else entering the precincts, Beria was in arrogant good humor.

The presidium met. The membership had been enlarged for the occasion, because of the supposed requirements of the agenda, and included Voroshilov, as well as other top military men who had entered the plot as more than willing co-partners. The first item on the agenda, put forward by Khrushchev himself, was 'the matter of Beria.' The words fell on the astounded security chief like a kick in the pit of the stomach. Turning round to Khrushchev, sitting immediately next to him on his left, he grabbed his hand agitatedly: 'What's going on, Nikita? What's this you're mumbling about?' The indictment went steadily on from speaker to speaker, the main charge being Beria's attempt to establish arbitrary rule, though a secondary charge also included the surprising allegation that in 1939 he had (indirectly) worked for British Intelligence. Malenkov was so seized by panic when it came to his turn to sum up that Khrushchev

Bottom left: Lady Docker's fabulous limousine and luxurious life was a striking contrast to the drab existence of most Britons in the 1950s.
Top left: The floodlit Westminster Abbey in 1953.
Left: Cameraman and his subject experiment with color television in 1953. All commercial sets were monochrome in the 1950s.
Below: A British family watch an experimental color television set.

had to step in. The motion should then have been formally put, but Malenkov could stand the strain no longer. Frantically he pushed the secret button which summoned the military leaders waiting in an adjoining room. They had not obeyed the rule about surrendering arms, and it was with a purposeful 'Hands up!' that Marshal Zhukov advanced on Beria, who was promptly marched off under strict guard.

Arranging the custody of a man who was himself controller of the prisons and the police, and in ordering the trial of a man who was in charge of Russia's entire legal system, presented problems. But the conspirators were in no mood to be baulked; the trial was held and the bullets thudded home. Investigation and interrogation had turned up more than enough evidence to convict Beria on every possible count, including enough charges of rape to have provided most men with a full-time occupation.

Beria's arrest had been in June 1953; his execution did not follow until December. The Korean armistice was finally signed in July that year: with events in the USSR in such turmoil there was no inducement to look abroad to foreign ventures. Weapons and other hardware which might be needed for internal use were not likely to be exported to North Korean allies and Chinese friends. The quantity and the quality of those received had also begun to be doubtful: the Russian MIG fighters, for example, had been completely outclassed in the later stages of the war by the American Sabre. It was time for peace in everybody's book.

The chief problem was one of face. Almost half the Chinese and Korean prisoners held in the south were refusing to go home, but their governments could not bring themselves to admit such a thing might be true. Synghman Rhee part solved and part increased the problem by letting loose all the twenty-five thousand in his personal custody. There were cries of 'bad faith' from the other side, but at last on 2 July 1953 the armistice was signed.

Among the United Nations prisoners who came home was Lieutenant-Colonel Carne of the Gloucesters, over forty pounds lighter from lack of food and the strain of solitary confinement. The official citation for his VC rightly said of this gently patient man, whose hobby in retirement is still fishing, that he had shown 'powers of leadership which can seldom have been surpassed in the history of our army.'

In retrospect the Korean War is no longer regarded as a Russian attempt to conquer the world, but as a 'miscalculation' and a sideshow. Yet close on six million Americans were involved either directly or indirectly in the fighting, and some thirty-five thousand were killed and one hundred thousand wounded. On the other side, some four million Koreans were rendered homeless, and some two million North Koreans and Chinese were killed. The disparity in casualties is significant. The indifference of the Chinese command in throwing in their troops to gain a position at any cost marked the dehumanization of war to a new stage: napalm was used against them as if against an insect plague.

What captured the mind of America, however, in the new-style war was the concept of brainwashing, from the Chinese *hsi nao* (wash-brain). Some seven thousand Americans had been taken prisoner, of whom about a third had died (admittedly in very bad conditions), and none had escaped (again admittedly in conditions which gave them no chance and no goal to escape to). Harder to explain was the collaboration of one in three of the men with their captors, from accusing the American command of practicing germ warfare to the writing of letters home acknowledging they had been on the wrong side. Using the methods developed by the KGB, the Chinese had for the first time in warfare made a systematic application of a formal technique of extracting information, reducing the prisoners to apathy, and turning them against their government to the extent of being able to use them for propaganda purposes.

Emphasizing the degree to which the men were at their mercy, the Chinese had humiliated them by enforcing obedience to senseless petty rules, degraded them by preventing their practice of personal hygiene and housing them in verminous cells, and had reduced their physical condition by starvation, deprivation of sleep, forced marches, and even drugs to induce illness. As a refinement, there was sensory deprivation (SD), in which continuous light or darkness, loose clothing which reduces the ability to feel, and noise had been used. It was perhaps less surprising that so many gave in, than that so many resisted. Even some of those who gave in kept the inner spark of resistance alive by making gestures when photographed which had an obscene significance lost on their captors (even though many of the interrogators had been educated in America), or wrote their letters home with references to imaginary relatives which showed that they were not writing freely.

The scientists, however, were intrigued. The Turkish contingent in Korea, for example, had utterly refused to collaborate, and had come through in remarkably good shape. Finding out why, and how all recruits could be battle-hardened for future wars became a new branch of psychological science during the 1950s, and by the end of the decade considerable progress had been made, not only in the more negative aspect of making men stand up to capture, but in equipping them better mentally on the fighting field, so that they were less likely to be captured. Many of the methods had ancient roots; what was new was the exactitude of the application. The rivalry of the Australians and Americans serving alongside each other in Korea had brought out the best in both, and the phenomenon was analyzed to gauge how the greatest advantage could be gained from widely differing types of unit being put to compete with one another. It was also found that the best small grouping of soldiers was four to five men, who should be kept together in all circumstances – a fact that had long ago been known instinctively to Dumas in creating D'Artagnan and the three musketeers.

Enthusiasm for the manipulation of the human psyche became such that the Central Intelligence Agency embarked on a program

Far left: Salvador Dali with his new painting 'Christ on the Cross.'
Left: President Tito of Yugoslavia gives an address in Belgrade.
Bottom left: King Hussein of Jordan is enthroned in 1953.
Below: Former Secretary of State George C Marshall just prior to receiving the Nobel Peace Prize in 1953.

Week ending April 18 1953   EVERY THURSDAY 3½ᴰ

Picturegoer
THE NATIONAL FILM WEEKLY

John Fitzgerald's
Current Release
starts in this issue

Joan Collins

involving nearly two hundred private scientist and eighty research institutions, many at im portant universities. There were attempts to modify human behavior by using drugs on subjects who might be willing, unwilling or even unconscious that any such experiment was being carried out. So-called 'safe houses' were estab lished in San Francisco and New York, staffed with prostitutes and embellished with th trappings of the trade, such as bedrooms with red curtains and Toulouse-Lautrec pictures Sexual psychopaths resorting to these establish ments were then spied upon with two-way mirrors and recording equipment. The aim wa said to be the discovery of how far their taste might be changed.

The work was very much 'under cover,' and the combination of secrecy and power induced the lunatic recklessness which led to LSD being administered to Dr Frank Olson in 1953 Unaware what was happening to him, Olson committed suicide a week later by jumping from the bedroom window of his New York hotel. As a civilian employee of the American army, Olson was of more account to the author ities than the unfortunates of the CIA brothels but although questions were asked, it was no until 1977 that full information became avail able. Documents which had been believed destroyed were discovered by Admiral Stansfield Turner when, as the newly-appointed director of the CIA, he had instituted a search among the agency's financial records. This revealed details of many such experiments on students schizophrenics and normal members of the public, which were in fact continued until 1973

The main American aim, apart from the salvation of sexual deviants, was to find drugs to ensure victory in future wars by creating con fusion and bewilderment among the enemy The end of the Korean War certainly created bewilderment enough among Americans them selves. They hardly noticed that South Korea the country they had gone to war to defend

PICTUREGOER April 18 19

n't mind being my fourth wife—we go out together more than most Hollywood couples"

Above: Humphrey Bogart and his wife Lauren Bacall were still big box-office in the mid-1950s.
Top left: Film magazine features British movie star Joan Collins.
Left: Joe Loss, British bandleader, Ava Gardner and Frank Sinatra at ringside in Paris for the Turpin-Humez fight.

took no part in the signing ceremony – on the orders of Synghman Rhee – but they were used to wars which ended in splendid conquest. Now the peace terms, after so much expenditure of blood and money, virtually restored the status quo on the uneasy 38th parallel and released China to concentrate on Vietnam.

In frustration at failing to carry the battle home, energy was turned to other measures. A rider to an appropriations bill reached Eisenhower which would have committed America to stopping at once all contributions to the United Nations if Communist China were ever admitted. He baulked at signing, and the rider was converted to a resolution by Congress that the erring country should be for ever excluded. The President committed himself to 'an active part in opposing her admission.' In fulfilment of his election pledge to root out 'pinkish influence,' issued an Executive Order in April which made the head of each government agency responsible for dismissing any personnel who were disloyal or 'poor security' risks. To safeguard their own positions, department heads naturally interpreted the pro-

visions broadly. There needed to be no formal evidence of disloyalty, but suspected addiction to drugs or alcohol or perverse sexual practices was enough. Misfortune and misbehavior were equally condemned and a mental or criminal record disqualified the individual for employment. Even the mere suspicion of being a liar, being considered a person of unclean habits, or with an eccentric turn of mind – a practising nudist, for example – brought the dreaded ban. Nearly seven thousand people lost their jobs, without hope of protest, since they were neither required nor allowed to defend themselves – they were not convicted, merely suspect.

Among the more important figures caught in this 'net' was J Robert Oppenheimer, the 'father of the atom bomb.' In December 1953 almost exactly a year after the explosion of the first hydrogen bomb at Eniwetok on 1 November 1952, he was suspended as a security risk but refused to resign. A special panel headed by Gordon Gray judged him to be 'loyal,' but voted two to one against his reinstatement. As a 'fellow traveler' till 1942, he had made financial contributions to the Party and, when questioned in 1943 by Colonel Ed Lansdale, among others, had refused for four months to disclose the name of the person who had approached him for information. He had already delayed eight months before telling the authorities an approach had been made.

In the diplomatic field, Charles 'Chip' Bohlen – loathed by McCarthy because he had been interpreter for Roosevelt at Yalta – barely made it to Moscow as the new American ambassador, even though Eisenhower put all his weight behind the appointment. The very head of the State Department himself, John Foster Dulles, lived in fear of McCarthy turning his guns against him, for had he not been willing to testify to the flawless reputation of Alger Hiss? In consequence Dulles allowed McCarthy to usurp the department's authority to such a degree that the world overseas mocked at his behavior. The Senator's henchmen, Cohn and Schine, were sent to ferret out suspect volumes in the libraries of the United States Information Service abroad, and came up with inflammatory works ranging from Dashiell Hammett to Ralph Waldo Emerson and Henry David Thoreau.

In Congress there were endless wrangles over the supposed 'secret agreements' at Yalta and Potsdam with the Communists, which Eisenhower himself had supported in 1952 before becoming President and seeing the records for himself. As a result, the so-called 'Bricker Amendment' was passed aimed at limiting the President's treaty-making powers, and making approval by legislatures of all forty-eight states essential before a treaty became valid. It was not eventually thrown out until February 1954. Such drastic clipping of presidential powers was unthinkable for Eisenhower, but had a more moderate measure been passed, the committal to retaliation in Vietnam after the Tonkin Gulf incident in 1964 would have been less fatally easy.

Finally there were the Communists, committed card carrying Communists who openly admitted to being such, to be dealt with. Under the McCarran Act they were already compelled to register, but 'registration' carried increasingly discouraging hazards. Governor Allan Shivers of Texas was by 1954 urging the death penalty in his state for all Communists, and Senator Hubert Humphrey introduced a bill in Congress making party membership a crime. Even in the modified form in which it was eventually passed, the earnest candidates who registered would find themselves liable to five years' jail-sentence and a fine of $10,000 (£4000). The lines of people were not long.

In such an atmosphere Churchill's speech of 11 May 1953, calling for talks with Russia's new regime, fell on horrified ears as far as Dulles was concerned. Relations between Britain and America were in any case a little strained. Eisenhower did not want the kind of close personal communication that Churchill had established with Roosevelt during the war years and wished to resume now that he was once more Prime Minister. Neither did he want to go in December to the much-postponed Bermuda Conference with Churchill and the representatives of France, since he saw the proposed 'summit' as offering the French one more excuse to drag her feet over entrance into the European Defense Community. Despite a Dulles threat that the United States could not avoid an 'agonizing reappraisal' of her own European commitments if the EDC agreement was not soon ratified, France was even more fearful of being left alone in the community with Germany as a more than equal partner. She wanted a twenty-year preliminary guarantee from Britain that her troops would be kept in Europe at their existing strength.

Two years before Eisenhower had tried everything 'including argument, cajolery and sheer prayer, to get Winston to say a kind word about EDC.' He was now dumbfounded, for Churchill suddenly told Georges Bidault, the French Foreign Minister, that either EDC was accepted or 'he for one was going to urge the unilateral rearmament of Germany.' The sudden volte-face on the point was linked with Churchill's persistent raising of the Egyptian question with Eisenhower. To the President's renewed embarrassment, the Prime Minister said outright in the presence of the French who had so long been linked with Britain in controlling Egypt that he wished to discuss the problem with the Americans alone.

In July playboy King Farouk had been rolled off his throne by the military takeover of General Neguib, and sent into hurried exile with his portmanteau of pornographic photographs, his sultry Queen Narriman, and the little boy prince who had enjoyed a brief technical reign before the declaration of the republic. Already rising nationalism in the country had led to the premature unilateral ending of the 1936 Anglo-Egyptian Treaty, eventually compelling Britain to withdraw her troops from the Canal Zone in October 1954. With an eye to future dangers, Churchill wanted to involve American interest in ensuring that the United Nations should decide when peace was threatened in the canal area, and when British troops should come back to the Suez base.

To Eisenhower this smacked of colonialism. His sympathies were with the new Egyptian military regime, partly because he was a soldier, and partly because no American ever seems to finish fighting the War of Independence by proxy everywhere in the world. Dulles was, by

the early links of his international legal practice, in sympathy with the Continent rather than Britain, and was in any case bent on reversing the attitude of the Truman administration, which had strongly favored the Israel lobby. The whole contretemps was symbolized by Eisenhower's personal gift that year to Neguib of a plated .38 caliber pistol, which evoked indignant comment and cartoons in the British press. There was little 'special relationship' between the Prime Minister and the President at this juncture.

Eisenhower was not the only one experiencing difficulty in his relationships with Churchill. As early as 1947, following the debacle of the Conservative defeat of 1945, the 'Shadow Cabinet' had felt that Churchill was 'a little bit out of touch with some of what might be called the modern tendencies in politics.' The Conservative Chief Whip, deputed to make a tactful suggestion that he might like to retire, was met by a peremptory 'stomping' on the floor by Churchill with his stick. In 1951 speaking to Lord Moran of his reception on a visit to Liverpool, he said, 'There was rapture in their eyes. They brought out their children. I'm not conceited, but they wanted to touch me.' Argument was powerless against divine right, and his ministers were reluctant to cross him even in trifles. Summoned to see him at 9.30 a.m. in the morning, and being impressed into joining him in refreshment, Lord Butler managed to settle for port rather than the Prime Minister's whisky, but even so had entered into a permanent understanding with the butler, cemented with a tip of $1.25 (50p) which enabled him merely to sip from the glass in front of him without an obligatory refill. Only in this way could he tactfully fulfill his social obligations.

In June 1953, however, age took a hand. Entertaining the Italian Premier to dinner at Number Ten, Churchill made an amusing speech, but could not rise when the time came to leave the table. On his feet at length, his step was uncertain, his speech slurred, and he had lost the power of movement on his right side. It was a stroke, but no such word entered the public statement, any more than it had done on the first occasion in 1949, or the second in 1950: the Prime Minister had been told by his doctors to 'rest.'

It would have presented an ideal opportunity for his Cabinet colleagues to ease him into retirement, had not Anthony Eden – the understudy who had spent so many years in the wings waiting his promotion to the leading role – fallen seriously ill himself. At that critical moment he was undergoing a major operation in Boston in the United States. Churchill won the race for recuperation, scored a personal triumph with his speech at the Conservative Party Conference in October, and decided to stay on until the Queen returned from her Coronation Commonwealth Tour. This was to start in November – and continue until the following May. When she did return, July seemed a better date. In July there were reasons for thinking September preferable, and the end of 1954 saw him still firmly in the saddle. He was exercising a full personal rule, and when, early

in 1954, the railwaymen had made pay demands calculated to upset the balance of the economy and hasten the slide into inflation which was to shoot away dangerously in 1955, he did not hesitate. Butler was astonished on arriving at his office one morning to be summoned, not to the negotiating table in his role as Chancellor of the Exchequer in charge of balancing the economy, but to Churchill's presence. The rail crisis was over. 'Never mind, old chap,' the great man consoled him, 'we [meaning Churchill and Walter Monckton, the Minister of Labour] settled the rail strike last night, without deciding to keep you up, on their terms.'

1954

In September 1954 the British eventually agreed not to withdraw their current forces against the will of the enlarged Brussels Treaty powers, and the announcement to this effect was described by Eisenhower as 'electric' in its impact. Eden also negotiated in October 1954, much against the Prime Minister's wish, the final evacuation of British troops from the Canal Zone, which the end of the Anglo-Egyptian treaty had made almost an automatic step.

The main preoccupation in 1954, however, for both America and Britain was Vietnam, at the opposite end of the Dulles defense perimeter from Korea, where the position had just been shored up at such cost. Vietnam was costly, too. Already by 1952 aid authorized by Truman had reached the level of $400,000,000 (£160,000,000) a year.

Focus of the situation was Ho Chi Minh. His wizened face only plumping into life on the T-shirts stretched across a million young chests

as a cult hero of the 1960s, he was an unlikely object of adoration. He had begun his agitation for Vietnamese independence from French rule at the Versailles Conference in 1919, where his appeal fell on completely deaf ears. For some thirty years he directed operations in Vietnam from exile, and when attempts were made to get him extradited from Hong Kong, it was Sir Stafford Cripps who acted as his lawyer. At one time he made a living as a retoucher of photographs, and he certainly became an expert in retouching his own image to as many forms as he had aliases.

He had returned home in 1940, and claimed to have sampled thirty of Chiang Kai-shek's prisons in little more than a year, since the Chinese Nationalist leader had no idea of allowing Vietnam, as a former Chinese possession, to become independent after the war. From 1944 he had fought against the Japanese in North Vietnam, making himself a reputation

Above: Film producer Mike Todd and his wife Elizabeth Taylor with Eddie Fisher, the singer, and his film star wife Debbie Reynolds at Epsom Derby. Fisher later divorced Reynolds to marry Taylor.
Top right: Senator Joe McCarthy and his wife read some critical comments on his anti-Communist activities in the Daily Worker, the American Communist journal.
Center right: Roy Cohn, McCarthy's intrepid aide, on the witness stand.
Bottom right: Secretary of the Army Stevens and General Young with Cohn and McCarthy, whose investigation of subversion within the military led to the Senator's downfall.

among the people which was reinforced and confirmed when Japanese rule collapsed by – of all people – the Americans.

Not until the 1970s did it become widely known how affirmative a role had been played by the predecessor of the CIA, the Office of Strategic Services. Major (later Colonel) Archimedes Patti assisted Ho in composing the wording of the Vietnamese Declaration of Independence, modeled on that of America, and photographs survive of him standing alongside the subsequently celebrated General Giap as the Communist flag fluttered officially for the first time over Hanoi. Roosevelt's antipathy to the restoration of French rule in Indo-China had taken a form that would have surprised him.

Disapproval of the French still made Americans bite on the bullet every time that money and supplies had to be sent, at French insistence, to them and not the Emperor Bao Dai's native regime. Not that they could be enthusiastic about the Emperor either. Known only to the people of the part of Vietnam of which he had been the original ruler, he was tainted by collaboration with the Japanese, and his only recommendation was that he could hardly be counted a French puppet ruler. He did not care for ruling anything and spent his time in the livelier fashionable resorts of Europe.

The French, with their concept of the close-knit French Union, rather than the loose ties of the Commonwealth, found it unthinkable to give Vietnam the kind of independence Britain had given India. Apart from someone like André Malraux, with his poetic ideas of Indo-China, they did not care much about Vietnam itself. But, if Vietnam went, how could they maintain their hold on the Mediterranean possessions – Tunisia, Morocco and – above all – Algeria, for which they did care?

Onto this scene came John Foster Dulles with no trace of divided mind. In an article published in *Life* in 1952 – 'The Policy of Boldness' – he had early formulated the doctrine of massive retaliation which dominated the American political arena until he left it. The 'free world,' he wrote, 'must have the means to retaliate instantly against open aggression by Red armies, so that if it occurred anywhere, we could and would strike back where it hurts, by means of our own choosing.' America had no alternative, since she was 'marked down for destruction by those who today control one third of the world.' After this it was perhaps understandable, if not diplomatically pardonable, that Eden should have allowed himself to hope out loud to Eisenhower that Dulles would not be his Secretary of State. His hope was unfulfilled, and despite the lesson of Korea, the views of Dulles remained unchanged. Eisenhower graphically expressed his own view of the situation in the 'domino theory' – 'You have a row of dominoes set up. You knock over the first one, and what will happen to the last one is that it will go over very quickly.'

In this particular instance the striking back was to be done by the French. Cheered on by the might of American money and supplies, they were not only prepared but eager to confront the Vietminh, and issue a challenge for the

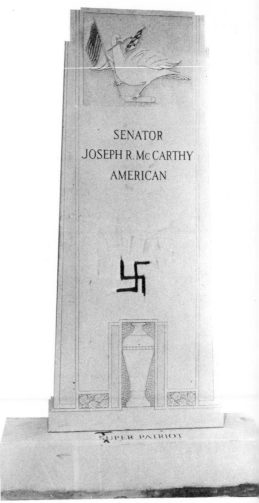

on the valley of Dien Bien Phu – the name meaning 'big frontier administration center' – as an ideal position for a hedgehog fortress. As a practical soldier, Eisenhower scratched his head at the choice. It was about ten miles from the Laotian border in steaming jungle country, a couple of hundred miles from Haiphong, the main supply base. Opium grown in the area helped supply funds for the Vietminh, and their communication trails ran through it, but the French had no hope of cutting these simply by holding the fortress, even if they held it till doomsday. The choice seemed to owe more to the euphoria induced by the fact that America was now disbursing four-fifths of the cost of the operations in Vietnam.

Low hills surrounded the valley of Dien Bien Phu, ideal for siting artillery to fire directly down into the fortress. But the Vietminh had no guns, nor were there roads to enable them to be brought to the site. Even should small weapons be brought in, the French were confident they could immediately be blasted out by the unending heavy artillery reinforcements which could be brought in by air, together with troops and other supplies. The same pattern would be followed as had evolved on the single previous occasion when the guerrillas had attacked a fully-prepared French position. The only problem for the French had then been disposing of

two thousand corpses piled before their artillery emplacements. Only this time the scale would be bigger.

The French officers drank their wine from home on a mess table complete with its silverware, and looked forward to meeting the evasive enemy on their terms. The central camp was defended by a skillfully constructed system of outposts, and even General Giap would be hard put to it to find the thirty battalions it would need to encircle the valley completely from the heights.

Morale was excellent among the ten to twelve thousand men of the garrison. Even when, on 11 March, forty thousand Vietminh took up their positions with their forward troops less than half a mile from the fortifications, there was only slight unease at the unexpected maneuver. Food and ammunition for this comparatively mass movement of troops had been brought in by bicycles fitted with specially strengthened frames to enable them to carry a load of up to four hundred and fifty pounds. Among the thousands upon thousands of cyclists were many carrying oddly misshapen packs of metal – the parts of dismantled guns. Under cover of darkness these were dragged into positions hollowed out of the ring of hills which made them highly resistant to return fire. They were sited with their muzzles lined directly on the fortress and its airstrip.

The garrison quickly became more uneasy

as the slurred chink-chink of rhythmically wielded metal cutting into earth grew louder: the Vietminh were digging their way ever closer, like undermining termites. Then came the shock of the opening bombardment, so powerful that the French artillery commander, Colonel Piroth, took a hand grenade and committed suicide in the agony of his realization of the extent to which he had underestimated the enemy potential.

On 13 March the real assault began. Suicide parties opened the way by blowing up the French barbed wire defenses. In the first three days of bitter fighting there were five thousand Vietminh killed and wounded. French casualties were also heavy, and the constant bombardment prevented aircraft from landing, so that stores and ammunition, and reinforcing troops, could only be dropped by parachute. In itself this was not serious. So long as they came in sufficient quantity, it did not matter how, but they did not. Thirty-eight of the aircraft on the daily run into Dien Bien Phu from Haiphong had been destroyed on the ground by Vietminh infiltrators. Making their way into the city area as civilians, they had evaded the defenses' perimeter and the guards at Cot-bi airport by coming up through the sewage system.

Civilian aircraft were hurriedly commandeered, and those that got through performed miracles. The bleary-eyed pilots were in the air for fifteen hours out of twenty-four. A notable

part was played by the American civilian pilots
of General Chennault's Chinese Air Transport
Company, ferrying munitions and supplies. In
the comparative lull of the next fortnight
retaliatory measures were taken which included
the deluging of the area north of the fortress
with a thousand gallons of napalm. It made no
difference. General Giap, his strength and resources tried to the utmost, guessed the significance of Dien Bien Phu. Khrushchev's memoirs
reveal how desperate the position of the Vietminh was. On a visit to the Kremlin, Chou
En-lai buttonholed him to confide that the
situation was 'hopeless,' and that the Vietminh
were prepared for a retreat to the Chinese
border. There they hoped that the Chinese
would come to their aid with troops, as well as
military supplies, as they had with Kim Il
Sung in Korea, but Chou En-lai shook his head.
'We've already lost too many men in Korea –
that war cost us dearly. We're in no condition to
get involved in another war at this time.'
Characteristically Khrushchev came up with a
practical solution: the Chinese leaders should
simply not let the Vietnamese know they had
decided to let them go down the drain. If the
Vietminh managed to hold out just the same,
they would never know the difference, and, if
they did not – well, nothing was lost by silence.

The French were also rushing for more help.
They hoped for a carrier-based air strike by the
Americans. Georges Bidault, the Foreign Minister, discussed the possibility, and according to
Maurice Schumann, Bidault's deputy, the question of the use of atomic weapons was also discussed. René Pleven, the Defense Minister, is
adamant that the French government never

asked for them, but did Dulles offer them? 'He didn't really offer,' says Schumann, 'He made a suggestion and asked a question, but he actually uttered the two fatal words, "atomic bomb."' He added that Bidault at once responded as if this was something not to be taken seriously, but Schumann's account of what Dulles said has the ring of individual authenticity. If Dulles were going to say it, that is what he would have said. In January–February the Berlin Conference had ended in deadlock on the problems of German reunification and European security, and the only move forward had been the convening of a conference on the Far East at Geneva to open on 26 April. It must have at least crossed his mind that, if the French lost Dien Bien Phu they would not have much of a hand to play at the conference. Neither would the United States. The only possibility of an ace was the obliteration of the opposition by an atomic explosion.

While he dithered mentally with the prospect, by 30 March the Vietminh were once more on the attack from the now perfected system of trenches and earthworks they had been working on during the relative calm after the first onslaught. By mid-April the French were finding it impossible to evacuate their wounded, artillery fire on the airstrip preventing any landings at all, and a thousand wounded men were having to be cared for in deep dug-outs. Outside, defensive positions were being fought over time and time again, only to fall inexorably into enemy hands on the only time it mattered – the last.

The Vietminh now had the Chinese Communist General Li Chen-hou stationed at Giap's

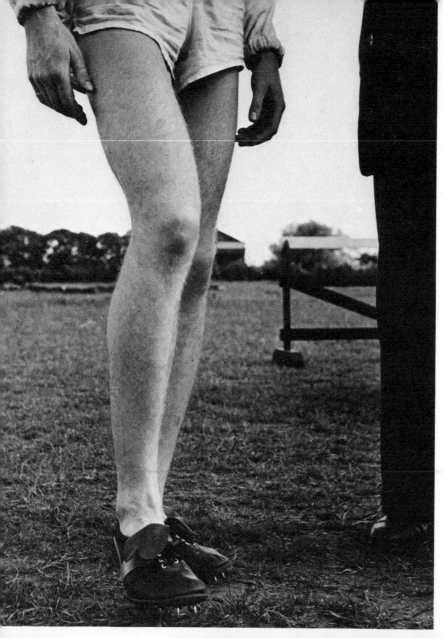

headquarters, and a ruthless progression wa
maintained in the conduct of the siege. On th
French side the commander was fifty-year-old
General Christian Fernand Marie de la Croix d
Castries. In World War II had had led tha
smartest of French regiments – the 3rd Spahis -
in North Africa with panache and gallantry
Now he brought the same qualities to Dien Bien
Phu, and looking back on the battle, nothing i
more moving than to turn to the maps of the
fortress on which the strongpoints bear women'
names: Dominique, Eliane, Claudine, Huguette
and Isabelle.

These were the five surviving when the fina
onslaught came at ten o'clock on the night of
1 May 1954. The names were all French, but
except for the officers the men who defended
them were not. Half were Vietnamese, and the
rest Moroccans and Senegalese from France's
colonial forces, and Foreign Legionaires -
mainly German. That night they were on edge.
waiting as always for the artillery barrage that
preceded attack. This time it did not come.
Human waves rose from out of the silence of the
trenches close in on the French positions. The
defenders threw grenades, unable to miss their
targets at so short a distance, but the Communist troops came on. They met them with
bayonet thrusts, and they still came on. They
drew knives and went for their throats, and four
of the five outposts fell.

Supporting aircraft had battered at the Vietminh trenches in vain. All that remained was the
little outpost of Isabelle to the south, and the
central redoubt of General de Castries' headquarters. It took twenty hours of continuous
fighting, the defenders outnumbered ten to one,
before the quick successive radio messages:
'They are a few yards away . . . they have broken
through everywhere . . . the Vietminh have
reached the general's command post. Farewell.'

Isabelle, too, disappeared into dark silence.

Reconnaissance planes that night of 7 May saw only the fires and explosions of the ammunition dumps destroyed at the command of General de Castries. The next day long lines of men trudging towards Vietminh-held territory told their own story. Some one thousand four hundred seriously wounded men remained in the underground 'hospital' of the fortress, and with them – one woman – a French Air Force nurse who had landed early in the siege to evacuate casualties, but whose aircraft had been destroyed by Communist artillery fire. Lieutenant Genevieve de Galarde-Tarraube was allowed by the Vietminh to continue her work.

In the midst of the siege the British government had issued a statement that it was 'not prepared to give any undertakings about United Kingdom military action in Indo-China in advance of the results of the Geneva Conference.' This began, as a kind of hors d'oeuvres, with another inconclusive series of discussions on the reunification of Korea. On 4 May the Vietminh delegation flew in, and three days later Dien Bien Phu fell. The timing was perfect. In fact the French resources were not exhausted, everyone simply assumed they were; the Vietminh resources were exhausted, but only their own allies knew it, and the psychological effect of the fall of the fortress completed the rout.

The Communists were also able to present a united front. While even at a personal level Eden and Dulles could not tolerate each other, and it showed. Noted even among the elite for his superb charm of manner and his exquisite tailoring, Eden was in complete contrast to the crumpled Yankee who exposed yards of concertinad sock when he sat down.

Their views were equally far apart. As a trained diplomat, Eden believed, maybe even a

Top left: The legs that broke the 'unbreakable' four-minute mile barrier: Roger Bannister's.
Left: A British coffee bar in Notting Hill in 1954.
Above: Workers in the City of London wear masks to protect them against the smog on the Embankment in 1954.
Right: A scene from the popular British musical comedy The Boy Friend *when Joan Sterndale-Bennett and Ann Rogers sang 'Poor Little Pierrot.'*

little too much, in the power of sweet reason-ableness, but he also believed that, with what-ever mixed motives, the Russians and the Chinese wanted peace. Peace in itself might then so modify the situation as to make it self-sustaining. Dulles, on the other hand, had noted in a private jotting at the end of 1953 that he believed Malenkov's peace campaign to be 'phony.' When he had failed, before the fall of Dien Bien Phu, to edge Eden into taking up a belligerent stance which could be portrayed to Eisenhower (and thence to Congress) as justify-ing American hardline intervention, he had had Australia and New Zealand sounded out. In agreement with London they declined.

The Communists also knew that American opinion behind him was divided. Richard Nixon had spoken during the siege on 16 April to the American Society of Newspaper Editors of the need 'to take a risk now by putting our boys in,' but Lyndon Johnson stood on the other side, as did most Democrats. More con-clusively, though Eisenhower might speak of being unwilling to take action without Britain 'by our side,' his fundamental attitude after Korea had been voiced in a press conference in February when he had said of Indochina that he

could 'not conceive of a greater tragedy for America than to get heavily involved now in an all-out war in any of those regions, particularly with large units.'

The news that the 'provisional demarcation line' suggested by the West for the ceasefire agreement was along the 17th parallel, when relayed by the Russian delegate, Molotov, was greeted with chortles of glee by Khrushchev. Expecting much harsher terms, he promptly put in a demand for the 15th, just for good measure. In practice, he backed Chou En-lai, representing China at her first participation in a major conference as a world power. The Vietminh were pressurized into giving up some twenty per cent of their gains in order to get the matter quickly settled before Dulles managed to organ-ize direct American intervention.

All Vietminh forces were to be regrouped to the north of the line and all French Union forces to the south, pending elections that were to be held within two years – by the summer of 1956. The South Vietnamese were not signatories to the July agreement, which ended not only the Vietnam hostilities, but the overflow in Cam-bodia and Laos. Neither were the Americans. The United States made a unilateral declaration

Above: Another scene from The Boy Friend *when Lord Brockhurst tells the girls of the finishing school that 'Everything's nicer in Nice.'*
Above right: It wasn't so nice in French Indo-China, as French troops prepared for another Viet Minh offensive at Dien Bien Phu.
Above far right: French parachutists drop into Dien Bien Phu as reinforcements for the beleaguered garrison fortress.
Right: As the French involvement in Vietnam was petering out, the British in Malaya continued their successful guerrilla search and destroy operations.

Left: Jacques Baeyens of the French delegation in Geneva tells the conference of the fall of Dien Bien Phu in May 1954.
Below: A few wounded were transported from Dien Bien Phu to Luang Prapang in Laos. The majority of French troops were either killed or taken prisoner by the Viet Minh.
Right: The Premier of newly-constructed South Vietnam, Ngo Dinh Diem, urges his armies to continue the fight against the Communists after the partition of Vietnam at the Geneva Conference of 1954.
Below right: French Defense Minister René Pleven, Brigadier de Castries and C-in-C René Cogny in North Vietnam prior to the French withdrawal after the Geneva Conference.

that it would 'refrain from threat or use of force to disturb the agreements,' and would 'view any renewal of aggression in violation of the aforesaid agreement with grave concern and as seriously threatening international peace and security.'

The gravity of the phrasing was an indication of the extent to which America was becoming committed to confrontation in Vietnam with the Sino-Soviet monolith of Communism. There were actually more than hair-cracks in that impressive facade. When Khrushchev went to Peking in the autumn of 1954 the kissings on the cheek and the confidences exchanged were already forced. When he and Mao basked together round the Chinese leader's swimming pool they eyed each other rather like a couple of overweight bull seals sizing each other up for battles to come, and when Khrushchev returned to the comrades in Moscow, he told them categorically: 'Conflict with China is inevitable.'

In the West the siege of Dien Bien Phu had roused concentrated interest, especially the lone figure of the French nurse marooned in the fortress, the 'Angel of Dien Bien Phu.' In the succeeding negotiations public interest flagged since, not unnaturally, there were few who were exactly certain of the location of the 17th parallel. Not even Eisenhower was absorbed in

the crisis to the exclusion of all else, and foun
time to remark that the news of the fall of Die
Bien Phu had coincided with the announcemer
that the young London doctor, Roger Banniste
had achieved the long-attempted four-minut
mile. The very wording shows a change i
the image of athletics. Science entered in, an
the excitement was beginning to come less fror
the conflict of individuals than from the conte
of man against stop watch, and of another ma
– perhaps on the other side of the world – pittin
himself against the recorded figure.

America suffered a slight recession in 1953–
barely more than a hiccough compared wit
that to come in the early 1970s. Like the goo
general that he was, Eisenhower concentrated
great deal of effort on communications. H
managed at last to get approval for the S
Lawrence Seaway project past both houses c
Congress, aided by the threat from an exasper
ated Canada that she would go it alone if th
United States did not make up its mind. He wa
also concerned with the state of America
roads, on which the new prosperity was sendin
such hordes of cars that, with the existing sys
tem, they were likely to stand bumper to bumpe
in an unmoving mass in no time at all. The grea
forty-one thousand mile $76,000,000,00
(£30,400,000,000) federal highways scheme h
put into operation came as a welcome amenit
for the average automobile owner, but for th
President it was a precautionary measure in th
case of atomic war, when transport column
for the military would need to move fast, an
when millions of refugees might have to b
evacuated from the cities in double quick time
The development of the hydrogen bomb ha

Above: Jitterbugging and
pony tails were still popular
in 1954.
Right: Jitterbugging to a
Rock-and-Roll British band.
Top right: Pick-up lane of a
supermarket in a Yonkers,
NY shopping center, typical
of hundreds springing up all
across the United States in
the mid-1950s.
Far right: Ann Rogers doing
a number in the musical
comedy The Boy Friend,
the first British musical to
entrance citizens of the
United States in decades.

been approved by Truman on 31 January 1950, and the first perfected specimen was exploded on 1 November 1952, but quite unknown to the general public. At the beginning of the decade there had been a boom in atomic shelters built in the gardens of the more well-to-do, and a certain one-upmanship crept into press reports of the amount of time that a family of four might manage to survive without contact with contaminated air in their underground bunkers. Firms vied in the excellence of the bathing and sanitary arrangements provided in their models, and proud owners boasted of the wines laid in to make the time in seclusion pass more enjoyably. It was not until 2 February 1954 that Eisenhower announced officially his confirmation of the reports of witnesses which had filtered through. The cavity left in the bottom of the Pacific after the explosion had been one hundred seventy-five feet deep and a mile in diameter. Sales of back-garden atom shelters suffered a sharp decline: you had to be a Rockefeller to afford one a hundred seventy-five feet deep and if you ever surfaced, what sort of world would you come up to? A similar degree of secrecy had also been observed in Britain, where the Labour government had begun manufacture of the H-bomb under ingenious financial wraps in 1952, the actual announcement of the work not being made until the Defense White Paper of 1955, and the British weapon not being detonated till May 1957.

It should not be imagined that worries about these developments dampened the spirits of the 1950s. Rather the reverse. This was not the time of proliferation and contamination. If the worst happened, and most of the time people felt it would not, then it would all be quick and very final, and if it were going to, then there could be no better argument for having a good time first.

Predictably the situation touched off a little nostalgia. There were glimmerings in England of the revival of croquet, that Victorian game designed for malice at the Vicarage, and the hit of the year on the stage was *The Boy Friend*, Sandy Wilson's excursion into the 1920s. Dior's H-line was a softened sheath, with a suggestion of a waist, and *Punch* recorded that the old class distinctions were coming back into fabrics. From being a novelty, synthetic fabrics had become widespread and cheap, and the inexpensive natural fabrics of the war years – such as cotton and denim – were considered fit only for 'beach-wear, house-coats, and morning frocks.' How evocative is the term 'morning frocks': only the woman who did not work outside the home, and who changed for the afternoon social round, before changing again for the evening, had a use for morning-frocks! The fabrics now the fashion, according to *Punch*, were 'shantung, surah, wild silk, lace, taffeta, grosgrain, richly printed silks.' In this world of elegance Elizabeth Arden was still refusing to train for beauty service any candidate below twenty-five: by the 1960s anyone of twenty-five was too old.

Youth was beginning to move. In politics they were still what their elders contemptuously called 'the Silent Generation,' but in the world

111

of their pleasures they were poised for change. As in all change, there was an element of the sinister. The new dance, first seen at the tail end of 1953 was 'The Creep' one of the few dances one could still manage to do in the heavy soled shoes which were *de rigueur* to wear with the Edwardian-style suits still in favor with boys. Although rendered attractive by being condemned as 'hideous' by the older generation, the Creep did not last long.

The new music was to last a lot longer, but came in with no fanfare. The first 'Rock' record was 'Sh-Boom' in the version by The Chords, and so unprepared were the fans for the simultaneous challenge of the powerfully insistent instrumental beat and the improvization of the words, that they had to be 'broken in' to liking it by a tidied up version produced by The Crew Cuts. The latter name, pointing up the overhang of the World War image of the short-haired male ideal, if not crewcut at least well-brilliantined, is an indication of the gulf that was soon to exist between the old popular music scene of balladeers Perry Como and Eddie Fisher, and the coming world of Rock.

The roots of Rock probably go down deepest to Country and Western. Highlight the instrumental sound, accentuate the rhythms, and highpower the singer, and one has the makings of rock. In 1953 one Country and Western group, The Saddlemen, were looking for a new image. They tried calling themselves Bill Haley and his Comets. On 12 April 1954 they did a recording session, and 'Shake, rattle and roll' did exactly that on a million discs. At the same session they cut another number, 'Rock around the clock,' which was a bit slower in take-off, but once put on the soundtrack of the MGM film *Blackboard Jungle*, dealing with the attractive theme of juvenile schoolroom revolt, it became the first record to sell over the million mark in British stores alone. Haley was white, unusual for a rhythm man, and he had a more relaxed air than previous stars. His little group of five or six music men also broke new ground in using special recording effects to get the timbre they wanted, and started the division between 'studio' and 'live' sound which was to become such a feature of Pop. The showing of the film *Blackboard Jungle* was accompanied in

Top far left: Some London secretaries take a lunch break.
Bottom far left: Judy Garland in the chorus line of A Star Is Born, *her last great picture which was released in 1954.*
Center left top: Frankie Laine was a popular singer in the early and mid-1950s.
Above: Pietro Annigoni was an Italian artist who later did a portrait of Queen Elizabeth.
Left: Frankie Laine singing 'Mule Train' in Liverpool.

113

Above: Singer Nat 'King' Cole and 'comedic
Henny Youngman.
Below: Doris Day as 'Calamity Jane'.
Right: Jeff Chandler and Maureen O'Hara
'War Arrow'.
Below right: New York Yankee Joe DiMagg
kisses Marilyn Monroe after their marriage.

England by unprecedented scenes. The youthfu
audiences had found a new direction for Jiv
which was a long way from the Creep, and the
set it on its way right there in the theaters. The
danced in the aisles to the new pulsating rhythm
and when the packed audiences could not fin
room, because of the seats, they ripped the
out, and managers were soon calculating the
increased takings against the cost of repair
America, for once taking its cue from across th
Atlantic, soon made up for lost time, and in th
spring of 1955 'Rock around the clock' eve
sent Princeton University campus into a riot.

Rock and Roll was on its way. The name itse
was rather older than its first realized e
pression; it was first used in 'album notes' writte
by the disc jockey himself in 1951 for 'Ala
Freed's Top 15.' The name Alan Freed becam
well-known throughout the 1950s, not merel
for his expertise as a 'jockey,' but for the roc
concerts he promoted and the songs he himse
wrote, or part wrote, including 'Sincerely' an
'Maybellene.' But it was the jockeys who too
the lead everywhere, for the recording was th
essence of the new music to the extent that o
the living stage the performers often on
mouthed the words to their own already famou
discs. It was the jockeys who decided the e
posure on air time to be given to any particula
disc, and the fans only went to concerts for

King
cates

three years as M-G-M's kingpin, Gable heads the
who are leaving Leo. Who waits to take his place?

by ELIZABETH FORREST

In *Mogambo* with Ava Gardner
(above, on the *Lone Star* set)
Gable proved he was still a top
personality at the box office

ut of touch with modern artistic developments
s it had feared. Churchill accepted the gift as
a remarkable example of modern art. It cer-
ainly combines force with candor.' In private
e complained to Lord Beaverbrook that it
howed him as though he were 'a drinking sot,'
nd it was discreetly hidden from his view.
3ut the knowledge of its existence still so 'preyed
n his mind' that Lady Churchill promised that
t would 'never see the light of day again.'
Following her death in 1978 it was revealed that
t had been burned within a couple of years of
ts being painted.

Among the memorable literary events of 1954
vas the radio play *Under Milk Wood* by Dylan
Thomas, and his broadcast, recorded the pre-
ious year, when the lavish alcoholic hospitality
xtended to him by his American hosts gave the
inal tilt to his already precarious health and
nded in his death in New York. On the air five
nonths afterwards, the program celebrated the
ininhibited enthusiasm of Americans of the
eriod for every possible aspect of culture from

ceramics to the modern Turkish novel, and the consequent stream across the Atlantic of 'poets, catarrhal troubadours, lyrical one-night-standers, dollar-mad nightingales, remittances bards from at home, myself among them boring with the worst.'

Meanwhile Senator McCarthy went indestructibly on, reaching such stature that he had been dubbed 'the second most powerful man in America.' Since Eisenhower remained silent, convinced that to speak against him would make his fellow senators automatically close ranks against presidential interference, many were beginning to think of him as the first.

Yet he was beginning to make mistakes. In 1953 McCarthy had gone to town on the 'blood trade with a mortal enemy' which Britain was conducting, according to Robert F Kennedy, who was listed in contemporary reports as 'one of the Senator's investigators.' During 1952, in the midst of the Korean War, Britain had supposedly been transporting troops along the Chinese coast: the accusation conjured up visions of thousands upon thousands of Red warriors being carried to slaughter American boys (no one seemed to reflect that they would also have been slaughtering British boys) while the shekels poured into British tills. In astonishment Anthony Nutting, Joint Foreign Under-Secretary, declared the 'allegations completely unfounded.' This, however, did not satisfy McCarthy or Kennedy who held that there was 'no excuse for denials.' The actual basis for the allegations shows excellently the way the senator worked. It turned out that two British ships were concerned. In one case an indignant captain had been held at gunpoint while a small number of unarmed soldiers had been mar-

shaled on board his ship under guard, and that his complaints when he reached Hong Kong had almost equaled McCarthy's. In the case of the other, the owners agreed that troops to any number might have been transported in her, and in her two sister ships as well, but since the Chinese had taken forcible possession of all three, there was not much their dispossessed owners could do.

The McCarthy attack against an ally, openly impinging on an area of foreign policy, and one in which America's allies were few, not to speak of the absurdity of the charge itself, was enough to provide the administration with food for thought. The great newsman, Ed Murrow, fresh from his broadcasts from the foxholes of Korea, also weighed in against McCarthy to some effect. But the Senator was too strongly entrenched, less in the strength of his case than in the fears of his opponents.

He now turned on the army – his greatest mistake of all. In January 1954 a young dentist, Irving Peress, had been called up. When it came to the standard loyalty questionnaire, he refused to answer some of the questions, and asked for and received his discharge, which the army had already decided to give following their own investigations. The sequence of events seemed impeccable to an outside observer, even adopting McCarthy's standards, but the Senator was implacable. Because dentists were routinely rated as officers with the rank of major, Peress

had been given that rank during his brief weeks in uniform. McCarthy wanted to know 'who promoted Peress?' demanded punishment of the non-existent culprits, and for Peress himself, ordered a court martial. Nor was he satisfied when told that Peress, having left the army, could hardly be recalled and that no grounds existed for a court martial, even had he still been under army jurisdiction. This time the note of ridicule in the comeback was stronger, and the descriptive phrase used by Senator Ralph E Flanders of Vermont, that all the Senator had managed to come up with in his army investigation was a 'pink army dentist,' stuck in the public mind.

Even more memorable, in that they sounded like a music-hall act, were two well-heeled young men in the McCarthy menagerie. Roy Cohn was a bright, fast-talking lawyer, with a taste for inside information which made him a useful informant for the veteran gossip columnist Walter Winchell. He became chief counsel for McCarthy's Permanent Investigations Subcommittee, and had the Senator create for his considerably less bright friend, G David Schine, the grand-sounding, but unsalaried post, of chief consultant in psychological warfare. It was these two who had been McCarthy's emissaries in the book-burning and book-pulping mission to Europe, which had already started a gale of laughter against McCarthy there, where even the US High Commission's Public Affairs

Above extreme left:
G David Schine, one of McCarthy's aides, is greeted by the Senator when he testified at the Army hearings.
Above center left: Marilyn Monroe in pedal pushers.
Left: Organdy pleats were popular in womens' fashion in 1954.
Above left: A cocktail dress by Jacques Fath in 1954.
Above: A close-fitting day dress by Heinz in 1954.

Division in Germany had referred to them as 'two junketeering gumshoes.' Eisenhower had also been roused by their eighteen-day trip to denounce the 'book-burners,' and had urged his hearers to read whatever they liked so long as what they read 'didn't offend against their own ideas of decency.'

Undisturbed the two junior McCarthyites still continued to work for the Senator until the desolate day in November 1953 when Schine was himself called up to do national service. Cohn went into action to ensure that his friend had it easy. The most exalted names in the military hierarchy found themselves harassed to find a way to secure Schine an immediate commission. Should he be sent overseas, Cohn threatened to 'wreck the army,' and insisted on a posting cosily nearby in New York State, where a limousine could collect Schine on his special weekend passes and re-deliver him after their reunions.

At length the army, which Schine had pledged himself to 'modernize' in those intervals between weekend passes, took the offensive, and McCarthy was accused of exerting improper pressure on behalf of Schine. It was poetic justice that the Senator did not even like Schine, whom he tolerated as a friend of Cohn's, apparently unconscious of the kind of ribald suggestion which the association of the pair had occasioned, and which was to surface indirectly in the hearings.

For fifty-seven days in a series of thirty-six sessions the television cameras looked down on the Senator as the damning evidence was given of what had been done to make Schine's military service the kind of cushy number that every ex-draftee would have given his eye-teeth for and had never had. There were a lot of veterans watching. The questioning of McCarthy got so close that he himself began pleading the Fifth Amendment (about self-incrimination), the defense measure he had so roundly condemned in others. Stepping deeper in the mire, he tried to bring in the name of a young lawyer in the firm of the cross-questioning counsel, who had briefly belonged to a leftist legal organization. The young man had no connection with the case, and the only purpose of bringing up his name as far as viewers could see was to deflect attention from himself. As Eisenhower commented wryly, the whole affair 'finally [ended] in a near fist fight between Roy Cohn and the counsel for the Democratic members of the sub-Committee.'

The Senate passed a resolution relating to the conduct of the Senator from Wisconsin, that it was 'contrary to senatorial traditions and tends to bring the Senate into disrepute, and such conduct is hereby condemned.' It had been moved by Flanders. In itself the resolution was a near mortal blow, but McCarthy also lost his committee chairmanship because of the change in the composition of the Senate – now under Democratic control – caused by the year's congressional elections. There was no hope of a resurrection; and he died in 1957 as an alcoholic. But there are still many Americans who would agree with John Wayne in the interview he gave to Alexander Walker in London in 1960. 'McCarthy was a friend of mine. Whether he went overboard or not, he was of value to my country. A number of liberals think he started the witch-hunt. I think he was witch-hunted himself.'

What was the value? No one was ever successfully prosecuted, following the investigations by McCarthy, for undermining the American constitution with malice aforethought. Moreover all those who were huddled into quiet by his hectoring, because they were just that little bit 'liberal' in the fashionable trend of their youth, were often less afraid of admitting they were wrong than of revealing they had been none too quick on the uptake. It takes courage to confess, as Archimedes Patti did, concerning his helpfulness to Ho Chi Minh in drafting the Vietnamese constitution in the very phrases of the American one, that 'I, perhaps, was somewhat naive at that point of time.' McCarthyism was perhaps the price of not being so naive second time around. It also illustrates a strange volatility, of which America sometimes seems capable, and the results of such a campaign in a time of depression rather than boom might have been different. 'I really believe,' said Alistair Cooke in a radio interview in Britain in 1978, 'they could have torn up the Constitution.'

120

1955

The year 1955 saw one or two notable sideways moves in politics. The first came when a teetering Malenkov resigned in February, confessing to agricultural troubles in the Soviet paradise which were all his fault. It was one of the ironies of history that 'agricultural difficulties' were to be at least in part the cause of the downfall of the man who was now nudging him from power, Nikita Khrushchev, although the leading role went nominally to Bulganin. All the same, Malenkov was allowed to keep his head on his shoulders, a blessing which he owed partly to the fact that the new regime wished to present a more acceptable face to the world, and partly to the fact that his second wife, Elena, was

Khrushchev's sister. Khrushchev omits to tell in his memoirs how she took the demotion of her husband: it would be amusing to think that she nagged, and that this was why in 1957 Malenkov was given the comically remote job of manager of Ust-Kameno-Gorsk power station.

Another notable political change was in Britain. Churchill had decided to use the £150,000 ($375,000) cheque raised by the Birthday Presentation Fund mainly to endow his country home at Chartwell 'as a museum containing relics and mementoes of my long life.' However this was election year and the physical challenge of campaigning was one which it was

Above: Casey Stengel, manager of the New York Yankees, shows Burmese Premier U Nu how to hold a baseball bat.

self-evident he could not meet, otherwise even the clinching arguments put forward by Harold Macmillan might still have been brushed aside. Reluctant yet, he told Lord Moran, his physician, 'They would be wise to keep me at the top where I did very little, but where they could get my advice.' Besides an instinctive clinging to power, there is no doubt he felt he still had something to give, and, quite possibly, knew Eden well enough to have reservations about the succession. So long 'understood,' it could not now be changed, and in any case – still at the top or not – he did not intend that the new government should be deprived of his advice.

Eden kept Butler at the Chancellery, pro-

moted Macmillan to the Foreign Office, and, still debonair in the gravity of his new role, increased his majority in the general election from seventeen to fifty-nine. For the voters the years of the restored Churchill government had been a boom time. This was, as usual, attributed by the Conservatives to their own good management, and by the Labour opposition to their having profited by the fruition of the measures they had undertaken before 1951, aided by the luck of favorable changes in the terms of world trade, especially falls in the cost of raw materials.

It was a time of change for Labour, too. Attlee had stepped down in favor of Hugh Gaitskell, whose intellect and sophisticated

Above: Russia's B and K team, Bulganin and Khrushchev, at the Geneva Conference in 1955.

ideas brought him close to the 'left-wing' of the Conservative party, as personified by Butler. Their almost joint outlook was so widely recognized as to give it the nickname of Butskellism. Attlee had considered retirement earlier, in 1951, and Herbert Morrison, who felt as entitled to the succession as ever Eden could do, was convinced that Attlee postponed his decision only to prevent his becoming premier. Those few years meant that he was inevitably past the age when he could be seriously considered for the job. It had the element of tragedy, and reflected one of the constant divisions in the party between those who come up the 'university' and those that come up the 'trade union' way. Nevertheless as the crisis with Persia had shown, it was unavoidable. As Foreign Minister, Ernie Bevin had sometimes found the names of the countries he dealt with difficult to pronounce, but as one civil servant feelingly remarked, he had at least known where they were.

The spring of 1955 also saw a meeting of twenty-nine Afro-Asian nations in April at Bandung in Indonesia. The new nations of the Third World were celebrating their coming of age party, waving the flags of a nationalism disconcerting to an era which thought of it as a relic of the past, and pricking the balloons of conceit of both the Communist and 'free' worlds. They were shouting 'a plague on both your houses' in alarm and evident annoyance at what was happening in the Pacific and Indian Ocean areas.

After his failure to mobilize direct intervention in Vietnam, Dulles had brought about the formation in September 1954 of the South-East Asia Treaty Organization, rounding up Australia, France, New Zealand, Pakistan, the Philippines, Thailand, the United Kingdom and the United States, with South Vietnam, Cambodia and Laos as protocol states. Nothing could be more impressive – on paper – but when it came to aggressive power, they were passing one set of false teeth around among them, and that belonging to America. Britain, especially, with the scattered links of her Commonwealth, was chary of provoking further troubles, such as those she was still coping with in Malaya, by entering into anything that looked like a war-like alliance. Senator Knowland, the nick-named 'Senator for Formosa,' was not alone in America in growling over her as 'an undependable ally.'

In Vietnam the Americans took over the White Man's Burden from the French in 1954 without in the least realizing what they were doing. Dulles, eager to have what he called 'a clean base' against Communism, never dreamt that to the majority of Vietnamese the Americans were merely the face behind the French mask; they made no differentiation. Eisenhower subsequently said that, if elections had been held at the end of the fighting in 1954 Ho Chi Minh would have got eighty per cent of the votes which was possibly an overestimate: what he and everyone else underestimated, in the light of what they knew to be their own undoubted good intentions, was the dislike, inherent in ancient prejudice, and in the new nationalism

p left: Sir Alexander
eming, the discoverer of
nicillin.
bove: London newspapers
eculate about the
gagement of Princess
argaret and Group
aptain Peter Townsend.
r left bottom: Peter
ownsend in Chelsea after
ning with Princess
argaret.
eft: Princess Margaret in
pensive mood after it was
cided that her wedding to
e divorced aviator Peter
ownsend would not take
ace.
ight: Princess Margaret
views troops in Belfast
ith Peter Townsend behind
er. This photograph was
ken eight years before the
edding was called off.

of white faces. Arthur Larson describes one endearing incident which symbolizes the 1950s attitude to Vietnam. Little plastic gramophones were made for the USIA, at a cost of some fifty cents each, which were to be dropped in thousands over Vietnam in 1957. They were operated by turning a handle to play tiny records of inspiring messages from the South Vietnamese Prime Minister, Ngo Dinh Diem. When samples were produced in the Cabinet room, everyone from President downward had to have a turn at the handle.

Dulles had not even waited till the pens were poised to sign the July agreement in Vietnam in July 1954. Air force general Ed Lansdale was sent in on 1 June at the head of a secret military and political mission. Graham Greene's 'quiet American' was at work. On the military side, he assisted the organization of anti-guerrilla operations in South Vietnam, and on the political side aided the development of the administration. But his activities were not limited to the South. He had already established contacts in the North with anti-Communist leaders and their supporters who, under the Geneva arrangements, would have to move southward. In consultation with them, he arranged 'stay-behinds' to act as information channels as to what was happening under the newly-established Communist government. These agents were also entrusted with generally sabotaging the regime.

Their operations included hindering transport and communication arrangements, by such means as sugar in the petrol tanks of buses and lorries, and the spreading of 'black propaganda,' such as telling shopkeepers of supposed Communist plans to tax certain goods on the basis of their inventoried stock, and so persuading them to shut up shop and flee southward, bringing local commercial life to a standstill.

In the 1950s there was a kind of youthful exuberance in such activities, and a certainty of the rightness of the struggle against the Communist enemy. There was no agonizing of conscience that the regime operated against had been tacitly recognized at Geneva. There were no such feelings either when Communist-supported Jacobo Arbenz came to power in Guatemala in 1954. Dulles, conscious of a threat to Panama, sent arms to rebels lurking on the border, and a successful coup was engineered to establish a more 'suitable' regime. Richard Helms is again said to have been active here, and the move certainly helped to stabilize the situation in the area to the relief of many neighboring governments. To quote Hugh Sidey in *Time* in 1977, Helms was 'faster, sharper and, yes, at times more brutal' than his opponents, 'if he had not been he would have been fired.' Yet in 1977, this real-life Bond was dragged from retirement, and given a suspended sentence plus $2000 (£800) fine for misleading the Senate about the CIA's endeavors to keep Allende from becoming President of Chile. Such was the change in atmosphere between the 1950s and the 1970s.

In Vietnam in 1954 the Americans kept the Emperor Bao Dai as a figurehead for the sake of continuity. They were looking, however, for

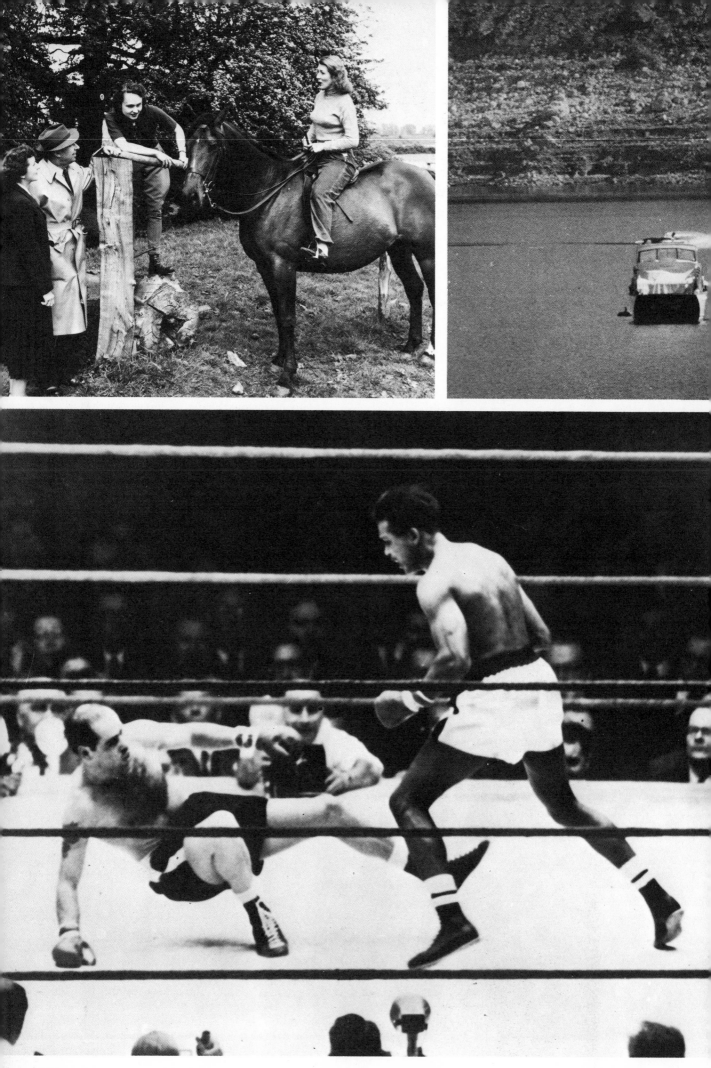

someone more reputable to be in actual control and eventually take over. The difficulty was that the people of the country were as alien as if they came from an unknown planet. Khrushchev experienced the same sense of utter frustration when confronted in Peking with inscrutable Chairman Mao, demanding the gift of a new university or new highway with no sense of anything due in return. He had to remind himself forcibly that he was dealing with a human being and a brother Communist. The Americans could not find any such intellectual binding basis as Communism, and eventually began to forget that the Vietnamese were fellow human beings either.

In the circumstances they fell with gratitude on Ngo Dinh Diem. He had actually spent some time in America and had greatly impressed many people there, including his co-religionist, Catholic Senator Mike Mansfield. Now in his early fifties, Diem was so high-principled that he had refused office from the Japanese in 1945, from Ho Chi Minh in 1946, and from the French Commissioner-General in 1947, and in 1949 had gone into exile voluntarily. From the time of his first resignation in 1933, when Bao Dai had turned down his early proposals of reform, he had lived some twenty years in retirement.

Besides being somewhat rusty in practical politics, Diem had the additional disadvantages of being an aloof bachelor of the aristocratic mandarin class, and of being a Roman Catholic in a country where only about fifteen per cent shared his faith. He was also cursed with a tribe of relatives as voracious and bloodthirsty as the East had ever mustered. Of his four brothers, one was Archbishop of Hué and a politico-religious activist; one was at his right-hand as 'political adviser'; one was his ambassador in London; and the fourth, Ngo Dinh Nhu, literally moved in on him in the presidential palace, as well as mentally dominating him. It was Ngo Dinh Nhu who developed the curious creed of 'Personalism,' a blend of anti-

Communism and Confucianized Catholicism which was rigidly moralizing. It also included a strong element of feminism in order to please Madame Ngo Dinh Nhu. She subsequently sponsored legislation outlawing abortion, beauty contests, boxing, concubinage, contraception, jazz and Western dancing, polygamy and prostitution. More Catholic than the Pope himself, she eventually roundly condemned John XXIII for diverging from her code. Her Women's Solidarity Movement, with its twelve hundred thousand members engaged in spying among the South Vietnamese in all fields, was a worthy adjunct of her husband's Special Forces – funded by the CIA – and other political police organizations which were to come to be used more against the loyal South Vietnamese than the Communist enemy.

From being Prime Minister, Diem became President in 1955 by a referendum which established a republic. His reputation for patriotic integrity might have achieved a genuine majority vote, but, to the embarrassment of his American sponsors, his majority was so overwhelming as to be obviously rigged. But, at least he could be counted on never to negotiate with the Vietminh, for yet another of his brothers had died at their hands, having been buried alive.

For a time it looked as if he might succeed in creating a viable state, despite his family and the excesses of the religious sects of South Vietnam, such as the Cao Dai, who combined Catholicism and Buddhism with exotic trimmings, and had a disorderly rabble of military followers. Diem attempted social and economic reform, struggled to re-settle the million refugees from the north, and tried to consolidate a state which was being supported almost entirely with American funds. However the guerrilla menace meant that ever-stronger measures had to be taken against them, which inevitably had side-effects, often bearing more heavily on the loyal peasantry than on those who were their intended target. The elections of the Geneva agreements could not be held with a victory for Ho Chi Minh throughout Vietnam. The American liberal conscience was uneasy, but a vote for Ho Chi Minh was believed to be a vote for the very Soviet-Chinese bloc which was refusing to countenance elections in Germany and Korea, because it was realized that there they would not mean a victory for Communism.

The people of North Vietnam had more to worry about than elections in which they now knew they would have to put the 'right' mark on the ballot paper. Even according to the

Above: Cantinflas rides his bicycle in London's Chelsea during the filming of Around the World in Eighty Days.
Above right: Anuerin Beva addresses the Labour Party conference at Margate in 1955.
Right: The Shah of Iran and Queen Soraya leave London after their state visit to Britain in 1955.

egime itself, the 'people's democratic rights' ad not been 'respected.' In particular the 'land e-allocation' campaign had led to a reign of rror. People's Agricultural Reform Tribunals ad been classifying people with minute por- ons of land as 'landlords,' since it was difficult therwise to find land in the over-populated elta area to 're-allocate.' Labor camps, prison, nd quite often execution followed condem- ation at kangaroo courts. A prisoner sentenced o death faced his end in public, and was very icky if he were simply shot, the majority en- uring torture first. At the height of the cam- aign, news began to trickle north of Diem's nd distribution efforts in South Vietnam, and e Communist government admitted its 'grave nistakes' in November 1956, promising 'demo- ratization' of the regime.

The North Vietnamese government was con- erned to have a stable potentially prosperous tate to the south of them. At the time of emarcation, they had taken some fifty thousand nthusiastic young Communist sympathizers orthward for special training, and at the end f the 1950s they gradually infiltrated South ietnam. This created a growing problem in ietnam, one which was to be faced by Kennedy hen he took over from Eisenhower in 1961.

Another point of abrasion, this time directly between the United States and China, was the offshore islands – Quemoy, Matsu and the Tachens – which had always belonged to China, and were now held by the troops of Chiang Kai-shek as stepping-stones for the reconquest of the mainland from Taiwan. The concept of reconquest grew more fanciful every day, and the little specks on the map were periodically bombarded by the Communists with live shells or dud propaganda through loudspeakers, according to the current attitude of the Chinese government towards Dulles. Sometimes they would appear to be considering their own rather better chances of using the islands as stepping stones for their conquest of Taiwan. Dulles would then warn Eisenhower that atomic weapons would be the only effective weapon to defend the islands against assault from mainland airfields, and would gloomily prophesy that 'before this problem is solved, there is at least an even chance that the United States will have to go to war.' Eisenhower thought the chances rather better than that, and promptly asked and received by an overwhelming majority from Congress 'unlimited authority to act in the Formosa Strait' calculating that China would overhear and subside. In the end the Tachens were evacuated and became Chinese and the other two remained in Chiang's hands. The main importance of the episode, or rather, continuing series of episodes in the 1950s, was the Eisenhower request to Congress, which was seen by later commentators as opening the way for the exercise of a presidential licence to make war in subsequent administrations, most notably in Vietnam.

Yet by 1955 it was the brightening prospect of peace which absorbed the world. The Soviet H-bomb tests in September 1954 had convinced Eisenhower of the need to negotiate, and, at the American request a meeting of heads of state 'at the summit' was arranged for July in Geneva.

In the 1970s news of 'yet another' summit is more likely to summon a wide yawn rather than avid interest, but in the mid-1950s scarcely anyone actually knew what the Soviet leaders looked like in the flesh. Equally important, though so often forgotten, the Soviet leaders saw the West for the first time. Stalin had hardly stepped beyond his web in the Soviet Union through the whole of his long life. To Western eyes the Russians looked odd, for this was the year when 'pleats' had disappeared from the trousers of the well-dressed man, who was aiming at a trim waistline, and was soon to be discarding cuffs, and experimenting with the daring idea of slant pockets. The Russians' trousers had deep cuffs, the legs so wide that they flapped in the breeze, and fitted 'where they touched' they were so poorly tailored. As a concession to summer the material was a curious mauvish lilac.

It is an eye-opening revelation of the chronic inefficiency of intelligence services that Eisenhower had assumed, from Bulganin's title, that he was the 'real boss.' It was to him that he unfolded his 'Open Skies' plan for mutual aerial inspection by the two powers of their atomic and other war preparations. It even seemed as if Bulganin might eventually be persuaded to agree, and Eisenhower felt optimistic as he walked to the cocktail lounge with Khrushchev. 'I don't agree with the chairman,' said Khrushchev, with a warm smile and a cold voice, and Ike 'wasted no more time probing Mr Bulganin.' Maurice Macmillan, there with Eden to represent Britain, found it a mystery that this 'fat, vulgar man, with his ceaseless flow of talk' could be the successor of the czars in ruling so vast and populous a country, but picked up the genuine desire of the Russian for peace, and his impatience with the Chinese drain on Russian industrial and military power, and realization that China might become more dangerous than convenient as an ally.

Since the days of Britain's imperial power were over, Khrushchev concentrated unerringly on the Americans, but for once his native cunning somewhat failed him. Seeing Dulles passing notes to the President before Eisenhower risked an opinion in the discussions, he tended to dismiss him as a puppet of the Secretary of State. For the latter Khrushchev had a healthy respect, remarking later, in his memoirs, that Dulles had always known how far to push us,' but had never pushed too far. It was a mistake the British government tended to make, too, and it is true that Eisenhower was not a conference man. He hated things 'being sprung upon' him. But, it takes more than saw-

Left: Glubb Pasha and some of the members of Jordan's Arab Legion which he commands.
Right: Ruby Murray on BBC television in 1955. This young Irish girl was extremely popular in Britain.
Below: Sam Snead, captain of the US team, defeated his opponent, Dave Thomas, in the Ryder Cup competition of 1955. However he lost this hole to Thomas!
Bottom center: One of the first portable TVs is displayed in 1955. It had a nine-inch screen.
Bottom extreme right: A British 'Teddy Boy' jives to a Rock-and-Roll band.

dust between the ears to make a five-star general, and one who could marshal allies to win a war. Nor was it only that he had, as Richard Rovere of *The New Yorker* said, a 'unique ability to convince people that he has no talent for duplicity,' though his likeability – even Adlai Stevenson admitted, 'I like Ike,' – was an enormous asset. Above all he was brilliant in the quality of his common sense when it came to action during his first administration. Common sense is something which appears so obvious when exercized that it never strikes anyone as brilliant. But for that quality, the 1950s might not have been looked back on with nostalgia: there might have been no one to look back.

In the event, it was Eisenhower himself who very nearly failed to see even the end of his own first term. Reading Macmillan's diary record of the lunch to which the President entertained the British at his villa during the Geneva Conference, it was surprising that his heart attack did not occur there. 'A disgusting meal,' noted Macmillan, 'of large meat slices, hacked out' and served with 'marmalade and jam.' Eisenhower did not care for sweet courses, and concentrated on large amounts of soldier-in-the-field-type first courses. His Waterloo came on 23 September 1955 after 'a huge hamburger sandwich generously garnished with Bermuda (raw) onion and accompanied by a pot of coffee,' when he disregarded the initial discomfort of a coronary as indigestion and went on to play a round of golf.

Once he was off the danger list, the thoughts of everyone turned to whether the attack ruled out a second term, and it throws light on the encouraging medical progress of the 1950s that the question arose at all. Only a few years before a coronary meant the immediate end, or a regime so sedentary as to make the end preferable. Now, with new drugs, complemented by a regimen of moderate exercise, men were recovering to a life sometimes more active than before the attack, and books proliferated in the new age of do-it-yourself health care to tell them exactly how it was to be done.

In 1955 immense relief was also given to t
mothers of the world by the development of
polio vaccine at the University of Michigan
Jonas E Salk and his staff. The tables of dea
and disablement, with the figures that ro
annually as the population grew more congest
and infection easier, were soon no longer
exist. The coming of the warm weather and t
sight of children splashing round in swimmi
pools had lost the power to make a woman
heart miss a beat, as she wondered whether
would be one of her kids next.

The year also brought another medic
innovation. In *Free and Female* in 197
Barbara Seaman wrote of the casualties of t
new freedom of sex that came in the 1960s a
1970s. The 'train gradually carrying us awa
from Victorian morality' became runaway un
in the backlash of the later 1970s, when restrain
again began to be imposed. But in 1955 t
moment when the moral brakes really starte
to go was when Gregory Pincus of the Worcest
Foundation for Experimental Biology and Joh
Rock of the Reproductive Study Center
Brookline, Massachusetts, discovered wh
rapidly became known as simply 'the pill.' N
cleared for public distribution until 1960,
came into a ready-made climate. World War
had contributed to a loosening of moral stand
ards in the middle range of society where the
had been strongest. The new popularization
psychology, with its advocacy of doing wha
came naturally because it might even be harmf
if you did not, made its impact. The new pro
perity, particularly in its new mobility, provide
opportunity. Young people could no longer b

ept under the parental eye, and the parents ould also more easily escape the restricting resence of the young. The only sanction that emained, in view of the unreliable nature of xisting contraceptives, was fear of the consequences. Dr Pincus removed the only one that nost people feared, and left them to discover nat there might be others of which they had ever thought.

In the field of more orthodox science, it was ne year of the death of Albert Einstein, the reator of the theory of relativity, and of Sir lexander Fleming, the discoverer of penicillin, ut the word that was on everyone's lips was automation.' Suddenly the captains of industry vere talking about computer-controlled machine tools, and automatic machinery with or vithout transfer or feedback mechanisms, and ven people in jobs far removed from factories ound that their weekly pay-packet (payment y check being still as uncommon as possession f a bank account) was beginning to be worked ut by a computer. The demands of the Welfare tate in Britain, with an ever-increasing number f deductions from wages to be calculated on n ever more complex basis, was making omputerization essential. Moreover even the omputers found the weekly performance a train, and the changeover to monthly paychecks was on its way.

Delight at having the labor taken out of their asks by the new computerization was tempered or many by nervousness that the job itself might lisappear, as machines took over the work that up to then had been performed by hand. George Meany, now President of the merged American Federation of Labor and Congress of Industrial Organizations created this year, and mercifully known as the AFL-CIO, was optimistic. Looking with pride at his membership figures, now at a record eighteen million he was optimistic. 'The new techniques offer promise of higher living standards for all, greater leisure, and more pleasant working conditions.' He had not calculated that, as the blue collars turned white, leveling off in his membership figures until the 1960s, and after that a marked decline took place.

In Britain the unions imbued with the spirit of the 1930s and the fear of depression and redundancies, made certain what they most feared in the long-term took place. As Macmillan said of this period: 'Now we had full employment – some would say artificially full employment – but prices were all the time rising.' The artificiality arose in either preventing by union power the installation of the new machinery, or allowing it to be installed providing the workforce remained at the same level. Indirectly this increased the flow of immigrant workers, with the ultimate prospect of great unemployment as harsh reality stepped in during the 1970s, when world pressures beyond union control became effective. In the meantime the party continued.

In effect trade unionism was widening its powers. In the prewar period, there had been an increase in the local 'red-brick' universities, and in the postwar period there was a great proliferation of the 'plate-glass' universities. The new kind of student was epitomized in the

Top left: Teddy boys and the rough trade gather in the Club Martinique in Newcastle.
Left: A Digby Morton pencil dress in 1955.
Extreme left bottom: Dancers in action at the Club Martinique.
Below: Miss Great Britain of 1955 displays her 'Guys and Dolls' skirt, named after the famous Broadway musical.

Kingsley Amis novel *Lucky Jim* in 1954. The mass of incoming students was too large to be assimilated to any existing pattern, their backgrounds were completely different from those of the students in the older institutions of an earlier generation. They had trade union links, and when they went out on the market, they strengthened the movement's upward growth into teaching, local government, social work, and the new nationalized industries. By the mid-1950s there was a new middle class which relied for its existence on the continuation of the whole framework created by the spate of postwar social legislation. As they mellowed and put down roots, they were to be the people who tended to vote Liberal, because their origins suggested that it was treason to vote 'Tory,' but who really wanted the benefits for themselves that only Conservatism could bring. It was not until the 1970s that the Conservative Party, as a whole, began to realize the true nature of this new section of the electorate.

British Royalty was another institution that was changing its image. The talk of the Royal Academy was the portrait of the Queen by Pietro Annigoni, painted for the ancient Fishmongers' Company, in Garter robes against an Italianate landscape background. Everyone who was anyone rushed to have themselves equally flatteringly recorded in the same style. Both inside and outside this select company, the gossip of the year concerned the Queen's sister, Margaret.

Towards the end of the war George VI, very much a plain man himself, decided to widen the choice of candidates for court appointments which until then had been confined to members of the Establishment, by taking in some of the men who, though of less exalted birth, had done a yeoman stint in their country's service. Among the 'possibles' was a tall, dark, handsome young man, a fighter pilot who had brought down the first German bomber to crash on British soil in the war, and who had

Above left: Stirling Moss, champion motor racer, checks the engine of his Cooper before a race.
Above: Donald Campbell in his Bluebird during the London Boat Show.
Right: American high school cheerleaders in saddle shoes and white bucks which were very popular in the early 1950s.

een 'one of the few' of the Battle of Britain, in
hich he had himself been shot down and
ounded. He even shared the King's disability
f a stammer. His background also checked out.
not 'top drawer,' he was not much more than
ne drawer down – he was a cousin of the
pposition leader, Hugh Gaitskell – and was
uitably married, with a pleasing wife and two
oung sons already in existence or in the offing.
roup Captain Peter Townsend was appointed.
  Princess Margaret was then fourteen, but she
as growing up, and, as Townsend has recorded,
s marriage was disintegrating quite indepen-
ently, and ended in divorce. The Princess's
mpathy with his loneliness cemented their
isting friendship, and the couple were in love.
eaction inside the Court was curious. Such
ings did not happen, so everyone continued to
ehave as if it had not, and, with the King now
ead, Townsend remained within the even more
timate little 'Court' of the Queen Mother's
ousehold at Clarence House. It needed an

outside reaction to set events moving, and it came on Coronation Day. Members of the Press noticed the 'charming little gesture' with which the Princess brushed a bit of fluff off the Group Captain's uniform, and the American reporters did not stay silent. The story made the New York headlines. It was a smaller world than when the American stories of Edward VIII's romance with Mrs Simpson had been kept under wraps in Britain while the Continent and America freely gossiped. It took the best part of two weeks still, but on 14 June the story hit the London press.

The Establishment made its classic response: separation. By a dispensation of Providence, the Queen Mother was due to visit Rhodesia, together with Margaret, and this gave a head start to the testing period of a year's existence apart. Just in case the lovers should rush into each other's arms the moment the Princess returned, Townsend was despatched two days beforehand to the embassy in Brussels as 'air attaché.' Given a choice of Brussels, Johannesburg or Singapore, Townsend had picked the nearest, for which the newspapers were duly grateful.

True love endured, but so did the Royal Marriages Act, passed by George III in 1772 to ensure that none of his descendants should marry before the age of twenty-five without the consent of their sovereign. It would be two years before Margaret reached her twenty-fifth birthday – in 1955. Even then, though she might dispense with her sister's consent, Margaret would in that case have to get the agreement of the British and Dominions' parliaments. It was

'you win, I lose' situation, and the hope lay the greater marital freedom of the 1950s, en even Anthony Eden had been divorced fore marrying, as his second wife, Churchill's ce. The real stumbling-block, however, ough everyone pussyfooted round it, was that e divorce had taken place after Townsend's pointment as equerry and the development of e couple's friendship. Someone so close to e Queen as Margaret could not be allowed to ke up a position in which, even in the way of chnicality, she could be smeared as a 'home-ecker.'

In the spring of 1955 Margaret was des-tched on yet another tour, this time to the ribbean. On her return the hunt was on, and porters followed the couple in droves, like ghts of seagulls following the progress of a ough, for every least titbit of information. All rough the summer the reporters remained at e ready, with rumor growing wilder with the nds and falling leaves of autumn. The court mained rigid, and when an announcement me from Clarence House on 14 October, it as the ultimate in absurdities, an announcement say that 'no announcement was at present ntemplated.'

Speculation ranged from Prince Philip having d such a row with his sister-in-law that all the lace servants had fled in fear and trembling, rough the Queen having threatened one or th the lovers with the Tower, to the Arch-shop of Canterbury having thundered about communication. It was at least true that the incess had seen the Archbishop, having in ct dined with him and a select company of the more weighty of his fellow bishops, but as missionaries they had apparently lost their cunning. Or so the rumor went. Rumor had it, too, that the Cabinet had met and that a Bill of Renunciation had been prepared.

What was certain was that the price of her intended marriage had been made clear to the Princess in a way which outdid all but the very wildest stories. She would lose the royal rights to a title and the succession to the throne; she would lose the income paid to her as part of the Civil List approved by Parliament for maintenance of the lesser members of the Royal Family; and she would no longer be accepted in communion with her Church.

On 31 October came a real statement at last. The Princess announced her intention not to marry the Group Captain 'mindful of the Church's teaching that Christian marriage is indissoluble.' She saw the decade out unwed, the nation gave a universal 'Ah!' and in the following year David Cooksey's prizewinning photograph of her in the *Daily Express* showed her 'Smiling Through' a veiling of raindrops on the window of her limousine. The Group Captain returned to Brussels, and was eventually consoled by his marriage in 1959 to Marie-Luce Jamagne, the young Belgian girl whom he had met there soon after his first banishment when she fell from her show-jumper practically at his feet.

A case that curiously criss-crossed with the royal romance was the Foreign Office scandal of the two diplomats, both of whom had been in sensitive posts in Washington, Guy Burgess and Donald Maclean. Soviet agents since the 1930s, they both disappeared from England and turned up in Russia in 1951, obviously having been warned that suspicion had fallen on them. The Establishment had already been undermined and much of its power dissipated in the 1950s, but there still remained a grudging respect for the traditional virtues of Eton and Oxbridge – loyalty and dedication to service in the cause of sovereign and country: the Burgess–Maclean affair shattered the last bastion of its defenses.

Press and public were eager to discover the identify of the 'third man' who had done the 'tipping off,' and since the loud-mouthed, drunken exhibitionist Burgess had been a chum of 'Kim' Philby at Cambridge, suspicions led to Washington again. There Philby was representing the British Secret Intelligence Service (MI6), working in cooperation with the American CIA and FBI, and had welcomed Burgess to stay in his house, when the latter had arrived in the capital on his assignment as Second Secretary of the British Embassy in 1950.

By early summer 1951, Philby had become concerned, in the role of Soviet agent which he had entered upon in 1934, with the danger that

Below: The ship Theron *loaded with supplies and even a light aircraft for its journey to the Antarctic in 1955.*
Right: Bertrand Russell, the great philosopher, gives a lecture warning of the dangers of nuclear warfare.

Maclean was about to be 'blown.' He wanted Burgess to go back to Britain to help in the arrangements for getting Maclean out of the USA, and was hoisted with his own petard when the shady couple made a joint bolt and left the trail to himself as wide as a motorway. The ruse by which he had had Burgess sent back to England by an indignant Ambassador Franks – abusing the privilege of CD plates by getting caught speeding in Virginia three times in one day – seemed rather less of a good idea.

He was recalled to London and, following interrogation, asked to resign. One of his interrogators was the celebrated William Skardon, who with the silken, sympathetic courtesy of his interest, had laid bare his mind with scalpel-precise questions breaking through his defenses until he incriminated himself. Although asked to resign, Philby remained in a kind of non-proven limbo. In 1954, however, Vladimir Petrov defected in Sydney, when he was recalled to Moscow to answer charges connected with his involvement in Beria's plotting to take supreme power in the Soviet Union. During the press furore, the *Daily Express* referred to a 'security officer' who had served in the British embassy in Washington and had been asked to resign. The wording was discreet because English libel law would have enabled Philby to sue, but the press swarmed out to his home at Crowborough in Sussex. This lay between Uckfield, where Princess Margaret was hiding out with friends and Eridge, where Peter Townsend was doing the same. The press devoted either the morning or the afternoon to chasing one of the parties to the romance, taking a lunchtime break on their way to the other to look up Philby, who evaded them for the most part by skulking in Ashdown Forest during the middle hours of the day.

At last he was named in the House of Commons, where 'privilege' allowed Colonel Marcus Lipton, Member of Parliament for Brixton to do so. Harold Macmillan declared that there was no evidence of Philby having betrayed British interests, though he was now formally dismissed from the Foreign Service because of his associations with Burgess. The next year he went to Beirut as correspondent for *The Observer*, finally slipping into Russia in 1963 after the arrest of George Blake – the 'fourth man' – blazoned his role yet more emphatically. In the Beirut years he is said to have still been working for the Secret Intelligence Service.

The story is one of such incompetence that it is calculated to make any Briton squirm with embarrassment, and in his own account of events published in 1968, Philby – while gently deprecating his own 'brilliance' – underlines every stupidity with effect. The total effect, however, is possibly too overwhelming. The blunders Philby admits to are in retrospect so great that it suggests he made many others. Afflicted from infancy with a stammer, he needed to compensate for being deprived of the chance to excel directly in politics, which were his main interest in life. His chance of even a secondary role in the eventual triumph of the Communist Party, with which he had completely identified himself, was destroyed by the col-

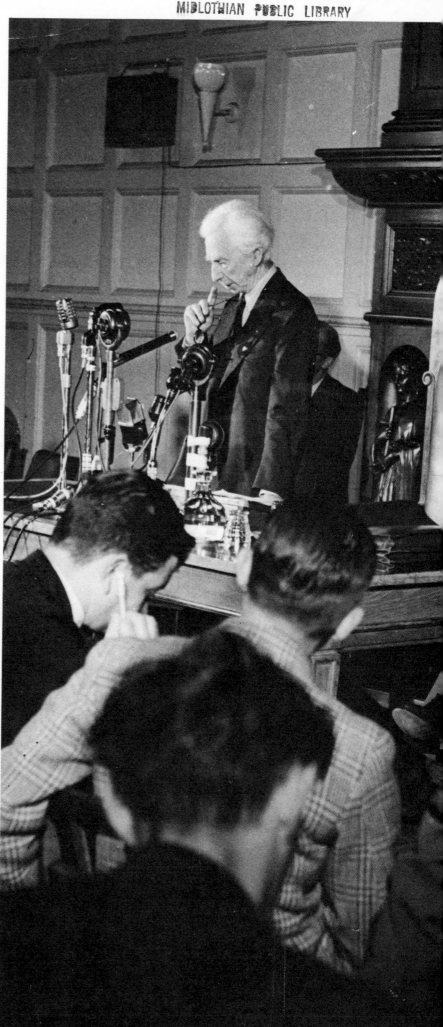

143

lapse of support for the Party among his more intelligent contemporaries. He found a role for himself as the only one to 'stay the course,' as he expresses it, when the excesses of Stalinism deterred the others. The purity of the cause would survive such aberrations. By 1968 he had still 'no doubt about the verdict of history,' but was forced to admit that the advances he had hoped to see in his lifetime 'may have to wait a generation or two.' To admit that in print, suggests that he had begun to wonder whether it might not be more than one or two.

It is also permissible to wonder at the resolute 'blind eye' turned by the British government is an ever mounting number of clues; the statement by Macmillan; and the reluctance to release Philby from service even during the Beirut period. One is reminded that the most valuable agent of all is the enemy agent whom you can use because he does not know he has been rumbled. Maybe Harold Adrian Russell Philby was merely being humored in the kind of little-girl Brownie game which uses the Kipling name of Kim for its leaders, and which he so clung to in the make-believe name he adopted for himself. Even if this were true, it is unlikely that it could ever be admitted, and we shall probably never know – even in these days of candid memoirs.

In sport there was something of a revival of the 1930s mania for speed records, with Donald Campbell taking his turbo-jet hydroplane *Bluebird* up to 202.32 miles per hour on Ullswater, and up to 216.2 on Lake Mead in Nevada, but speed records were fast outrunning the purse of individuals, and becoming the province of governments and technicians. One record, of interest as being still unbroken in the 1970s, is that of two French locomotives of the SNCF – electric locomotives BB 9004 and CC 7107 – which on successive days in 1955 attained 205.6 miles per hour over one and a quarter miles at Morceur. In motor racing the man of the year was Stirling Moss, the first Englishman to win the Mille Miglia in Italy, and the first Englishman to win the British Grand Prix at Aintree – beating the legendary Fangio to do so – since it was held at Brooklands in 1926. In boxing one more British heavyweight failed to make it, Don Cockell suffering a technical knock-out at the hands of Rocky Marciano in the ninth round. Rocky had dominated the scene since his knock-out of Jersey Joe Walcott in the thirteenth round in 1952, and appeared indestructible, but was to retire in 1956. In the circumstances, there seemed a certain realism in the decision of the BBC television to try out a new type of ring floor, claimed to minimize

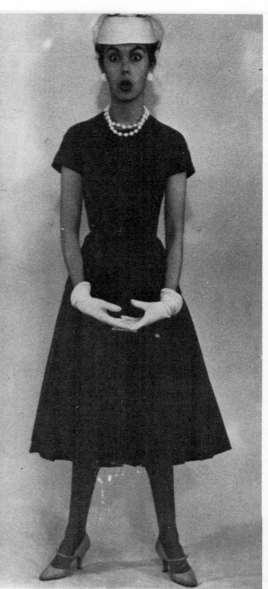

Above: A frilly underskirt is sexily displayed.
Right: Christian Dior's new A-line dress.
Far right: Graham

Sutherland was finishing his portrait of Churchill in 1955. The painting was destroyed by the Prime Minister after he received it.

the shock to a boxer's head when he was knocked down.

Probably the *cause célèbre* of the year was the shooting by Ruth Ellis, a twenty-eight-year-old model, of her faithless lover, David Blakeley, a racing driver some three years her junior. She was not endeared to modest matrons by being a divorcee and the mother of two children, and the degree of premeditation together with the number of shots she had fired into her lover's body, went against her. The location, outside a pub on Hampstead Heath on Easter Monday, was also less than refined. She consequently hanged. However the fact that she had been a good-looking woman in the prime of life, obviously who had been out of her mind with jealousy, helped Sydney Silverman get his bill for the abolition of the death penalty through the practically all-male House of Commons in 1956. It fell foul of the House of Lords, however, and the measure was not passed for another decade.

In more orthodox entertainment this was the year of the first independent (commercial) television channel in Britain. On the night of the opening the BBC cunningly made use of the remaining drawing power of radio by arranging for beloved Grace Archer, heroine of *The Archers*, the serialized 'everyday story of country folk,' to be burned to death. Tears and outrage came from throughout the land, and the BBC's defense of its right to be realistic was rendered somewhat hollow by the convenience of its timing to nobble the opposition. Television marked the year by axing all its panel games, except the American adopted 'What's my Line?' which owed its survival less to its intrinsic entertainment value than the hope that panelist Gilbert Harding would exceed even his usual irascibility in being rude to the subjects or his fellow panelists. The new craze, again American-inspired, was to have the audience participate in quizzes with big giveaways, as in 'Double Your Money.' The prizes were never so great as they were in the States where quizzes became a manipulative industry, with attractive contestants groomed for audience appeal, coached in how to raise the tension when giving the answers on which a fortune depended, and – when popular enough – given the answers to keep them in the show until it seemed time to get rid of them. There the steam was taken out of it when Charles van Doren, whose erudition had astounded the whole country, turned out to be a fake. He had resisted confession in a cliff-hanging way that resembled his handling of the questions fed to him, but the breaking point came when another competitor showed how it was done by posting answers to the questions before the program was screened.

On the larger screen the film-makers were setting puzzles for the exhibitors with their competing new processes – Paramount's Vista-Vision, 20th Century Fox's CinemaScope, and the nightmare complexities of Cinerama. In Britain the Rank Organization had some six hundred cinemas to adapt with variable ana-morphic lenses and screens which could cope with the lot. Even at that the film of the year was no spectacular, but *Marty*, the story of 'a fat, ugly little man,' as he called himself, who felt rejected by everybody. He found himself a girl-friend at last, who did not please his mother or his friends, and whose looks classified her as a 'dog,' but with whom he found life fun. It was a realistic landmark in American film-making, in that it showed an acceptance of life as it is and two people making something worth-while out of it: had the film been made a decade earlier, there would have been a miraculous conversion of Marty to a handsome hero, and the woman would have been inevitably a beauty. Even as it was, it is significant that it was an adaptation of a television play by Paddy Chayefsky. The fertilization of the large by the smaller screen had begun.

Other films included the fiery Anna Magnani in *Rose Tattoo*, the Halas and Batchelor cartoon version of *Animal Farm*, a remake of *A Star is Born*, with Judy Garland and James Mason, and Laurence Olivier's *Richard III*, clustered with the star names of John Gielgud, Cedric Hardwicke, Ralph Richardson and Claire Bloom. The war made something of a comeback with *The Dam Busters*, with Richard Todd as the VC Wing Commander Guy Gibson who dropped the bouncing bombs (designed by Dr Barnes Wallis, who was played by Michael Redgrave) to destroy the Möhne Dam, and *The Colditz Story*, telling of the prisoner-of-war camp for recidivist escapees that no other camp could hold, had a theme revived for a television series in the 1970s. Marilyn Monroe appeared in *The Seven Year Itch*, once more having the luck to hit a good writer and a good story. At the time, if there had been a world vote of cinema-goers for the most luscious female film star, it seems inescapable that the palm would have been awarded to 'La Lollo,' Gina Lollobrigida. Yet, looking back on her film titles in the 1950s –

Les Belles des Nuits, Infidelity, Beat the Devil, Crossed Swords, and *Bread, Love and Dreams* – none rings a very loud bell. She also failed to die young and tragically.

Tunes running round the heads of 1955 included the 'Dam Busters March'; still a favorite on radio request programs, the insistent theme tune of the film 'Love is a Many-Splendored Thing,' in which Jennifer Jones looked out wistfully in the guise of an Eurasian doctor, and the pulsing melodies of *Carmen Jones*, the Dorothy Dandridge 'colored' film version of Bizet's opera, which competed with the rustic harmonies of the film musical *Seven Brides for Seven Brothers*. An oddity of the year was 'The Happy Wanderer' which made its first appearance at the Welsh Eisteddford in 1953, and ran on in the hit parade for over twelve months from 1954 to 1955 in a recording by the Oberdkirchen Girls Choir. Also a run-away hit was 'Softly, softly,' a breathy little tune which made the name of British singer Ruby Murray, who never achieved a second success of similar magnitude, but remained a nostalgic name. Petula Clark was another name of the year, which later suffered eclipse before rising again in France and returning home, still to be in lights in the 1970s.

Fashion had taken on a somewhat hectic note. Dior launched an A-line early in the year, and a Y-line in the autumn: Paris was finding it harder to keep its lead. The Y-line had a wide-spread shoulder effect, with a panel down the front over a very full short skirt. The short, day-length dress, was now *de rigueur* for evenings, too, in the fast-moving mid-1950s. It got its special occasion quality from expensive fabrics rounded out into an almost crinoline shape over frilly nylon petticoats.

By March the clouds of the Middle East crisis which was to dominate the rest of the year were gathering. The legendary Englishman, Glubb Pasha, the fatherly figure who had guided the young King Hussein of Jordan in the early years of his reign, was dismissed from his beloved Arab Legion. France began her retreat from North Africa – Morocco was recognized as independent at the beginning of the month and Tunisia towards the end, and Algeria began to tremble in the balance. On Cyprus, where Greek Cypriots were demanding *enosis* 'union with Greece,' the black-veiled 'top-hat' headdress of Archbishop Makarios nodded with ever-greater emphasis in their support, until he was deported into Napoleonic exile in the Seychelles by an exasperated British government.

The British people concentrated with their usual annual hopefulness on the Budget. Harold Macmillan, now Chancellor of the Exchequer, tapped on his battered black despatch box with his magic wand and produced Premium Bonds. 'Investors' would buy bonds which would retain their face value but earn no interest: instead a low rate of interest would be allowed to accumulate for distribution in monthly prizes to those holding lucky numbers. Inflation ensured that the investors lost considerably when they cashed in any bonds, and that the government made a bundle on a huge loan at the minimal interest of four per cent: the prizes ranged from £25 ($62.50) to £1000 ($2500) with a limit of £500 ($1250) on individual holdings of bonds. Harold Wilson, on behalf of the Opposition, denounced the scheme on moral grounds as a 'squalid raffle.' As Macmillan was wrily to note, when the chance came, Wilson did not abolish this tremendously popular gamble, but merely increased the prizes!

Back in Moscow, Bulganin and Khrushchev, had developed a taste for foreign travel. Like holidaymakers everywhere they had used the

Top extreme left:
Archbishop Makarios of Cyprus bids for support among Greeks overseas.
Center: Six members of the EOKA organization captured in Cyprus.
Bottom left: A Greek Cypriot barrow boy shot during the uprising in Nicosia.
Above: West Indian immigrants to Britain arrived at a rate of 3000 per month in 1956.
Left: Bulganin and Khrushchev on their visit to Britain in 1956 wave goodbye as the bearded Soviet atomic chief Dr Ivan Kurchatov and A N Tupolev, the aircraft designer, observe.

151

winter to thumb through the brochures, and fancied Britain. As an advance guard, Khrushchev despatched his brother-in-law, Malenkov, for a tour of the country's power stations. The timing – Britain was to start the world's first atomic power station at Calder Hall in May – was apposite, and Malenkov and his team of over a dozen experts made sure they visited the site. The ex-Prime Minister also made a cultural tour, and distinguished himself by singing Auld Lang Syne at the birthplace of Robert Burns, and repeated a number of the poet's verses from memory, in Russian. 'B and K,' as they were soon known, followed him in April, having in the interval since their last appearance improved their tailoring. The highlight of their visit was a reception by the Queen, which left Khrushchev 'very impressed,' especially with her 'gentle, calm voice' and her lack of pretention, she was 'completely without the haughtiness that you'd expect of royalty.' He had presumably expected to find her like the Red Queen in *Alice*, shouting 'Off with his head!' at regular intervals. A close second among his pleasures was the changing of the guard. 'Such a colorful ceremony!' he enthused, 'I could see why it was such a great tourist attraction.'

Attractive to the Secret Service was the Soviet cruiser, the *Ordjonikidze*, on which the Russian pair had arrived. A Russian sailor on watch saw a frogman close to the ship in Portsmouth harbor, and although the intruder took evasive action before the watchman could do anything about it, Commander Lionel Crabb – a Royal Navy Volunteer Reserve diver noted for his World War II exploits – disappeared. In the House of Commons Sir Anthony Eden had a rough time replying to questions, government responsibility was disclaimed, and the Russians received an apology. In the coming months other topics took over the front pages, until in June a headless body was

Cairo to Arabs everywhere to follow Egypt's example in throwing off the yoke of foreign occupation. He created the vision of an Arab Empire taking in Algeria, Libya, Morocco and Tunisia to the West; stretching southward to Moslem states of eastern Africa and northward beyond Palestine to Iraq, Jordan and Syria; and eastward to the Gulf States. At least a hundred and twenty-five million people, with oil resources to make them into one of the wealthiest as well as the largest states in the world.

It was a vision with a flaw. Such empires are built by conquest and bloodshed, and like the pharaohs with their great monumental inscriptions recording 'prestige' battles which we know from other sources never took place, Nasser had no appetite for the realities of bloodshed. The trait is an attractive one: even today, for example, a robbery in Egypt that leads to the death or serious injury of the victim is so rare that a whole police force is sent into a huddle when it happens. This was what made Eden's broadcast comparison of Nasser, at the time of the Suez intervention, with Hitler so incongruous. In 1956 Nasser had only a fraction of the tanks, and aircraft supplied to him by Russia in operational order. His mind was on his great monumental project, 'our new pyramid' as he described it to the London *Times* reporter – the high dam at Aswan, and the funds needed to accomplish it. He needed a substantial sum, and he fancied his chances in making Soviet Russia and the United States bid against one another for the privilege of making the loan, and so preventing his going over to the other side. Astute enough to know that increasing dependence on

Russia meant increasing dominance by Russia, whereas America could more safely have its toes stepped on, he sent his unfortunate ambassador for one more go at Dulles.

The ambassador was very much on the American side, and pleaded with the Secretary of State not to turn down the loan request because he had had the Russian offer of finance 'right here in my pocket.' It was the wrong move. Dulles, his feet up on the table in front of him, suddenly lost patience, and told him that if the Egyptians already had the cash, then they did not need any of America's – 'My offer is withdrawn!' In an equal fit of temper, Nasser nationalized the Suez Canal (which he had always intended to do anyway), seeing this as a way to immediate funds which would enable him to do without further Soviet entanglement.

At Number Ten Downing Street, Sir Anthony Eden was entertaining the King of Iraq and his Prime Minister, Nuri as Said, to dinner when the news came through. The little gathering dispersed in a hurry as Nuri adjured his host 'Hit him, hit him hard and hit him now.' The Iraqi Premier – whose body was to be dragged through the streets of his capital in the eventual aftermath of Suez – had no love for Nasser. Eden decided that he would 'hit him,' but 'hitting him hard' and 'now' were rather more difficult. Britain was hardly better prepared for hostilities than Nasser himself. Nationalization was announced on 26 July, and the emissaries of Britain and France shuttled between their respective capitals like wet hens. The British had throughout been hampered by the need to sustain the special relationship with America. Dulles both wanted to remain dominant in the

157

negotiations and to refrain from making any decisive move in America's presidential election year. He had opposed putting the matter in United Nations hands because one canal might lead to another in which America had an even more vital interest – Panama – and it was not until a couple of days before the showdown that Eisenhower himself, according to Arthur Larson, 'told the British and the French that the matter should be handled through the United Nations, and that they should take no direct action.' Even colonial possessions and satellites resent being 'told,' and anyway by that time it was too late.

The French who, as the original builders of the canal, had retained a vital interest, were close in cahoots with the Israelis. Leaving aside their right to be where they were, the Israelis were unlikely to stay there very long if they ignored what was happening round their borders. There had been numerous recent 'fedayeen' raids across their southern frontier, their only outlet to the Red Sea at Eilat was under Egyptian blockage, and broadcasts from Cairo proclaimed that Nasser would choose his moment to strike finally, and declared a 'state of war' already to exist. A pre-emptive attack was strategic sense, even if contrary to United Nations ground rules, and the French were prepared to go it alone with Israel even if the UK held back. If the venture were successful, Britain would then have abided by the rules and France would have the spoils – the worst of the available worlds.

In mid-October at Chequers, the secluded official country home of the British premier, joint action with France was agreed. Israel would attack across Sinai, Britain and France would then order both Egypt and Israel to draw back from the Canal Zone and intervene to protect it. On the dark wings of the fog that

ttled over Paris on the night of 22 October,
e Israeli leaders themselves flew in – David Ben
urion, Moshe Dayan and Peres – for a final
ttlement of the details at a house on the Paris
utskirts at Sèvres. The attack was to be made
the half-light of the evening a week later – on
October.

The Israelis rolled across the Sinai peninsula
a rate that surprised Dayan. For five days
ere was continuous bombardment of the
gyptian positions while Britain ferried armor
d landing craft from Malta nearly a thousand
iles away, and on 5 November the British and
rench went in. Port Said and a third of the
anal Zone was occupied.

The British and French had assumed that, if
e Americans did nothing to help, they would
least be neutral, and not act against them.
stead, Eisenhower and Dulles drew up a
nited Nations resolution calling for a cease-
re and asking members to refrain from force in
e Middle East. 'We just do not do things like
at any more,' said Eisenhower, when he
eant, 'We do not let our allies do things like
at any more without our instructions.' The
N resolution might have been resisted, but the
ower of the dollar could not. Britain had to
olster sterling by borrowing from the Inter-
ational Monetary Fund, and the loans would
ot be available if she continued the fighting
lthough she was legally entitled to them),
ecause America could block them by invoking
rtain technical procedures.

On 6 November Eden told the cabinet that a
asefire had been ordered, and a UN force
as to be raised and sent in. On 23 November
e left for a three-week holiday in Jamaica,
ffering from 'over-strain,' and on his return
the end of the year found himself facing
nterruptions, catcalls and ironical laughter' in
e Commons. The Opposition, some from

principle and some from hope of a chance of toppling the government, had shifted their position from an initial attitude of support. The Russians, too, were laughing – at the split in the Anglo-American alliance: Churchill's 'special relationship' with America was in ruins. It was not through lack of the Ex-Premier's advice, however, for he had invited himself to lunch at Chequers that fateful October. His first reaction when the crisis broke had been that it served Eden right, he had inherited 'what he let me in for.' The three hours of the car journey from Chartwell were beguiled by the dictation of a series of queries and suggestions on the crisis to be retailed to Eden on arrival.

Also on the receiving end of unwelcome advice during the crisis was Nasser. As he surveyed the bombarded remains of his Soviet-supplied air force in the midst of the battle, Khrushchev told him bluntly to hurry up and make his peace with Britain and France. He did not stand a chance against them alone, and Russia was not risking a third world war for the sake of Egypt's Suez Canal. If there were to be a war, said the practical Khrushchev, the Soviet Union 'would choose a more appropriate time and place.'

In truth Khrushchev had been in need of the light relief of being able to side in a public show of virtue with America on the Suez issue. In Russia's own colonial domain the 'natives were uncommonly restless' that year. As long as the summer of 1953 demonstrations by the workers of East Berlin against increased work norms had developed into riots involving up to fifty thousand people. Sixteen had been killed when Soviet troops quelled the disturbances. The claim by Dulles that the mere announcement by the United States 'that it wants and expects liberation to occur would change, in an electrifying way, the mood of the captive peoples,' had not led him to arrange any support of a practical kind for the change in mood, whether inspired by American expectations or Soviet exploitation. Quiet was restored, and although Khrushchev felt the need to make a quick round trip to Yugoslavia in 1955 to try

Extreme left: Three British athletes train for the Melbourne Olympic Games 1956.

Left: Twin teenagers play records in their London flat.

Right: American Robert Morrow wins the 100 meter event in the Olympic Games in Melbourne.

Below left: Hugh Gaitskell, leader of Britain's Labour Party with Alfred Robins and James Griffiths leave Downing Street after a meeting with Anthony Eden.

Below: Lady Docker sorts out her mail at Claridge House.

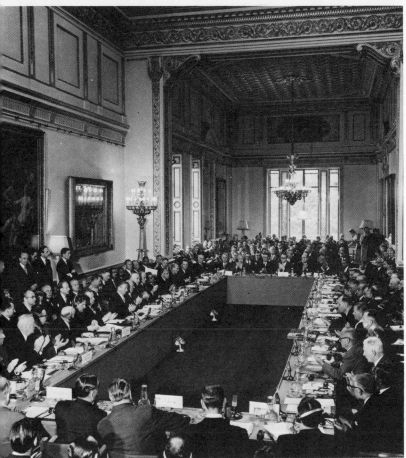

and patch up relations there, the ripples in the Soviet pond seemed to have died down.

The Poles waited until 1956 to 'have a go,' and although the riots in Poznan were suppressed that June, over fifty people were killed and some three hundred ended up in the hospital. The Polish government went so far as to confess 'it was a grave warning to us,' and in October Wladyslav Gomulka – not long out of jail, where he had been held for five years without trial as a Titoist – took over as first secretary of the Communist Party. He roundly said that the Poznan riots had not been due to 'imperialist agents, but were simply due to many years of 'deep discontent among the working classes.' The chickens born of Khrushchev's Party Congress attack on Stalinism were coming home to roost.

The ferment had also spread to Hungary. The country's borders with neutral Austria, and the slightly disaffected Czechoslovakia and Rumania, made it worrying for the Kremlin: its long border with Yugoslavia gave them a heart attack. In Poland Khrushchev would have sent in troops if Marshal Rokossovsky, then Polish Minister of Defense, had not warned them the Polish army was itself hostile. Now, here were the Hungarians able to call in Tito through the back door, and Tito again able to look directly to the West for aid – if it came to it. In Budapest some two hundred thousand

163

demonstrators swept Imre Nagy, the Hungarian popular leader into power, backed by the army and the police. The Russians were asked to withdraw their troops, and in a flurry of 'will we won't we,' decided they would. Then, a sudden switch sent them back in again in force under the screen of the Suez crisis in the first few days of November. Budapest was encircled by Soviet tanks, and at dawn the attack took place. At eight o'clock, with the final despairing words 'Help Hungary!... help us!... help us!' Budapest radio went off the air. Later freedom stations broadcast the call time and again: What is the United Nations doing? What is the United Nations doing?'

The United Nations, having failed to take action when Nasser seized the Suez Canal by force in clear violation of his treaty obligations, was preventing Britain and France taking action to restore the situation in the only way remaining to ensure that an international waterway remained international instead of subject to the aims of Nasser's political expansionism. In effect the United Nations concentrated its attention on the wrong side in the matter of a disputed waterway, because it could count on one superpower (America) to back it, rather than on the right side in defense of Hungary, a small nation being entirely crushed by the other superpower (Russia). Tito had also turned fainthearted. The violence of the Hungarian popular revolt, with which he initially sympathized, had made him nervous about the lid coming off in his own country. He grew embarrassed at having Imre Nagy tucked up for refuge in the Yugoslav embassy in Budapest. Of course nothing would happen to Nagy if

Far left: Egyptian children wander through a bombed street in Port Said before the Anglo-French invasion.
Below left: John Foster Dulles, US Secretary of State who disapproved of the Anglo-French invasion.
Left: The ruins of Port Said, the Egyptian port which the invaders seized after its bombing.
Below: Arab residents of Gaza are rounded up by Israeli troops after Israel seized the Gaza Strip during its invasion of Egypt.

he left his sanctuary, Tito was reassured by the new Hungarian government. Tito is said to have been enraged when Nagy was arrested the moment he stepped over the threshold: how he felt when Nagy was then taken out and shot is not recorded.

The occasion for it all, the Aswan Dam project? The Russians came up with the necessary cash. Purely out of the goodness of their hearts, as Khrushchev reassures us in his memoirs, for the Russians wanted nothing that Egypt had – nothing, that is, except 'regular deliveries of their best long-fiber cotton, rice and other goods.' The compulsory export of these items in return for the loan bore down harshly on poverty-stricken Egypt, who could have sold them to better advantage in the West. She also no longer had even her share of the Canal revenues, the waterway having been solidly blocked, and as a Christmas Eve expression of the country's frustration, the statue of de Lesseps – the builder of the canal – was blown up.

Left: Israeli forces interrogate Egyptian and Palestinian residents of the Gaza Strip after its seizure.
Below left: Labour politician Aneurin Bevan exhorts the crowd in Trafalgar Square to oppose their country's attack on Egypt. The British public was divided down the middle on this question.
Right: Rock and roll knew no national boundaries in 1956.
Below: The 1956 Chrysler would have to use more expensive gasoline after the Suez Crisis.

America ended the year politically on a relaxed note, with Eisenhower home and dry for a second term. By taking an Olympian stance, he had secured his own position above the election-eering fray, but a momentary interest arose in the possible ditching of Nixon as his running mate. By now Eisenhower had growing reserva-tions about his Vice-President being 'too politi-cal,' which was the very aspect of him which appealed to ardent party workers who were prompt to put the Nixon name on the ticket. It was an unbeatable combination, and the Democrats in their reaction set out to parody the Republican slogan of 'Peace, Progress, Prosperity' by making it war, retreat and poverty within their own party. Adlai Stevenson had to cope with an alienated Truman first trying to drive the party into nominating Averell Harriman, and then, when the Ex-President failed in this tactic, making an out-right attack on his own candidacy. During the campaign itself, Stevenson's pledge to re-open negotiations with the USSR went down badly with a nation which could see what was happening in Poland and Hungary for itself, and, already once a loser, his chances diminished as voting day approached. Eisenhower polled a million votes more than in 1952, and Stevenson a couple of million less, but for the first time in history a newly-elected President failed to have at least one house of Congress on his side – both were now in the hands of the Democrats. One other candidate finally declared out of the political race in 1956 was Hitler, who was officially declared dead by West Germany on 25 October.

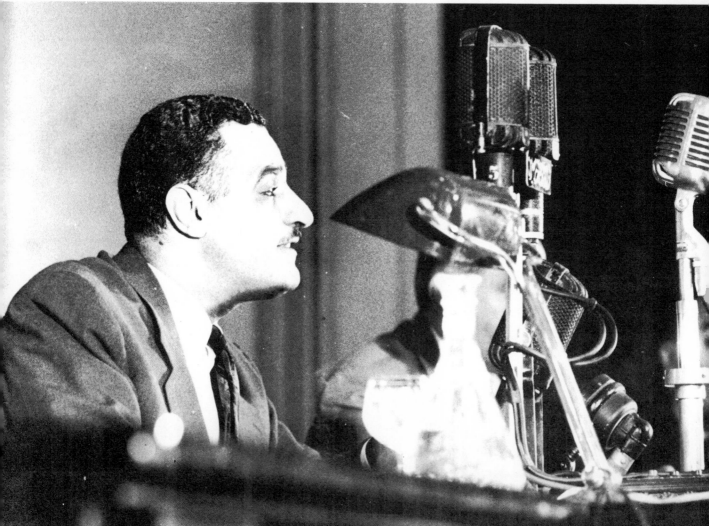

The XVIth Olympic Games of the modern era, and the first to be seen in the southern hemisphere, were held in Australia, with its Prime Minister, Robert Menzies, as President. Quarantine regulations meant that the equestrian events had to be held in Stockholm and the winter games were held in the Italian Dolomites. There were a few withdrawals by countries objecting to participating with the oppressor of Hungary, but it was Russia who, on her second appearance in the games, was the unofficial overall winner. She took thirty-seven gold medals as against the thirty-two of America, and the monopoly position which America had exercized since the revival of the games in 1896 – apart from the solitary German win in 1936 – was broken. The host country made the best showing in the water, and Dawn Fraser, as colorful in her love of life as in her swimming style, became a familiar personality throughout the world.

Even more artistic athletics were seen in London when the Bolshoi Ballet visited Covent Garden, but this time there was no revelation such as had accompanied the Diaghilev and Nijinsky era of half a century before. England now had her own Royal Ballet, and a dancer such as Margot Fonteyn had no rival anywhere. In another attempt to cement more friendly relations with Russia, which had been set in motion after the B and K visit, Anglo-Soviet athletics were organized in London this year, too. In the memory of the wider public, the most noted event was an unofficial one. Nina Ponomareva, set down in the paradise of London's West End department stores, and presumably short of roubles, made off with five hats. Looking back, it is hard to decide which is the more surprising, that she made such a beeline for hats – which were progressively less worn in the postwar years by women who wished to show off and preserve the good work of their hairdressers – or that she managed to select five which were stated in court to be worth collectively only £1 12s 11d. ($4.11). The fashion writers, who never lost an opportunity to plug the headgear industry, feeling that a third of their column-copy was gone when women opted for head-scarves, were still promoting annual changes of style in hats. Feathers had been in during the previous year, and in 1956 it was back to the garden. 'Never,' wrote Alison Adburgham 'since those old Edwardian summers has there been such a fair flowering.' Even allowing for inflation, poor Nina cannot have got many blooms for the equivalent of £1.65.

This was the year in which the waist rose, and the lower part of the dress, reluctant to leave the body line, ended in narrowed skirts a few inches above the ankle – Empire Dior. There was a rush to load the top effect with bat-wing sleeves, stoles, and the tiny jackets floating above the waistline as spencers, boleros or caracos – or whatever other name the designer could cull from the shuffled international cards of fashion. The long and narrowed skirtline did not linger, it was too elegant, too revivalist, too restricting.

Young women were now dreaming, not of

Top left: Port Said after the battle.
Bottom extreme left: Nasser in a news conference, days before Anglo-French attackers were obliged to halt their advance on Cairo.
Top: Labour supporters demand the ousting of Prime Minister Eden during the Suez Crisis.
Above: Harold Macmillan, with Rab Butler on his left, argue the Conservative point of view during the crisis.
Left: the beginnings of the crisis – youth demonstrate in Opera Square in Cairo, shouting 'Arm us to fight the British.'

changing places with studied models on the catwalk, but with Françoise Sagan. Her novel *Un Certain Sourire* (*A Certain Smile*), which appeared this year, had made her a cult figure. Like her, driving her high-powered blue 'Thunderbolt' with bare feet, so as to feel in perfect harmony when it raced up to 125 miles per hour, they wanted a more casual freedom. The clothes they wanted were the kind which struck a frisson through Dior, lovingly tending his collection of antique cachepots – those delicate china plant pots – in his secluded country residence. The winter sports resorts had once attracted the earnest performers in earnest outfits to match – navy, black and grey. Really bright colors for outdoor wear in stringent weather conditions had long been difficult to produce, and in the early postwar years the guardsmen in their magnificent scarlet uniforms, going through their paces at the trooping the color on Horse Guards Parade before their Sovereign, did not look forward to the rain. When they came to peel off, they looked as if they had had a bath in red ink. Now the chemists had won through, and by the mid-1950s the ski slopes could be brilliant with multi-colored pants, anoraks and parkas. At the fashion show, the hit item was less likely to be a ball gown

than the latest thing in scooter coats. In vinyl which imitated leather in white or palest pastel shades, the models for this year could be carelessly sponged without even the seams getting soggy, for – miracle of miracles – seams were now welded.

Ordinary fabrics, too, were becoming stain and water repellent, though makers were inclined to be optimistic, and 'shower coats' which damply took fright at anything more than half a dozen spots of rain were not unknown. Materials claimed to need no ironing could also be misleading, having a curious tendency to slit after a few wearings, and when it came to 'minimum ironing' many a housewife bending over an ironing board muttered that, if you had to iron at all, it did not make much difference whether it was minimum or maximum. The answer to a bachelor's prayers in those years was a drip-dry shirt. The best in their kind were immediately wearable when dry, others – well, anything drips dry if you leave it long enough, and it was at least difficult to fault the manufacturer on that. Another novelty, and one first appearing in 1956, was the coat lining which insulated against heat and cold by its treatment with a resin containing microscopic specks of aluminum.

Above: Soviet troops occupy Budapest and face the popular fury.
Top right: Despite the Soviet occupation and vicious repression, ordinary citizens continued to demonstrate their discontent.
Far right: Streets in Budapest were devastated by the Russian invasion of Hungary while the Suez Crisis continued.

Far from such mundane considerations, and embodying everything for the one occasion on which every girl still wanted to look formal, was the wedding outfit of Grace Kelly. Amidst a chorus of worldwide feminine sighs, she married her Prince Rainier twice – once in the palace throne room, and then again the next day in Monaco Cathedral. There were one thousand eight hundred journalists to cover the occasion, diplomatic representatives from two dozen countries, and assorted royalties – though not the prize catch of all, Elizabeth II of England – and a guard of honor including naval detachments supplied by both America and Britain.

Less fortunate in his choice of a bride was Arthur Miller, who had already shown an ageing lack of resilience in outlook in 1955 by emphasizing the importance of having one single theatrical center – Broadway – as the final crucible for testing dramatic excellence. The whole stream of theater was moving off Broadway in America, and away from London's West End. He was going to need all his resilience to cope with his new wife, Marilyn Monroe, fresh from her divorce in the previous year from the now retired baseball hero Joe DiMaggio. In 1956 she scored yet another hit in *Bus Stop*, and came over to England after her marriage to star with Sir Laurence Olivier in

The Sleeping Prince. Ill at ease with the blonde bundle, the British knight left her for once over awed, and the script flowed with all the zest of half-set glue. During her visit she was also included in the presentation line-up at the Royal Command film performance, *The Battle of the River Plate*. The re-creation of the World War II naval engagement was by some considered less enthralling than the outcome of the battle to retain Marilyn within the upper confines of her dress when she curtseyed to the Queen.

A footnote to the fashion era was written when Sir Bernard Docker was given his cards as chairman of the great weapons firm, the Birmingham Small Arms Company. His wife, Norah, had set the pattern in a kind of larger-than-life style of living, especially aboard their yacht *Shemara*, which was avidly followed in the tabloid press. That was how every working woman, slaving over a hot stove, dreamed of behaving if only her husband filled in his football pool coupon rightly and they hit the jackpot. Lady Docker even liked her limousines to be covered with all the trimmings, and when it came to seat covers, she chose neither material nor leather, but fur – zebra to be precise. Queried on this unusual selection – merely as a point of curiosity, for the conversation lobby was not yet active in the normal ways of

ournalism – she replied immortally, that mink was 'too hot to sit on.'

In entertainment, this was a vintage year for creen musicals. *Carousel, Oklahoma, The King nd I,* and *Guys and Dolls,* with the sophisticated ast of Frank Sinatra, Marlon Brando, Jean immons and Vivian Blaine. *Around the World n Eighty Days,* with David Niven as Phineas ogg, struck a congenial note in a decade in vhich the world was shrinking with every year. Other major films of the year formed a quartet of udden obsession with moral values. Gregory eck, heart-throb of suburban housewives, moted as woodenly as the hull of his ship as aptain Ahab in Melville's whaling classic *Moby Dick,* with its overtones of good and evil. 'irginia McKenna recreated the horrors en- ured by women prisoners of war at the hands f the Japanese in Malaya during World War II the filmed version of Nevil Shute's *A Town ike Alice,* only to find the film disqualified at e Cannes film festival for fear of embarrassing e Japanese. Diana Dors, who through the ar years had sustained the spirits of the ser- ces with the vitality of her curves, showed that ne had the mind of an actress under the blonde air-do, and gave dramatic intensity to *Yield to e Night,* which owed much of its inspiration the Ruth Ellis case. Last of the four was

Anastasia, in which Ingrid Bergman played opposite a Yul Brynner, complete with negative haircut from his Siamese days, and broke with the Hollywood tradition of clarity by leaving it still unsure whether she was or was not a deliberate impostor.

Yet, the most important film of the year had no moral, no message, no music – it simply was the incarnation of the new generation. James Dean in *Rebel Without a Cause* was the 'crazy mixed-up kid' who assumed heroic proportions in the suddenness of his death in a car crash. He died before many of those who were to become his most ardent worshippers had even seen him, a phenomenon which began the easy passage of the generations, through recordings and films, across the boundaries which had once ruled firm lines between the youth of father and son, mother and daughter. By the 1970s, the teenager might have the same cult heroes – such as Humphrey Bogart – who had enthralled his parents, or even grandparents.

Life was extending its boundaries in time, and stumbling steps were being made in exploring its depth. It was in the 1950s that people had first to worry about what being alive really meant. Twenty-two, a happy wife, and soon to be a mother, Mrs Ellen Moore spent one hundred and sixty-nine days in a coma after a traffic accident before her seven pound twelve ounce baby boy was born. It was now possible to keep a body breathing and nourished, while everything that made life worth living ceased to function. The implications were terrifying. Terrifying, too, were the researches on the effect of radiation, especially such as might be expected in the event of atomic war. Gradually, as the material was published, it began to fuel the protest movement that started towards the end of the decade.

On the plus side in science was the award to the American John Bardeen, together with Brattain and Shockley, of a Nobel Prize for their invention of the transistor in 1948, the basis of the marvels of electronics in the modern world. In contrast to the sophistication of this invention was one of the tragedies of the decade, which duplicated in almost every aspect a disaster of half a century earlier. The *Andrea Doria*, like the *Titanic*, was a giant ship – twenty-nine thousand and eighty-three tons – and carried some one thousand seven hundred luxury passengers. She too was thought to be unsinkable, and yet sank rapidly after a collision southeast of Nantucket. The main difference in the two wrecks was that only eighteen were announced 'lost' and thirty-eight 'missing,' as against the almost total loss of the passenger complement of the earlier vessel. On this maiden voyage the *Andrea Doria* is also said to have carried enough valuables to make her still more worth recovery than her immense quantity of 'scrap metal,' and although the depth of the Atlantic where she lies still protects her, ingenious schemes are constantly devised for raising her, and she might one day see daylight again.

A restoration from an earlier time which fascinated many of the new archaeology addicts

Buckingham Palace for his ceremonial visit as the new Prime Minister. He recalls in his memoirs telling the Queen that he could not answer for his government lasting for more than six weeks. She reminded him of it six years later when he still held the seal of office. With typical new Edwardian panache, he celebrated his appointment by dining with the Chief Whip at the Turf Club, where they split a bottle of champagne and demolished a game pie. It was the opening of the Conservative Golden Age, based on his belief that 'unless we give opportunity to the strong and able we shall never have the means to provide real protection for the weak and old.' Butler was safely tucked away as Home Secretary in the new administration.

In Britain the consequences of Suez came to mean less the loss of Empire than the blessings of release from keeping eighty thousand troops on the Canal at a cost of £50,000,000 ($125,000,000) a year. The history-book importance of the waterway proved a myth, it was even becoming more economical to ship oil around the Cape in the new tankers than it ever had been to ship it through the canal. In short, as Iain McLeod wrote: 'The after-effects of Suez were neither as serious nor as permanent as was prophesied. Our intervention, though cut short, forestalled the development of a general war throughout the Middle East.' Had it not been cut short, none of the subsequent Arab-Israeli wars would have been possible either, and speculations along these lines were very possibly in the mind of Dulles as he lay in the Walter Reed Hospital recovering from a cancer operation. Selwyn Lloyd, the British Foreign Secretary, called in on him on 17 November 1956. It was then just after the ceasefire, with American pressure at its height for the complete withdrawal of British, French and Israeli forces. Why had the British not 'gone through with it' and quoshed Nasser, Dulles demanded of the astonished diplomat? When asked in return why he had not given his allies the tip-off, Dulles rejoined: 'Oh! I couldn't do anything like *that*!'

For a change, it was the Americans who were eager for a conference with the British in 1957, and the final communiqué at the Bermuda meeting in March announced that they had talked with the freedom and frankness permitted to old friends in a world of growing interdependence.' American intermediate range balistic missiles were to be sited in Britain. National pride was soothed by the plans for British personnel being trained to man them as soon as possible; the United States would become as near a member of the Baghdad Pact as could be managed without having to submit the arrangement to the wrangles of Congress; and some progress was made towards a limitation of nuclear testing, on Macmillan's initiative.

The Russians were also interested in a limitation of nuclear testing (having just finished a massive program of their own), and gave a great welcome to Harold Stassen, Eisenhower's special adviser on disarmament. Originally authorised to report to the President directly, he had abruptly been yanked by an indignant Dulles into the State Department's fold, but remained enthusiastically eager to astonish the world in

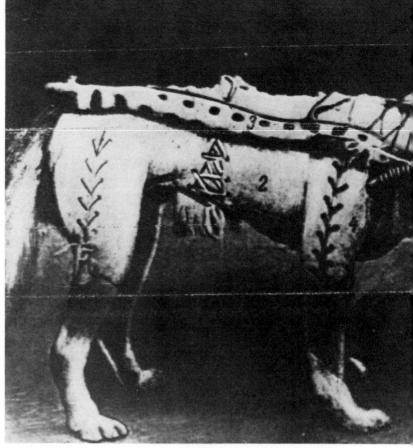

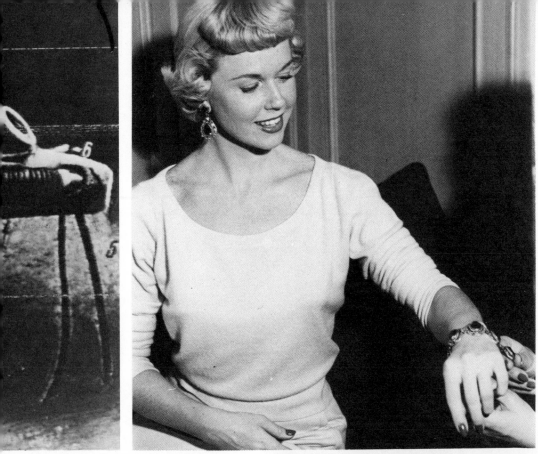

is peacemaking mission to Russia. He saw ritain and France as expendable in the duo-gue at the top and happily suggested calling a alt to supplies of fissile material to these second-ry allies before a sufficient stockpile had been chieved. The cable lines to North America ere white-hot with English and French exple-ves, and Stassen was airlifted home for con-ultations so engrossing that he never got around o going back. A dismayed Dulles was dissuaded om jumping aboard a plane at once to try and ort the affair out, and the furore died down.

Nevertheless, the world was increasingly eing governed by the might of the atom. The rst nuclear-powered submarine slid a snub ose into the sea at Groton, Connecticut, on 1 January 1954. Named after *Nautilus,* its ules Verne sci-fi predecessor, it was to cross the lorth Pole under the ice in 1958 in an awesome emonstration of its range and elusiveness. Soon ae new queens among warships were to be not nly nuclear-powered, but nuclear-armed. The uge fleets of conventional fighting ships moth-alled in the 1950s for potential future use were o be sliced into razor blades in the 1960s much o the distress of the admirals who lamented neir passing.

In 1959, the Camden yards in New Jersey aunched a civilian counterpart, the first atom owered merchant ship *Savannah.* It was an bvious step, but commercial dockyards re-nained wary. Accidents did happen with atoms nd not unnaturally harbor masters and custo-ner ship owners preferred to avoid a potential adiation hazard from tying up alongside.

In October 1957 the Number One pile of ritain's Windscale reactor overheated. Three ons of uranium sizzled menacingly, and the ctivity inside it multiplied by a factor of ten. he assistant manager was off duty coping ith a wife prostrate with Asian 'flu when it

happened. With true aplomb, he shoved some bread in the toaster and grabbed the first other edible item to hand – some bananas. 'This is it,' he said, handing over her survival rations and speeding for the door, 'I'll be back when I can.' But their hour had not yet come and no lives were lost. Only the thousand cows grazing the adjacent Lancashire pastures had cause to roll their eyes a bit, as Ministry men rushed to test their milk, but it was a near thing.

More horrendous rumors of atomic accidents were eventually to come from behind the Iron Curtain, but in 1957 the Soviet Union was pre-occupied with novels. In 1956 Vladimir Dudintsev had published his *Not by Bread Alone* during the doctrinal 'thaw.' The novel caused a sensation, and well-trained comrades, sure its appearance was only due to a slip in the censorship system, were quick to cover themselves. They attacked it bitterly. It took until May 1959 for Krushchev to announce that the author was not an enemy of the state, but had simply gone astray in the manner of his criticism.

Krushchev also thought that Boris Pasternak's *Doctor Zhivago* should have been allowed through the state presses, despite its double offence of mixing a positive Christian content with its anti-Marxist criticism. When Pasternak braved the opposition, and the book was published abroad, he was awarded a Nobel Prize – the first won by any Russian while still on the 'wrong' side of the Iron Curtain. He wrote a delighted letter of thanks, in which he expressed

the hope that he would be able to collect the
prize in person. The reaction of his fellow-
writers was one of disgust and contempt for his
'shameful and unpatriotic attitude.' 'Self-
enamored narcissist,' 'malevolent philistine,'
'pig that fouls its own sty' . . . these were among
the more printable terms of abuse thrown at him.

He was expelled from the Union of Soviet
Writers, and there was agitation that he be
thrown out of the country. If he went to Stockholm, it was clear it would not be on a return
ticket. For a man close to seventy the ordeal was
too much. He wrote a letter to Khrushchev,
recanting as abjectly as any Galileo. More
pathetic than all was his final claim that, 'No one
has put any pressure on me.' By 1960 he was
dead.

Beyond the bamboo curtain Mao Tse-tung
had his dissentors, too. In May 1956 he rediscovered an ancient Chinese proverb, 'Let a
hundred flowers bloom and a hundred schools
of thought contend.' The new liberalism brought
forth some odd 'flowers,' for a couple of dozen
new leaders aiming at a takeover had to be
rapidly put behind bars. Extraordinarily enough,
it was not the seat of a 'chairman' a number of
them were seeking, but the throne of an Emperor
and the restoration of a dynasty. Yet Mao was
unwilling to abandon his new-found saying, and
used it in a major speech to the Supreme State
Council in February 1957, in which he ridiculed
the Opposition which had once met the ideas of
Copernicus and Darwin in the West. Unlike

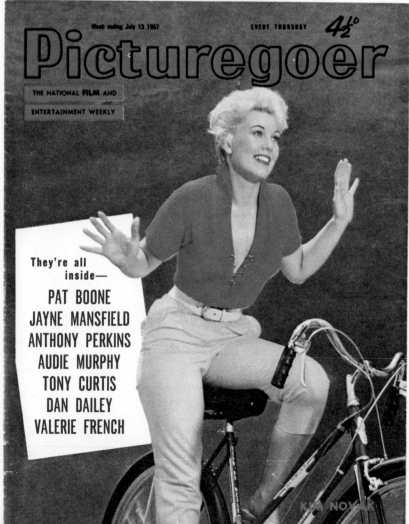

religion, Communism had no reason to fear discussion: 'as a scientific truth, Marxism fears no criticism.' The East was committed to the infallibility of scientific 'truth' just as the West was beginning to question it.

America's chief domestic troubles in 1957 were racial. Back in 1954 segregation in public schools — which in the States are 'public' — had been ruled unconstitutional by the Supreme Court. Separate was not equal. Southern-born, and having spent a substantial part of his life there, Eisenhower considered that the Court would have been better advised to rule that there should be 'equal opportunity' as an opening stage. In the armed services, where he had successfully completed the process of desegregation begun by Truman, the situation was perfectly containable. Outside that limited area it was not.

No one realized that more than Governor Orville Faubus of Arkansas. In some half dozen states of the deep South, the Supreme Court ruling had been nullified by abandoning a public school system and giving grants to private schools, or 'assigning' children to particular schools. When it came to the University of Alabama, and a young black woman braved showers of stones to drive in and register in 1956, she found herself on the sidewalk again by the end of the month. A special ruling in Autherine Lucy's favor by the Supreme Court did not stop her ultimate expulsion for supposedly having made 'baseless allegations' against the university authorities. The same year, Governor Earl Long (brother of famous Huey), had extended his state's apartheid-type legislation with an unanimous vote. Any personal and social contacts between the races were 'out.' This included dances, or any other social functions or entertainments, and the whole field of athletics, games, sports, and any other kind of contest.

In another half dozen states school integra-

184

tion had begun without trouble — including the Arkansas of Governor Faubus — and only in three others (Kentucky, Tennessee, and Texas) had protests and some violence resulted. That did not mean that there had not been the kind of ground swell which a little wind could fan into rolling coasters. In Little Rock, where black and white had lived peaceably for the last quarter of a century, only a fifth of the population was black, but the League of Central High School Mothers there had applied for an injunction against the School Board to prevent the admission of colored children. Any witness on their behalf was going to get newspaper coverage. When the chief witness turned out to be Governor Faubus, he swung the verdict in favor of segregation with his forecast of 'bloodshed and mob violence' and carried the court with him. When a higher court overruled the verdict, he declared a state of emergency on the day before the opening of the Fall term and two hundred men of the Arkansas National Guard were ordered out to keep nine colored children from entering the school on 3 September.

The situation continued to seethe and when, despite a hostile crowd of a thousand people, the nine were smuggled inside by a side door, three hundred white children came out through the front. At midday police cars had to take the nine scared youngsters back to their homes. It was now that Eisenhower finally spoke. He was criticized then, and has been since, for his failure to speak before, but nothing could have been more effective in ranging national public opinion behind him than the newspaper, radio and television coverage of those nine small, frightened faces, at one particular time and one particular place. Consonant with his motto of never using force unless you had to, but using all you had got when you did, he despatched a thousand paratroopers to cordon the streets round the

school. In his initial statements he had said it would 'be a sad day for this country — both at home and abroad — if schoolchildren can safely attend their classes only under the protection of armed guards.'

Faubus went into histrionics about 'bayonets in the backs of schoolgirls' to whip up support, but it was coyly smiling faces that the girls turned to the Federal troops when they got the chance. The last of them were not withdrawn until 27 November — two days after Eisenhower had been hit by a stroke which left him unable to speak. For him the price of the tension at Little Rock had been high. Thirty years later Governor Faubus was holding down a minor job in a bank, and one of the nine black children had been given a plum post in the Carter administration.

It was not only Little Rock which had laid Eisenhower low. Coincident with insuring that one small-town school could start operating on 24 September with black and white children side by side at their desks, Eisenhower had also to cope with a small Russian sputnik above his head. In public he stated that he was 'not one iota' worried, but the one hundred and eighty-four pound sphere circling the Earth every hour and a half and swinging its cargo of electronic hardware in an elliptical orbit hundred and forty to five hundred and sixty miles up, was in reality a serious headache. The sensation that Sputnik I caused worldwide on that 4 October 1957 is difficult to realize today, owing to the number of rockets and satellites that have been launched in its wake.

Almost as astonishing as the achievement was its source. At the time Russia was not even recognized as a technical and scientific competitor with America, the atom bomb being considered as merely pinched from its superior by devious means. Even in the context of Europe, Russia was thought of as the backwoodsman

"I'm Gonna Wash That Man Right Out Of My Hair," sung by Mitzi Gaynor, is one of *South Pacific's* bounciest, tuniest big routines

Left: Mitzi Gaynor sings *'I'm gonna wash that man right out of my hair'* in the musical, South Pacific.
Right: Bill Haley and the Comets were probably the first big time Rock and Roll band.
Below: Grace Kelly and Frank Sinatra pose for publicity shots before commencing work on the film High Society.
Below right: Bill Haley plays his number one hit, *'Rock around the Clock.'*

of the continent. The world gaped in wonder, amused that America had been outsmarted – Britain, at least, gained some consolation from the fact that the Russians could not track the sputnik without the help of the telescope at Jodrell Bank in Cheshire. It had been built for the Department of Radioastronomy at Manchester University, and was just being prepared for a leisurely first series of tests when the Soviet satellite was launched. The electrical work was completed in double-quick time by crews working round the clock, so that tabs could be kept on the satellite. In the clear skies of Australia thousands watched it pass from end to end of the continent, and every radio and television station in every country had its 'bleeping' — like some tireless, over-excited Morse operator — punctuating the news. To the Third World it was like a television commercial, broadcasting the superiority of Communism over Capitalism, on the vastness of the encircling screen of the sky.

Eisenhower was above all shaken by the military implications. In August the Soviet News Agency, Tass, had announced successful tests of 'a super long-distance intercontinental multistage ballistic rocket,' and a skeptical General Norstad — the Supreme Allied Commander, Europe — had described it a 'a technical development . . . still far from having any direct military application.' The initial vague Tass announcement was followed by hard facts: speed fifteen thousand miles per hour; altitude— up to six hundred miles; range – anywhere on Earth; degree of accuracy – within six to twelve miles of the target. With a hydrogen warhead, six to twelve miles was near enough for anybody, and with the Sputnik now dancing overhead, all the world knew that every last figure of the Russians specifications could be taken seriously.

To reinforce the message, the Russians had

the world staring up to the sky again on 3 November when Sputnik II appeared. Weighing half a ton, it took just a little longer in its orbit than its predecessor, rising over a thousand miles above the Earth. The Mullard Radio-Astronomy Observatory at Cambridge in England had 'diagnosed' its orbit within minutes by means of an array of strange shaped aerials on their roof, which already looked like something out of the year 2002. What they could not fathom was the presence of a passenger, a little dog. Anxious reporters besieged the Russian information service to find out its name, and the bewildered Russians, who had never thought to give it one, answered with the name of its samoyed-type – *laika*. A couple of days and two million miles later, the little creature's heart stopped. There was an end to the drill of eating and drinking – so much and no more – at the sound of a bell, and to being helplessly strapped in with its instruments clocking up its every breath and every throb of its pulse. The protests against this experimental use of an animal were loud – particularly so in Britain.

These 'heavenly twins' set Congress by the ears. After the first one, Senator Henry M Jackson (on behalf of the Democrats) spoke of it as 'a devastating blow' to American prestige, while Senator Styles Bridges (for the Republicans) regarded it as a sort of Dunkirk and called on the nation in Churchillian phrase for 'blood, sweat and tears' to make up the lost ground. After the second one, a panic surge went through the country, and Eisenhower had the television

cameras rushed into the White House on 8 November so that he could reassure millions of startled Americans. Desperate for something that could be *seen* as evidence of America's own progress in the field, he produced the nose cone of a Jupiter missile which had been 'hundreds of miles to outer space and back' and was 'completely intact.' The impression might have been greater if it had been less intact, for it did not look as if it had been anywhere.

America's 'Project Vanguard' was hurried at top speed. On 6 December the firing button of a seventy-two-foot long carrier rocket was pressed on Cocoa Beach at Cape Canaveral. Eyes followed the gush of flame one hundred and fifty feet skyward, then they fell to where the mini-satellite – a foot across and weighing thirty-two pounds – nestled snugly on the beach. Senator Lyndon B Johnson called this fiasco 'one of the best publicized and most humiliating in our history.' The future President was right. The world did laugh again, but at the same time it admired the courage of a thing openly done.

Soon the laughter was over and *Explorer,* America's first Earth satellite, winged its way skywards on 31 January – 1 February without a hitch. It did so at the behest of Hitler's former rocket engineer, Dr Wernher von Braun, New Zealand-born Dr William F Pickering, and Dr James Van Allen. Van Allen was to discover in May 1958, with the aid of the *Explorer* satellites, the famous radiation belts more than six hundred miles above the Earth, which it was feared might hinder space exploration: they showed up

Above: Lonnie Donegan entertains teenagers on 'The 6.05 Special' on BBC-TV.
Above right: Teenager and her amazed friend during a Elvis Presley concert in Philadelphia.
Right: Johnnie Ray 'doing his thing' in London.

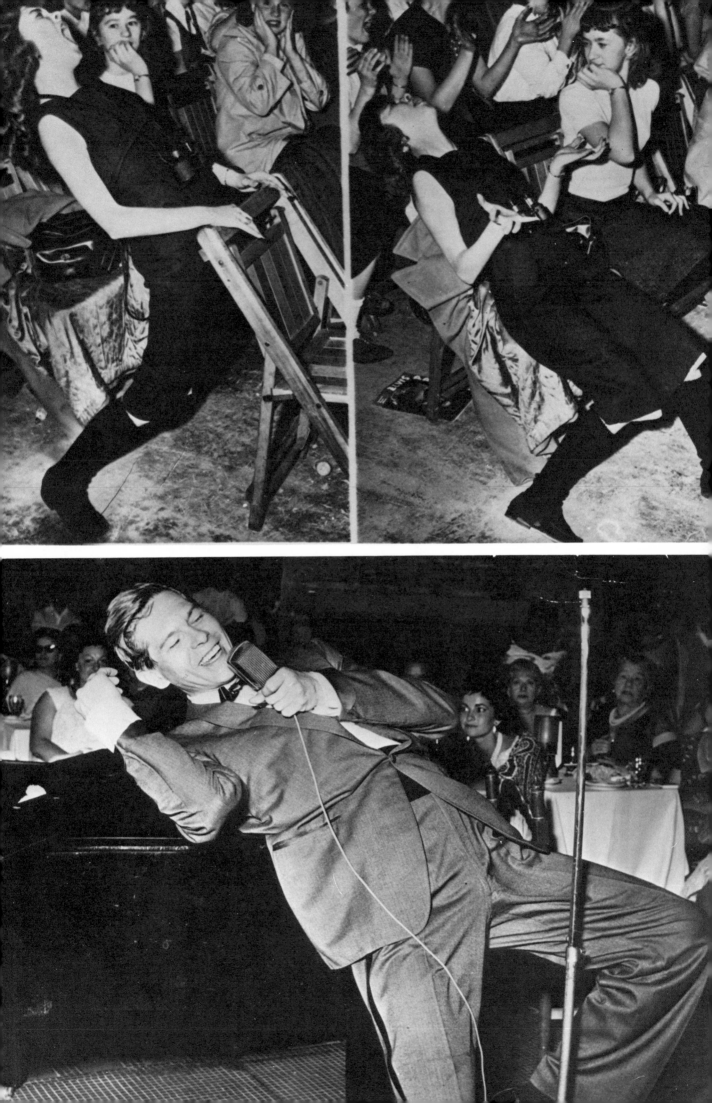

in ghostly fashion by jamming the satellite geiger counters like some Martian enemy.

Also pushed ahead with unerring speed was Eisenhower's $1,600,000,000 (£640,000,000) program for the development of education, focusing particularly on science and technology. An interesting sidelight on the Sputnik was later provided by James B Donovan, the lawyer who defended Colonel Abel, and who maintained his contacts with him up to the negotiation of his exchange for Gary Powers. He asked the master spy after the appearance of the Soviet satellite whether, allowing for the work of a few Soviet scientists, it was not 'a highly developed system of overt intelligence' which accounted 'more than any other single factor for the Soviet Union launching the first Sputnik'? Quiet for a moment, Abel then said 'I won't disagree.' He went on to complain that the work of Soviet scientists was too often overlooked in various fields, but that was the very point – America publishes and the USSR tends to be less accommodating. One Soviet-inspired publication which failed to find enough readers in this fateful year in America was the *Daily Worker*. From some twenty thousand readers before World War II, it had sunk to about seventy-five hundred in 1956, and when two thousand subscribers stopped ordering it in 1957, it did the decent thing and closed down on 26 December 1957.

Totally American in its origin, though nicknamed by San Francisco journalist Herb Caen on the model of the 'sputnik,' was the 'beatnik.' Jack Kerouac, submerged since the appearance in 1950 of *The Town and the City* in a litter of publishers' rejection slips, managed to get his novel *On the Road* on the bookstalls in 1957. It took the country by storm, and with reviews for and against, stayed in the bestseller lists for over a month. According to legend the book had been pumped out by typewriter during a three-week nonstop session in 1951 on a teletype roll, but had in reality been much worked over in the subsequent years. The hero 'Dean Moriarty,' an idealized projection of Kerouac's friend Neal Cassady, was seized upon as the footloose, restless cowboy of modern times, who had exchanged his horse and the great plains for an automobile and the freedom of the highways.

The young of the 1960s and 1970s, fleeing from jobs in the great corporations which had grown up in the 1950s, and would turn them into 'Organization Men,' at once identified with him. They wanted to be be among 'the only people' whom Kerouac approved, 'who burn, burn, burn like fabulous yellow roman candles exploding like spiders across the stars,' and are 'waiting for God to show his face.' Kerouac's French-Canadian, and even more his American Indian, origins appealed to them so much that this was the book that Mick Jagger found his class-mate reading beneath the shelter of a textbook during lesson time.

The previous year, in 1956, Kerouac's friend Allen Ginsberg had had his *Howl and other Poems* published by Lawrence Ferlinghetti of San Francisco's City Lights bookshop. After the newest pattern, only paperbacks were sold here, and the doors of the store were open from ten in the morning till midnight, so that poets and

writers of all kinds thronged it the day through. To the rest of the world it did not become known until the police raided it in 1957, two years after its opening, and charged the owner with bringing out an obscene book – Ginsberg's. By the time Ferlinghetti had defended the case and won an acquittal, his shop was a Mecca, and Ginsberg and authors such as William Burroughs of *Junkie* fame were notorious household words.

As early as 1952 John Clellon Holmes had written his pioneer article in *The New York Times*, 'This is the Beat Generation,' based on Kerouac's interpretation, as the original coiner of the phrase in 1948. Now it was really coming true. They were, according to Kerouac, the people 'who *really* knew where they were,' and who felt 'a weariness with all the forms, all the conventions of the world.' As a Roman Catholic, it later came to him with the force of a revelation that the word contained the mystic sense of 'beatitude.' The way to the beatific vision went through drink, but even more through drugs – benzedrine, marijuana, morphine – and on to the more exotic beckonings of the drugs of native cultures, such as peyote.

The mass media did not bother with the finer shades. Beatniks were news because they meant beards and jeans, alcohol and drugs in lurid excess, dirt and perverted desires – homosexuality and group sex. Kerouac had his share of the lot from time to time, but his admirers never quite caught up with the other side of him. The young man who did his writing within the

comforts of home, living on hand-outs from a mother working herself to death in a shoe factory; who wore the silk shirts she carefully ironed; and who celebrated in his books the alluring highways of freedom on which he was actually too nervous to learn to drive.

For Britain the most important event of 1957 was one in which she had no share. On 25 March the Treaty of Rome was signed, setting up the European Economic Community, alias the 'Common Market,' which was to begin its formal existence on 1 January 1958. In a 'memorandum' she pointed out that 'her particular interests and responsibilities in the Commonwealth' precluded her taking part in the suggested union, but hoped to be part of an associated 'free trade area.' Britain would not abandon her Commonwealth connections, whereas France apparently could sacrifice the interests of her colonies, but at the last moment the French whisked their possessions smartly inside the market while the British were not looking, totally discarding the concept of a free trade area.

It was irritating, but Britain was doing too well for the moment to want to be caught up in the Market machinery. It was on 20 July 1957 that Macmillan made his famous speech at Bedford: 'Let's be frank about it; most of our

192

eople have *never had it so good*. Go around the country, go to the industrial towns, go to the farms, and you will see a state of prosperity such we have never had in my lifetime – nor indeed er in the history of this country.' What most eople forget, in their memory of that much-peated phrase, is that he went on to wonder hether it was 'too good to last,' and asked 'Can e control inflation? That is the problem of ur time.'

In spite of the prosperity, the effects of inflaon were already making by-election results go wry for the Conservative government. Lord ailsham, the new Party chairman, had a medy for that at the conference in Brighton ring October. Rousing the constituency work-s to enthusiasm with his call to 'beat the day-ghts' out of Labour, he effectively adapted the venteenth-century poet John Donne: 'Let us y to the Labour Party: "Seek not to inquire r whom the bell tolls." It tolls for them.' To inforce the point, he rang a handbell, and the nage of the corpulent, chubby-faced figure aking that theatrical gesture so imprinted self on the public mind, that it probably robbed m of any chance in later scrambles for the remiership.

World fashion needed a similar rallying point.

It was literally disintegrating at its foundations, for the earlier 1950s had been a great period of 'foundation garments.' Corsets in regulation white and pink, with metal or whale-bone-type reinforcements, might have departed, but the new synthetic materials lent themselves to what was actually known a 'engineering construction'. A flat stomach and a not too-rounded rear required firm construction, and the breasts themselves were hoisted up and shaped to definite points.

As the 1950s progressed, however, the new life style made rapid inroads on the supremacy of the foundation. One of the most potent factors was the increasing acceptance of trousers for women, even in situations outside the boudoir, work or sport. Foundation garments required garters and stockings to anchor them, and also slips to screen their obtrusive lines from showing through a dress. They could not be worn satisfactorily under trousers.

Foundations were also at war with the new kind of existence which the top layer of society now enjoyed in sunny places, and to which the rest of society aspired, at least for a few weeks a year. There was a need to slip in and out of clothes more easily than such figure molders allowed – and mostly the accent was on 'out.'

The new natural style make-up was fully established in 1957, and the beauty salon was no longer visited for intensive action only above the neck. The young, svelte, sophisticate underwent top to toe treatment. Then she lingered over the choice of her beachwear in the elegant exclusivity of the Rome fashion houses which had stolen a march on Paris as the ultimate in snob value.

In 1957 it was the 'look of the year' to shine. Once a gleaming nosetip had been every woman's horror. Now she shone all over, like a lightly bronzed statue, and, in case male eyes should dazzle too dangerously, fashion decreed that the day of the bikini was over. The lady should wear a bloomer suit. For once the pundits were disobeyed, and the languid beauties on the beaches continued to be bikini-clad, much to the delight of the male population.

The mid-1950s were also the era of sunglasses. Squares, polygons and oblongs were commonplace, and the more daring allowed them to flare into exotic shapes, dazzling colors, and all kinds of decoration, from gilt stars to plastic flowers. They were worn everywhere, even at midnight, and had a significance beyond the obvious. They played the part of eighteenth-century masks and fans. A whole language lay in the way they were carelessly shifted above the hair line, seductively dangled over the side of a chair, or meaningfully rested in passing on a smiling lip. The 1950s needed sunglasses, for the

personality of its people was being stripped of
protective coverings. First names were rushed
upon strangers at a single stride, and to prove
real intimacy with top-notchers one had to have
access to nicknames and diminutives, and the
secret-code use of initials, which had spread
everywhere from America.

Another refuge from the pushing present was
the growing interest in the past. Museums once
thought it enough to put their treasures on
display in heavy, well-protected, display cases.
In 1957, at Jamestown in Virginia, they built a
complete replica of Fort James on the site of the
first permanent British settlement in America,
together with a reconstruction of the first
American factory – a glassworks – and models
of three sailing ships in which the pioneers
arrived. People could wander around the place,
walk among the exhibits and see how the people
of the past had lived. The visitors to the opening
festival included Elizabeth II and the Duke of
Edinburgh. It was the year of pioneer memories,
for a replica of the *Mayflower* sailed from
Plymouth in England to New York harbor
during the summer, and found its final birth as
yet another piece of walk-round history in the
national shrine at Plymouth, Massachusetts.

The change to a more positive attitude was
everywhere in the 1950s, even in the conservative field of medicine. Curing what went wrong
increasingly gave way to the idea of preventive

*Extreme left, top and
bottom: Attempts by Negro
students to enter all-white
schools in Little Rock,
Arkansas lead to violence
and riots as local citizens
tried to stop their
admittance. Here,
demonstrators are arrested.
Above: The Cadillac
Eldorado limousine replete
with fin-tail rear fenders,
open top, whitewall tires
and wire wheels in a 1957
auto show.
Left: General Sir Gerald
Templer salutes as the
Malayan flag is raised in
Kuala Lumpur during their
independence celebrations
on 31 July 1957. Templer
was instrumental in crushing
the Communist insurgency
before independence was
granted.*

Above: Segregationists climb the stairs of the Arkansas state capital to challenge Governor Faubus about admitting black students to previously all-white schools, a policy which had been declared unconstitutional.
Top right: Police arrest demonstrators on the first day of 'integrated' school in Little Rock.
Bottom right: This man was clubbed on the head when he tried to grab a soldier's rifle near the Central High School after nine Negro students were escorted into the newly integrated school.

medicine. In June 1957 the British Medical Research Council and the American Cancer Society collaborated on the subject of the relationship between smoking and cancer, 'one of direct cause and effect.' The message came over strongest in the haggard face of Humphrey Bogart in his wheel chair, the toughest guy of them all, who died that year.

Bodies were also being looked at in new ways. In America Douglass Howry had found a new use for war junk by putting one of his patients inside the gun turret of a B-52 bomber. Placed up to his neck in water, the patient then had an ultrasonic device focused on him as the turret revolved, and pictures of his inside arrangements were recognizable. Ian Donald was Professor of Midwifery at the University of Glasgow, and considered the use such a tool could be to him. The engineering firm of Babcock and Wilcox was using ultrasound to ensure that the vast boilers they were supplying to Britain's nuclear power stations were without a flaw, so he asked to carry out a few tests with their equipment. With a healthy piece of steak as 'control' and an assortment of cysts and tumors for comparison, he found that he could differentiate the various types of tissue. By 1957 he had, with the aid of engineer Tom Brown, evolved a machine to try on living patients. He subsequently enjoyed one of the happiest days of his life when a woman under a death sentence for cancer of the stomach was clearly shown to

have merely a large, and removable, ovaria cyst. The machine could also be used to diagno multiple births or reveal deformity in the unbor child and enable an abortion to be performe

Increasingly in the 1950s, as medical advanc preserved a less healthy generation, the proble was absence of children. The pioneer in artifici insemination had been the great British surgeo John Hunter, in 1790. The over-populate nineteenth century did not have much occasio for such a skill, but there was experimentatio in both Britain and the United States befor World War II. By the 1950s, it had becom frequent enough for legal problems to arise was it legal adultery? In 1957 a Scottish judg said no, the House of Lords could not make u its mind, and the Archbishop of Canterbu condemned the whole business. Even he, how ever, could hardly have foreseen that by 197 the controversy would be over whether it shoul be used to give children to lesbian couple

The film of the year in 1957 was *The Brid over the River Kwai,* which won an Oscar an another for the leading actor, Alec Guinness. had one of those sayings which pop up in a fil and recur in other settings in later years. Th Japanese commandant at the prisoner-of-wa camp dishes out ceaseless inhuman treatment the men, and Alec Guinness points out to hi the relevant paragraph in the Geneva Conve tion. Snatching at the document and slappin him across the face with it, the commanda replies: 'This is not a game of cricket.' John L Carré was to echo the phrase in 1963 in *The Sp Who Came in from the Cold,* as a keynote for th 1960s when life had become even less gentleman in all its aspects.

On stage it was a remarkable year for Britai A new major playwright, Harold Pinter, emerg ed with *The Birthday Party.* Reviewed by th London critics as a body, it came and went i about the space of a week, but the tale of Me and Petey's Eastbourne boardinghouse with i hauntingly repetitive dialogue was revived i 1965 and subsequently to great acclaim. In i techniques it was a landmark in its reflection the reverse influence of radio and television o the theater.

At the Royal Court Theater in London S Laurence Olivier gave a virtuoso performanc as Archie Rice, the music-hall comedian on th downward road, in John Osborne's *The Enter tainer,* and even the popular press gave wid coverage to Samuel Beckett's *Fin de Partie (End game).* It was a symbol of the new influence i drama emanating from Europe, so that Ber holdt Brecht was not the only familiar foreig name. A one-acter, it was played in the origin French, and was unbeatable for small-talk one upmanship. Even if the members of the audienc had last sniffed a French verb in schoolday they could not be caught out on the plot for was nonexistent; if they were asked what meant – well, the critics were in a free-for-a about that; and there was no need to fear laugh ing in the wrong place. Gloom hung thick ove the cast of four cripples: one unable to sit dow a second unable to stand up, and two unable t get out of dustbins. Only an Irish expatriate i Paris would get away with it on such a date

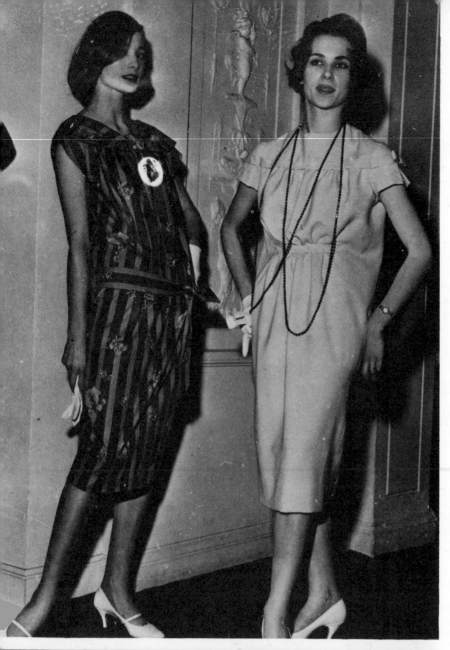

1 April 1959 – and collect a Nobel Prize as well.

Britain was also having difficulty with another Irish dramatist. Filled with fiery indignation over the iniquities of English spelling, George Bernard Shaw had made confusing provision for subsidizing its reform in his will. The tangle was eventually sorted out that year, but the remotest chance of success was ruled out by his stipulation that the new alphabet should contain at least forty letters, including sixteen vowels. English and American spelling marched on regardless of his wishes and it is not difficult to imagine what the nonagenarian Shaw would have thought of the title of the song 'Whole lotta shakin' goin' on,' which was Jerry Lee Lewis's hit of the year. It was in 1957, too, that the Everly Brothers made the grade with 'Bye bye love,' and Harry Belafonte created a vogue for West Indian calypso style and introduced a perennial Christmas favorite with the ballad 'Mary's boy child.' This new Caribbean element was a token of the widening field of Pop for another of the big sellers of the year was written and sung by Canadian, Paul Anka, whose 'Diana' was estimated to have sold nine million copies around the world. The eternal Elvis scored eight golds that year, of which the most familiar still is probably 'Jailhouse Rock,' also the title of his successful film of 1957.

The final hallmark for British television was stamped when the Queen's Christmas message came over the small screen for the first time. Palace officialdom had realized that, even for a Queen, people were not going to turn off their sets and switch on the radio, and that she was going to drop right out of the ratings if she did not adopt television as her medium.

The use of recording, rather than live production had been introduced in the United States in 1955, and with the development of a much less expensive process in Britain in 1957, it became standard practice. There was less spontaneity, more polish, the enormous widening of the camera eye for exterior shots, and a record for the future. Color television was also on its way in, both in America and in Britain.

Radio was not standing still either. There was increasing use of VHF, and the medium was playing its part in the cold war. In the spirit of the 'thaw' jamming of broadcasts from the West had been phased out during and after the Bulganin-Khrushchev visit to Britain. Even during the Polish troubles there was reluctance to admit that Communist perfection could not stand the blast of a few capitalist words from the Voice of America. Then, with the Hungarian revolt, the fist of the commissar came down on the buzzer – and stayed there. Yet there had been a respite, and the new technology had made it increasingly difficult to prevent those who really wanted to from tuning in on the program.

By 1957 Khrushchev was in trouble in more substantial ways than on the air waves. He was fairly knowledgeable in farming, and liked nothing better than promoting his popularity by being photographed with smiling peasants or looking at corn samples and cattle. Nevertheless, his Virgin Lands campaign did not allow for the fact that, in so old a country as Russia, there might be very good reason these great

Top left: The sack dress
made its debut in 1957.
Bottom left: This nightgown
was inspired by the film
Baby Doll.
Above: Sir Anthony Eden
leaves for an extended sea
journey after his resignation
as Prime Minister in
January 1957. Edward
Heath and Lord Home
stand to Eden's left.
Right: Eden leaves 10
Downing Street after
resigning due to ill-health
after the Suez fiasco.

eastern areas had been left uncultivated. The country was similar to that of the American West which the old pioneers had tried to farm, when it was suitable at best for rough grazing.

Dissent was not so efficiently organized as in his own campaign to displace Stalin, but Vyacheslav Molotov, the first Deputy Premier and former Foreign Minister, was keeping a grim-faced watch on the new leader. He did not like Khrushchev's policies abroad – in particular he had disliked his dallyings with Nasser and the relaxation of the grip on the satellites – and he did not care for any of his far-reaching plans for internal, agricultural, industrial and administrative reorganization. Joined with him in discontent were Malenkov, brooding over his power stations and his dispossession from the Premiership; Lazar Kaganovich, a manpower and transport specialist; and Dmitri Shepilov,

the former Editor of *Pravda*. The two hundred and fiftieth anniversary of the foundation of Leningrad by Peter the Great was coming up, and in June the Presidium met to discuss the celebrations to be held the next month. Following precedent, but without the military back-up which had disposed of Beria, Molotov made a surprise demand for Khrushchev's resignation. The docile Bulganin was in the chair, and Khrushchev used his quick wits to prevent a snap decision and have the matter postponed until the full session of the Central Committee.

Khrushchev used his breathing space to good effect. He marshalled his own adherents to isolate his opponents, and the file of major politbureau members making their exit from the inner council chamber grew long: Molotov, Shepilov, Kaganovich, Zhukov, Malenkov . . . . Khrushchev celebrated his triumph by a speech

against the 'anti-party' members at the Leningrad rejoicings in July, and had a few afterthoughts about the docility of Bulganin – in March 1958 he too was summarily dismissed. For the first time since Stalin, one man – Khrushchev – combined in himself the two top posts of First Secretary of the Communist Party and Prime Minister.

Alone on his pinnacle, Khrushchev now had to exert himself preternaturally to stay there. Russians enjoy a steak as much as the British and Americans – when they can get it – and one way to remain at the top was to increase meat production. The target for the province of Riazan in 1958 was an increase of up to seventy per cent. The result was a miserable five per cent. Lured by the prospect of political promotion, the regional party First Secretary decided to stake everything on raising the production for 1959 to one hundred per cent. As a result Riazan became the scene of a Soviet wild west.

Like the 'bad men' of the screen, the members of the local party committee rounded up animals from the private plots of the peasants, and made off with dairy herds and breeding stock from throughout the province. The promised target was still not reached, so secret emissaries were sent into neighboring regions to buy up animals to inflate the total. Since the authorities in those areas had also pledged greatly increased production, they indignantly set up road blocks to prevent the illicit purchases being taken 'over the border.' The rustlers responded by using country tracks to sneak the beasts away under the cover of darkness. By the end of the year the ambitious First Secretary of Riazan could point to a production increase of three hundred per cent. Nemesis came when the region was expected to improve yet further on supplies in 1960: output dropped to a fraction of what it had been in the first place, for there was nothing to breed from, no reserves and no supplies. Rather than face the consequences, the ingenious First Secretary preferred to shoot himself.

1958

Taking time by the forelock in 1958 was a middle-aged young man who looked into the future with bunched-up eyes. When Adlai Stevenson denied him the Vice-Presidential nomination in 1956, John F Kennedy had decided that it was the Presidency or nothing next time.

His chief aide was his brother, Robert, who had graduated in law in 1951, halfway down his class list of a hundred and twenty odd, before joining McCarthy's red-hunting sub-committee. By the time of the Cohn and Schine stage of the investigations, he had worked up his questioning technique to a needling point which once sent Cohn chasing him through the courtroom crowds, demanding whether he wanted a fight. Robert was a practical man, and when Stevenson campaigned, John Kennedy sent him along with a stack of notebooks to check on how it was done. In the event it was more useful as an exercise in how campaigning should not be done, as Steven-son shied from the flesh-pressing and the on-coming journalists, and became embroiled in the morass of professional politicking.

After Robert returned from this foray, and already accumulating presidential campaign staff were set to work on a detailed card-indexing of every useful contact and the planning of speaking tours, there was a need for something else to occupy the forefront of public interest until 1960. There was a tailor-made issue in Eisenhower's call in April 1957 for legislation against union corruption. After all, Estes Kefauver – who *had* nobbled the vice-presidential nominations in harness with Stevenson – had publicly won his spurs in jousting on the television screen with Costello. In 1957 Robert engaged in a three-year battle, as chief counsel for the Senate Select Committee on Improper Activities in the Labor or Management Field (alias the 'Rackets Committee'), until his resignation to become formal campaign-manager to his brother in 1959.

Above: University of Michigan halfback Dennis Fitzgerald goes over for a touchdown against Duke in Ann Arbor.
Top right: Rock-and-Roll star Jerry Lee Lewis and his 13-year old wife Myra.
Bottom right: Buddy Holly (center) and the Crickets were an extremely popular singing group.

202

The committee's Chairman, John L McClellan, the Democrat Senator from Arkansas, was a friend of Joseph Kennedy, senior. The target of its investigation was America's largest union, the bucolic-sounding International Brotherhood of Teamsters, which actually consisted of hard-bitten truckdrivers. The main charge was that gangsterdom had moved in on the union, even into its upper echelons, and that officials had made away with more than $10,000,000 (£4,000,000) since the early 1950s. The President was Dave Beck, who was quickly disposed of; his early proven iniquities ended with a sentence in December 1957 of a maximum of fifteen years. His successor was Jimmy Hoffa, a short and burly product of Detroit's underworld. The charges against him included bribery, telephone tapping (a sophisticated crime development of the 1950s), and pilfering some $3,000,000 (£1,200,000) from the 'health and welfare' fund of the union to pay off some Chicago gangsters.

Hoffa was wide open, but his lawyer was clever (up to the time of the hearings he had been a friend of Robert Kennedy, but not thereafter), and the teamster himself had a natural mother wit. He parried and sidestepped Kennedy's questions, which were delivered with a raging urge to convict that overreached itself. Hoffa even discovered that Robert Kennedy, who passed the union offices on his way home, would turn back to his own desk for another spell if he saw that his enemy was still at work. Thenceforward Hoffa instructed that his office lights should be left burning when he went home to bed, and chuckled at the thought of his accuser doing a turnabout when he caught sight of them. The jury acquitted Hoffa on successive counts in 1957 and 1958, and the teamster's lawyer offered to send Robert Kennedy a parachute if he felt like fulfilling his initial pledge – given in *overweening* confidence – that he would jump off the Capitol if he could not secure a conviction. Kennedy got Hoffa in the end, the union leader went to jail 1964-71, and in 1975 disappeared altogether. The FBI suggested that the Mafia had kidnapped and disposed of him.

While the fight in committee was conducted by Robert, John Kennedy was one of the sponsors of the Labor-Management Reporting and Disclosure Bill which received Eisenhower's assent in September 1959, and personally proposed the main amendments to it. The brothers cooperated similarly in the contemporaneous vote-gathering for the 1960 presidential election. The states were systematically quartered. Speeches were made at places no other candidate would even have heard of. Hands were shaken and links of personal commitment forged on such a scale that Hubert Humphrey confessed it made him feel like a corner grocery in competition with a supermarket chain. The impression of universal support was stage-managed by such dubious devices as holding back the crowd with a rope until, as the motorcade passed and the television cameras unspooled, it was dropped and the effect of a spontaneous surge of humanity was created. The 'image' of John Kennedy as already President-Elect, rather than as merely presidential material was being created. At the end of 1958, he even held the first meeting of his

203

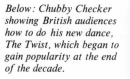

Below: Chubby Checker showing British audiences how to do his new dance, The Twist, which began to gain popularity at the end of the decade.

'Academic Advisory Committee' at a hotel in Cambridge, Massachusetts – the 'think-tank' was in operation.

In Britain, where elections occur less from lapse of time than from a sudden blockage in the system, it looked on 6 January 1959 as if one was imminent. The Chancellor of the Exchequer, Peter Thorneycroft, resigned, and was followed by Nigel Birch, Economic Secretary to the Treasury, and Enoch Powell, Financial Secretary to the Treasury. In view of the danger of inflation, Thorneycroft was intent that government expenditure for 1958-9 should not exceed expenditure for 1957-8 by even so much as Mr Micawber's proverbial sixpence. The rest of the Cabinet were willing to prune so that the excess would be less than £50,000,000 ($125,000,000) in modern Exchequer terms the equivalent of that sixpence.

There was an impasse, for to achieve a standstill, let alone achieve the further cuts which [we]re what Birch and Powell wanted, reductions [in] Family Allowances and other Welfare State [ite]ms were impending. Social legislation had [cr]eated a situation in which no government [co]uld risk cuts without also losing votes, and, in [th]is case, it would be succeeded by a government [pl]edged to restore and even increase such expen[di]ture. There was no longer a choice. For the [fir]st time it became apparent that a Conservative [go]vernment would never be able to do more [th]an moderate the speed of growth of the Wel[fa]re State during its alternating spells of office [w]ith Labour, unless it could find some funda[m]ental change of direction.

At the time the watershed was less apparent, [fo]r the master conjuror, Supermac (Macmillan) [h]imself, was at work. Parliament was in recess at the moment of crisis, leaving the Opposition powerless to do anything except declare their intention to press for a debate as soon as it reassembled. The Prime Minister, however, would not be there when it did. On 7 January he left for a six-week goodwill tour of the Commonwealth – India, Pakistan, Ceylon, Australia and New Zealand – declaring in famous phrase that recent events had caused him a little anxiety, 'so I thought the best thing to do was to settle up these little local differences and then turn to the wider vision of the Commonwealth.' He left the dependable 'Rab' Butler to 'mind the shop.' Lord Butler was once described as 'both irreproachable and unapproachable' but was one of Britain's most progressive leaders.

As the first Prime Minister to visit an independent India, he was greeted by a smiling Nehru who favorably recalled British rule, 'we have

Above left: The Everly Brothers, whose song Bye Bye Love *swept the Pop charts in 1957 and 1958. Many other hit songs followed.*
Above: Little Richard, another Pop singer, at Waterloo Station after a successful British tour.

earned much from you'; in Pakistan garlands overflowed from around his neck down his rms; in Ceylon the cheers were deafening; in New Zealand he appreciated the people's abounding energy and enterprise,' and in Australia he doubtless envied Robert Menzies in November the old campaigner was to win is fifth successive general election.

Elsewhere the Commonwealth picture was ess rosy. Britain had never had an 'Empire' in he true definition of wide dominions under irect rule by a massive home-based civil and military organization, having never had the money or the man power on a sufficient scale. The concepts of indirect rule through existing owers, and of trusteeship rather than exploita-ion, had screened the fundamental weakness of he whole system. Once the two world wars nded the unique naval power by which the mpire had been held together the end was nevitable.

The first major African country to become independent was Ghana in 1957, when Dr

Kwame Nkrumah, clad in gorgeous tribal robes, enlivened the Commonwealth Prime Ministers' Conference. The example was infectious. Colon-ial boundaries were rarely suitable for indepen-dent countries, depending often on the line at which the opposing forces of colonial powers had halted, rather than geographical, racial or economic reasons. Britain, unless she were pre-pared to face Malaya-style warfare through the whole of her African possessions was forced to hurry the process of independence instead of relying on gradual progress and to try to give the miscellaneous items a combined inter-supportive future by job-lot auction methods.

Southern Rhodesia, Northern Rhodesia and Nyasaland, which were planned to have a viable joint future with the coal and tobacco of the first, the copper of the second and the man power of the third, were pitchforked into the Central African Federation in 1953. Suspicion of the intentions of the Southern Rhodesian whites led to its breakup in 1962, and the two last-named became Zambia and Nyasaland. Another triple

Far left: President de Gaulle gives his famous victory salute before a speech in the Place de la République in Paris when he introduced the new Constitution of the Fifth Republic.
Above: De Gaulle addresses a packed throng in Algeria in June 1958.

union – Kenya, Uganda and Tanganyika – never got off the ground at all. Kenya posed a special problem with its European planters in the superb country of the White Highlands. The restive Kikuyu tribe formed the Mau-Mau ('Hidden Ones') secret society, and it took from 1952 to 1960 to suppress it. Aimed against whites, it also sliced up with *pangas* any blacks who were reluctant to support it, and the press overflowed with reports of its loathesome initiation ceremonies. Drinking the blood of sacrificial goats in cups formed from tropical flowers and decorated with the animals' unsocketed eyeballs, and swearing dark oaths in dim-lit tribal huts, raised more squeamishness then than now. Jomo 'beaded belt' Kenyatta was sentenced to seven years' imprisonment in 1953 for being the society's principal organizer, though earnest maiden ladies who had come to know him during his thirteen years in England still adamantly refused to believe that such a 'nice man' could have had anything to do with such things. His imprisonment was not onerous, and the authorities recognized that he 'used' it to his own advantage. It served as a reason to keep him in cold storage until – the emergency ended – he could be diplomatically released to power in 1961.

Yet another miscellaneous lot was the West Indian Federation, formed in 1958. Unfortunately, the islands differed widely temperamentally, were in competition economically, and were more interested in the mother country than their neighbors. This, too, fell apart in 1962.

France handled her colonial problems rather differently. In the same half-year that saw her involvement in Vietnam in 1954, the conflict in Algeria had begun. Part of the intensity with which France had plunged into Suez had arisen from her desire to cut off the arms supply to the Algerian rebels which flowed in from Nasser's Egypt. Syria, Lebanon, Indo-China, Tunisia and Morocco had all gone, but France was determined to hold on to Algeria, where she had invested massively, and where half a million Frenchmen had genuinely made their home, just as hundreds of thousands of Arabs had settled in France. Setting a seal on the 'crusade' was the oil of the Sahara, discovered in 1954, which began to flow into the tanks at Touggourt in 1958. Even the Communist anti-colonial creed faltered in the face of that oil.

De Gaulle had left office in 1946, but the delusions of grandeur with which he had filled his people during the brief time he held the provisional government in his hands from 1944, were at least partly responsible for the instability which saw fifteen French governments collapse between 1950 to 1958. Now the general sat at Colombey-les-deux-Eglises, setting out in painful longhand a slanted account of his heroic days, and diversifying his leisure by reading Hemingway's *The Old Man and the Sea* (1952). He drew the comparison between himself and the old fisherman battling with his fish. He felt his own battle had been lost.

In this he was wrong. The autumn of 1957 had seen France without a government at all for more than a month, and when Pierre Pflimlin

collected in the spring of 1958 yet one more hotchpotch cabinet – less supporters of himself than opponents of other candidates – Algeria came to crisis point. With such a weak regime, the European settlers, the 'colons,' feared betrayal. Excited crowds appeared in the square of the Forum, where the government administration building stood. Teenage schoolboys made the first assault – a foreshadowing of the 1960s unrest among the young – and an older student made off with the bust of 'Marianne.' These official portrayals of the spirit of the Republic are obligatory in French government buildings, and the heads are modeled on the favorite heroine of the time. Many French town halls have marble incarnations of the 'sex kitten,' Brigitte Bardot, who in 1958 was reaching a peak of popularity! The one now stolen was of an earlier period, but its significance was the same. Power was once more in the hands of the people, as embodied by the paratroopers who took over the building in scenes of wild enthusiasm, with the intoxicating refrain of the Marseillaise and talk of the formation of a 'Committee of Public Safety' to urge them on in the old-time spirit of Revolution.

The next day the would-be Prime Minister warned that France might be on 'the verge of civil war,' and President Coty appealed in broadcast after broadcast to the army in Algeria, his words receiving as much notice as the wafts of perfume for which his house was famous. The next day, de Gaulle announced that he was ready 'to assume the powers of the Republic,' which meant as much, or as little, as anyone liked to read into it. The Socialists, the Communists, and the trade unions, did not like what they read, and the army and the *colons* assumed that what the three forces of the left did not like must necessarily be what they would themselves like very much. The yells of *'Vive l'Algérie Française'* were more and more automatically followed by *'Vive de Gaulle.'*

De Gaulle was too wily to come to power on the backs of rebels if he could avoid it. Thus he waited at Colombey while the whole of France went into a revolutionary froth about him, and then on 19 May he held a 'press conference' in Paris. With 1200 journalists in attendance, the meeting took on the character of a royal reception. What had he meant by his statement of 15 May they asked with respectful daring? 'The powers of the Republic, when one assumes them, can only be those which the Republic itself has delegated. That is perfectly clear.' It was not, but who was going to look the towering general in the eye and say so? Nobody. The general progressed under convoy back to Colombey, still 'at the disposal of the country.'

The insurrection spread to Corsica. Paris newspapers were so censored that they were more white space than news, and copies of British papers were smuggled away from the police patrols who invaded the newsagents to be avidly read and passed from hand to hand. Above the buzzing flurry of the agitated politicians, the long shadow of the man at Colombey fell over the halls of power in the capital, the only unmoving factor in the desperate shift of events. To turn on the radio was to pick up Radio

Above: De Gaulle salutes as the Marseillaise is played during his three-day visit to Algeria in June 1958.
Right: President René Coty, the last President of the Fourth French Republic, stepped down in favor of de Gaulle after the coup d'état which flung the general into power.

208

Algiers sending out its sinister coded messages: 'The chapel will be lit up tonight,' 'The bottle of Muscadet has arrived,' and so on. Soon the *paras* would be masters in Paris, too, and the tumbrils would roll in a new revolution. Visitors came and went at Colombey in a frenzy of huddled diplomacy. Then, on the night of 26-27 May, Pflimlin met the general in secret at St Cloud.

The French parliament was under the general's heel, and he ground it in their faces. On 2 June he allowed himself a five-minute speech to tell them that his government would not outlast the night if they did not give him the 'mandate' he demanded. They gave it, and he returned to his Paris flat in the Hôtel La Pérouse, stern as ever. Yet there was a human being inside that giant frame. As the night porter took him up in the lift, he gave him a gentle slap on the shoulder. 'Albert,' he said, 'I've won.'

Algeria was a bit harder to win than the Paris parliament. The terrorists fighting for Moslem independence ripped through the fabric of France, and nearly robbed the capitol of its most famous landmark by putting a time bomb in the ladies' lavatory at the top of the Eiffel Tower.

By January 1959 de Gaulle consolidated his position by exchanging the Premiership for the Presidency, from which he could be less easily dislodged, but the Algerian war went on. Offers of 'the peace of the brave' failed and the attempt

to hive off the Sahara as a separate French dependency left France with oil only on her face. In a broadcast by the general on 10 September 1959 the words 'self-determination' were spoken, and though it was not going to happen in the 1950s, de Gaulle made the French accept it as probably only he could have done. Even if by then the voices which had been foremost in calling him to power, those of the *colons*, were now calling 'string him up,' and it was the Moslems who were beginning to shout *'Vive de Gaulle.'*

Absorption with Algeria did not divert de Gaulle's attention from other affairs overseas. The disturbance in the Middle East, with Nasser as the focus, did not subside with Suez. On 1 February 1958 Nasser took over the Presidency of Egypt-Syria – the United Arab Republic – and referred to the new state as 'part of the Arab nation,' serving notice to the world that there were more 'parts' to be added. King Hussein, knowing that his country formed a natural connecting corridor between Egypt and Syria, rushed to his cousin, King Faisal of Iraq for support. Together they founded the Arab Federation on 14 February. Nasser retorted with the announcement of his federal union with the Kingdom of Yemen, the little strip at the bottom of the spreading kaftan of the Saudi Arabian peninsula. King Ibn Saud (1880-1953) and his American oil company friends reacted as if their toes had been stepped on, as indeed they had.

Above: Pete Dawkins, Army captain and halfback in action against Penn State.
Left: Bill Carpenter, Army's lonely end, on this way downfield to catch a Dawkins pass.
Above right: Sam William Michigan State end, in action against Purdue.
Right: The 1958 Cadillac Coupe de Ville.

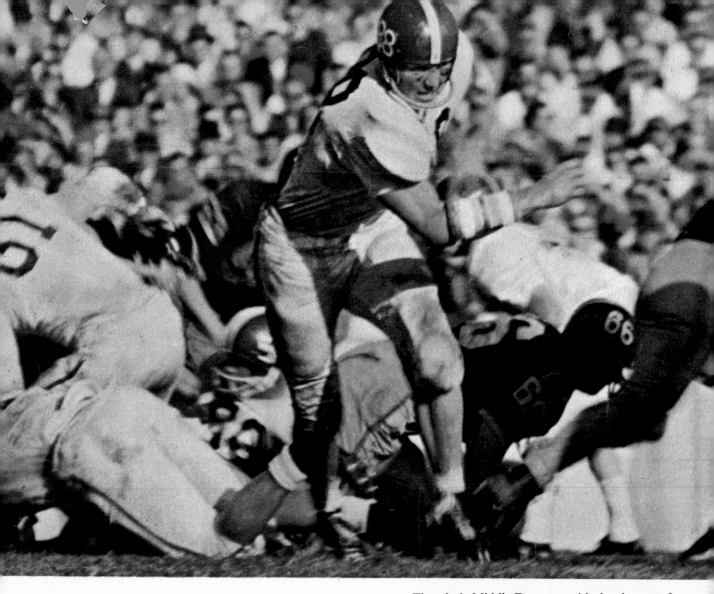

w measurement of greatness

The whole Middle East rang with the charges of plots and counterplots, with British Intelligence dragged in as a makeweight.

It seemed that Soviet arms were stacked away under every bed, and since the USSR had an appetite for oil as voracious as that of the United States, it was not difficult to see that Iraq would be the next Soviet target. In July 1958 there was an army revolt when disaffected troops were allowed to march through the capital with their guns loaded, and a number of more reliable units had been sent to bolster up Jordan. King

Faisal and his uncle were shot, the Prime Minister Nuri es Said was also murdered while attempting to escape disguised as a woman, and a number of inoffensive court ladies were killed. Apart from this the bloodshed was comparatively limited. The leader of the new Republic of Iraq was an idealist. General Abdul Kassem was said even to have forsworn marriage rather than dilute his love for the poverty-stricken masses, and in trying not to become too far engaged either with the Soviet Union or the West, he ended up a few years later – as idealists often do – facing a firing squad with his eyes defiantly unbandaged.

In Jordan beleaguered young King Hussein rode through crisis after crisis. Having called for the removal of British troops in 1957 because their presence invited attack, he now begged for their return because he would be attacked if they did not. On the wings of the same breath President Chamoun of the Lebanon appealed on 14 July for United States aid to prevent his own regime being toppled. Eisenhower had recovered from his stroke in 1957 within a matter of days, and could not resist the challenge of one last go at the most difficult of army exercises, a 'combined operation.' In a telephone conversation with Eisenhower on that same day, Macmillan accused him laughingly of 'doing a Suez' on me,' and the President set out to show how it should be done. President Chamoun got rather more than he bargained for.

On 15 July fifteen hundred Marines landed at Beirut, and within another five days Chamoun had about fifteen thousand American troops in

his country – one fighting man armed to the very teeth for every hundred of his own entire nation. Offshore he had the might of the United States Sixth Fleet of seventy warships headed by the giant aircraft carrier *Saratoga* – all sixty thousand beautiful tons of her – and including a guided missile ship, and over twenty-five destroyers who carved their way through the eastern Mediterranean fit to cause a tidal wave. Overhead Lockheed and Globemaster transports roared, and half a hundred jet fighters were sent screaming over Jordan to underline American approval of British landings there. Even beyond the immediate scene of action, the American war machine was in motion from the Pacific to the bases in Turkey, right on the Soviet frontier.

Britain, her Empire ever diminishing, was finding her part more difficult. Her troops had to be flown in over Israel, and the Israelis were as jumpy as horses surrounded by thunderflashes. To allow overflying would invite retaliation from their belligerent neighbors, to refuse would alienate those who would defend in the very likely event of their being attacked anyway. Macmillan at times doubted whether he should send troops at all, in view of the difficulty of trying to extricate them should the Jordanian army follow the example of their Iraqi brothers. Only the danger of the wildfire infection of Communist-inspired revolt spreading down into the Gulf, where Iraq bordered on the oilfields of Kuwait and Iran – the powerhouse of the economy of Britain and Europe – made the risk worth taking.

Macmillan gave the go-ahead and then sat tight. There would be outraged saintliness from the Opposition when it was discovered that he had done so without waiting for Israeli permission. On 17 July he had a one o'clock appointment with Hugh Gaitskell, the Labour leader, and he was not looking forward to it. Macmillan opened the interview with a careful lead-up to

Below: Pope John XXIII on the balcony at Castel Gandolfo since his election after the death of Pope Pius XII.

Above: Pope John was elected as an interim pope, but was the most influentia pope this century due to hi role in calling the Ecumenical Council in Rome.
Right: Pope Pius XII shortly before his death.

his confession of sin committed in mitigating circumstances, postponing from minute to minute the explosive admission. Then, in one of the blissful moments of a lifetime, the door opened and a hand placed in front of him a slip of paper: 'The Israeli government has agreed.' He was saved. By the time the Israelis 'disagreed' again, under Soviet pressure, the situation was in hand. In October the British withdrew from Jordan, as did the Americans from Lebanon, and the semblance of normality was resumed. By November Hussein could plan a trip to Switzerland, but was met at the border by two enemy Mig fighters. He and his British co-pilot switched the flightpath of his plane up and down like a roller coaster to dodge the machine-gun bullets. Thoughts of Swiss holidays were abandoned, and the King returned to Amman.

All the same, the immediate crisis was over, and only the cries of outrage from France – once the presiding power in Syria and Lebanon – quivered in the air. In the general confusion Britain and America had notified de Gaulle of their actions only after the event. The French naval squadron de Gaulle had sent dashing to the scene had not been included, and the French President took refuge in a lofty declaration that the whole Anglo-Saxon intervention had been entirely unnecessary. It boded ill for Britain, who was now beginning to do a U-turn on her attitude to the European Community. With a smile like cracked ice, de Gaulle was to raise successive road blocks to Britain's market applications in 1961 and 1967.

De Gaulle hated America even more than he hated Britain, however, and he saw Britain as merely a stalking horse for US influence in Europe. He could not wait to whip the French forces out of NATO on the pretext of needing them for Algeria, and in 1959 refused to allow the stockpiling of nuclear weapons in France unless they came under French control. The American Tactical Air Force promptly spread its wings and went to roost in Britain and Germany. He was indifferent. France was going to have her own atom bomb, a plan which was to come to fruition in the Sahara in 1960. Seeing no threat in the truncated remains of France's ancient enemy which formed the new West Germany, he made overtures to iron-faced Chancellor Adenauer.

Adenauer had no love for the British either – they had turfed him out of the burgomastership of Cologne during the Allied occupation for 'obstruction and noncooperation' – but he saw that Germany needed both Britain and America, and his response was cool. De Gaulle turned then to Russia, and met with Khrushchev at Rambouillet in 1960. But the two of them had little in common other than their knowledge of the 'Volga Boatsong' – and the outcome was unpromising. De Gaulle grew increasingly isolated in his policies.

Eisenhower's 'court' was also in difficulties in 1958. It had been the President's confident boast that no one in his administration had been 'involved in scandal or corruption.' It took Sherman Adams to prove him wrong. The stern New Englander, who had become Governor of New Hampshire in 1949 and Special Assistant to the

President in 1952, was regarded as a pillar of rectitude. It was he who had exclaimed in shock at the unauthorized actions of Britain at Suez: 'What your friends won't do to you behind your back!' Eisenhower could now well have said the same.

Although there is no official or constitutional provision for such an office as 'Special Assistant,' it is often far more influential than any Cabinet appointment. Yet, Sherman Adams had accepted gifts from textile manufacturer Bernard Goldfine, and in return was alleged to have tried to save Goldfine's skin when on various occasions he had been in trouble with the Federal Trade Commission. One time it had been a matter of misleading labels on Goldfine's goods, at another it had been a couple of property companies with which he had been involved and their failure to file the prescribed annual reports. Adams denied the charge of influence exercised in Goldfine's favor and admitted the gifts only as friendly tokens, claiming to have given similar items to Goldfine. This was not convincing when the Subcommittee on Legislative Oversight listed the hotel accommodation for which Goldfine paid over five years to the extent of $3096 (£1,238); the oriental rug priced at $2,400 (£960); and – the item which caught the public fancy – material for a vicuna coat – valued at $700 (£280).

214

UNCHIE

es exciting

g! **4^D**

*Top left and center:
Posters advertising a
popular American cigarette
and British candy bar.
Top and above: Two views
of the Mercury, built by
Ford Motors.
Far left bottom: Ford
automobile and other
American makes in Jeddah,
Saudi Arabia, where much
of the petroleum needed to
run them originated, share
the road with goats.
Left: Popular singer and
film star Dean Martin.*

Goldfine's evidence concerning his relationship with his 'dearest friend' of twenty years, was also unconvincing. The gifts to Adams had been listed on his income tax returns as 'business expenses,' which did not sound much like 'friendship.' There were also certified treasurer's or cashier's cheques for over $775,000 (£310,000) on issue to him, which had never been cashed. Such cheques do not carry the name of the purchaser and they could have been passed to government employees who, instead of compromising themselves by cashing them, might use them as collateral for a loan. Although Goldfine denied making any such use of them, and pleaded not guilty, it was recommended that he be cited for contempt of Congress.

Eisenhower stood firmly behind his friend, confident in his integrity, and claiming that Adams was a public servant whom he 'needed.' The verdict in the elections of 1958 showed a shift to the Democrats on the issue, and the Republican Party decided that Adams was not what they needed. He resigned. Public opinion was disturbed. As usual, it was less what had been revealed which worried them than what had not: there had been corruption somewhere, and on no small scale. They were also staggered that a man in a position of such influence as Adams should have associated with a man such as Goldfine had been shown to be. It was a sour note.

An even sourer one for the administration had been struck by Vice-President Nixon's tour of America's backyard – the Latin American countries. Goodwill tours tend to be back-page material, and, as Richard Nixon planned his itinerary through Uruguay, Argentina, Paraguay, Bolivia, Ecuador and Columbia. He re-

garded it as no more than a routine chore. In those countries it amounted to little more, although a growing pattern of abusive placards and hostile shouts became evident behind police barriers. Peru was a different matter. At Lima they threw more than insults. The missiles here were rotten fruit and eggs and, as the crowd warmed up, bottles and stones. A rock grazed Nixon's neck to emphasize the message of its thrower, 'Nixon go home.' A visit to San Marcos University had to be abandoned altogether. By the time he got to Venezuela, they were yelling not 'Go home,' but 'Muera Nixon' – 'Death to Nixon' – and meant it. Trouble began at the airport and continued with attacks on the motorcade. Rushing aside the motorcycle escort, rioters smashed the windows of the two cars in which Nixon and his wife were traveling, ripped up the American flag pennants, showered the procession with garbage, and spat on them.

On the day after Nixon and his wife returned, the Vice-President turned up at the Cabinet meeting to report on the tour. John Foster Dulles listened uneasily to a narrative which seemed to show that the further the American anti-Communist crusade was pushed in pursuit of 'brinkmanship,' the thicker Communists seemed to be springing up nearer home. Arthur Larson records him as characteristically scratching the top of his head as Nixon told the woeful tale, in a gesture reminiscent of a puzzled Stan Laurel.

Riots of another kind were first seen in Britain that year. Incidents in Nottingham on 23 August were followed next day by outbreaks in the Notting Hill area of London. In Victorian times the area was one of demure respectability,

but it had degenerated into rooming houses and makeshift apartments, with a street detritus of hooligans ready to flare into violence. Tension was focused by the association of white girls with colored youths, the acquisition of houses by colored owners and complaints of harassment by older white tenants, and the re-emergence of Sir Oswald Mosley. Before World War II this man had led the blackshirted British Union of Fascists, which in its present incarnation was the Union Movement, and had been distributing leaflets and holding meetings with the theme 'Stop Immigration Now.' The headlines were black when a so-called 'nigger-hunt' by nine white youths on 24 August led to the hospitalization of five colored men with injuries inflicted by iron bars and table legs. Stiff sentences of four years in prison put the chill of reason into the situation, but demand naturally increased that immigration be restricted although the colored population at this date was estimated to be only two hundred thousand.

Protest of a completely different kind was roused by increasing recognition of the hazard of the H-bomb, not merely in war, but when being ferried round by Royal Air Force and United States Air Force patrols. In America 'mechanical malformation' in a 'lock-in' system had resulted in a crater thirty-five feet deep and seventy-five feet wide where a South Carolina house had been. If this happened when an unarmed atomic bomb was accidentally dropped from a B-47 jet bomber, what would happen if . . . ? It was a question no one needed to answer. The Campaign for Nuclear Disarmament

Left: Five popular Western film stars. From the left, Ward Bond, Gary Cooper, Gene Autry, John Wayne and Gabby Hayes.
Bottom left: Ingrid Bergman and Curt Jurgens in China' during the filming of The Inn of the Sixth Happiness.
Right: Fred Astaire rehearses a number for his award winning television special, An Evening with Fred Astaire.
Below: The 1956 Nash Ambassador, soon to be phased out as an automobile and a motor company.
Bottom right: Doris Day in The Tunnel of Love.

more popularly known as the 'ban the bomb' movement, has been considered 'the founding father of all later protest movements' everywhere. It was led by Bertrand Russell, the pacifist peer, and Canon Collins of St Paul's Cathedral. A fifty-mile protest march was organized from London to the Atomic Weapons Research Establishment at Aldermaston in Berkshire, and some four thousand people set out on 4 April. In curious English fashion it became an annual event until 1964, though later marches went in the reverse direction. The next year the numbers were swollen to ten thousand and students with placards, women with prams, and children with dogs, supplied handy material for the media on their hard-up days. It had no effect in attaining its object, and in 1978 novelist J B Priestley was investigating why the movement – in which he had been an early activist – had petered out. The answer was surely that it became merely a publicity jamboree, full of hangers-on just out for the jaunt and that, even if Whitehall and the Pentagon had taken notice, the Kremlin and the Elysée would not. Had the protesters only known it, they were way out of date even in their diagnosis. In the United States' work on the neutron bomb – a device designed to annihilate people while preserving buildings intact was already under way in 1958.

A more harmless scientific exercise was the International Geophysical Year July 1957 to December 1958, when some sixty countries co-operated in research during the maximum sun-spot period. Most interesting to the layman were the Antarctic expeditions, of which the largest was the United States Navy's 'Operation Deep Freeze,' which had begun work in 1955 under veteran Admiral Richard Byrd. The scale was

221

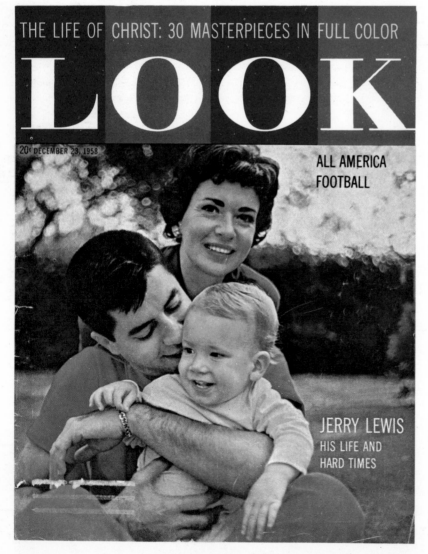

THE LIFE OF CHRIST: 30 MASTERPIECES IN FULL COLOR

LOOK

20¢ DECEMBER 23, 1958

ALL AMERICA FOOTBALL

JERRY LEWIS
HIS LIFE AND
HARD TIMES

enormous, over a million square miles being explored in Wilkes Land. The British contribution was the mechanized Trans-Antarctic Expedition led by Vivian Fuchs – twenty-two hundred miles from one end of the continent to the other in ninety-nine days, one day within his target limit of one hundred days. Cooperating with him was Sir Edmund Hillary, the conqueror of Everest, who was laying depots for the completion of the crossing from the other side. So few were the crises that the media were left to blow up Hillary's declaration, that he was 'hell-bent for the pole,' to meaning that he was abandoning his depot-laying role to engage in a race with Fuchs to get there first.

When he did get there, it made the overland effort – apart from the scientific readings which had been taken – seem pointless. As part of 'Operation Deepfreeze,' the Americans had flown in a team of 'Seabees' to build a South Pole base in a matter of weeks, which was supplied throughout from the air, and they were now able to give Hillary royal entertainment before giving him a 'lift' out by air. In the 1950s the world was a shrinking place, and there was now no wilderness anywhere. 'Great God!' Captain Scott's shaking hand had once traced in his journal, 'this is an awful place': now the region where he had died was almost the equivalent of Piccadilly Circus.

The world was shrinking for ordinary people as well as explorers. On 4 October 1958 British Overseas Airways Corporation started the world's first jet passenger service across the Atlantic with the Comet, and at the end of the year America's National Airlines began the first

hallmark consecrated by the work of Kerouac – blue jeans. Jeans had never ceased to be worn as working clothes since pioneer days, and their association with cowboys and the West had kept them alive when the nature of the work and play was not really so strenuous as to demand them, but now they were being worn as a symbol of revolt. The degree of the revolt was marked by the accompaniments – torn T-shirt or expensive silk, beaten-up sneakers or rich leather boots – but the essential mark of belonging was jeans.

The sudden instant spread of what he had initiated, and its transformation in the process, drew a cry of anguish from Kerouac that, 'All this was about to sprout out all over America even down to high school level and be attributed in part to my doing!' He underestimated. It was not only there, but London and Paris, and all points east and west.

New forms of sexuality were explored, and on the heels of the pioneers came the commercial exploiters, and a rising tide of pornographic pollution. In Britain there was, at one end of the scale, action against D H Lawrence's *Lady Chatterley's Lover,* which remained banned for obscenity in the unexpurgated edition until 1960, and corruption of police officers by dealers in such areas as Soho from the mid-1950s. After

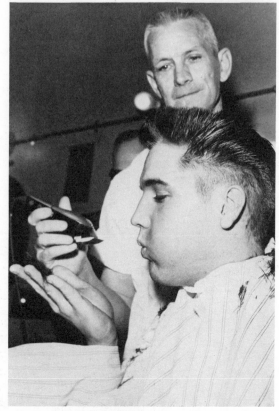

Top left: Elvis Presley flanked by starlets Dolores Hart and Valerie Allen carries an 18th century musket after he was drafted into the US Army in 1958.
Top center: Determined fräulein asks Private Presley for his autograph after his arrival to join US forces in Germany.
Above: Private Presley sported combat boots instead of blue suede shoes at roll call.
Far left bottom: Presley had to be guarded from enthusiastic German fans by MPs.
Left: Army barber administers a crewcut to Presley at Fort Chaffee where he underwent basic training.

the Obscene Publications Act of 1959 a special squad was set up, staffed exclusively by detectives, rather than local CID officers. More healthy was the openness of discussion of sexual matters now permissible, which was exemplified by the publication in 1958 of the Wolfenden Report on Homosexual Offences and Prostitution – once only spoken of in secret whispers – and legislation followed which legalized homosexual acts in private between consenting adults and drove soliciting women prostitutes from the streets – and into the networks of the call-girl system.

At the other extreme of concern, pious Catholics were much preoccupied with the election of a successor to Pope Pius XII, who died at the age of eighty-two in October. The white smoke which announces to the outside world that the Conclave in the Vatican has finally made up its mind did not emerge till the twelfth ballot. Their decision then, at least among the conservative, was probably influenced by the consideration that Pope John XXIII, as he was to be known, was in his seventy-seventh year and unlikely to have time or energy for revolution. They mis-

Top left: Prince Faisal of Iraq with Prince Abdul Illah, his Regent, before Faisal's assassination in 1958.
Above: Prince Faisal paints while at Harrow School in England before attaining power in Iraq.
Top right: Sugar Ray Robinson lands a left to the eye of Carmen Basilio during their middleweight title fight.
Left: Larry Page, Wee Willie Harris and model Sherry Newell in London's version of Tin Pan Alley.
Right: Pat Boone's song and film April Love *were popular in 1958.*

1959

America in 1959 was already in the grip of election fever. After all, there had been no such certainty of presidential change for the best part of half a century. Roosevelt had gone on being re-elected from 1932 until he died in office and they had had to change the rules. Truman might have run again and won, only deciding at a comparatively late stage he would not. Eisenhower could not be elected for a third term. The next President would be a new man – and since Richard Nixon did not appear to be getting the wholehearted endorsement as Eisenhower's heir – maybe the new President would be on a different party, and even the founder of a Democratic dynasty.

It was a heady vision and carried with it a positive desire for change. Eisenhower was old and tired, Kennedy would be almost the youngest man ever to hold the office and was the embodiment of energy. It was forgotten that it was Eisenhower who had proposed legislation for lowering the voting age to eighteen and Kennedy who had opposed it, and that energetic action by three Democratic Presidents had brought America into three wars in the twentieth century.

Eisenhower had never been articulate, even

before his stroke. Kennedy, with a team of speech writers headed by the contrapuntal Theodore Sorensen, would speak readily on any subject and roused the kind of fervor characteristic of revivalist Billy Graham on whom he was to call for Biblical stuffing to round out his inaugural address. Students, tired of the material wealth of the cocoons in which they had been raised, and eager for new causes, were ready to espouse that of the blacks. Little Rock had solved the problem of law and order, but not that of integration or much else. They counted on Kennedy to take up the challenge, but this was the one area that he was not to rush to establish an expert group to handle: it was still Eisenhower who passed in 1957 and 1959 the first Civil Rights bills since the Civil War. Rank and file unionists had wanted the unions cleaned up. Robert Kennedy admitted that, after his committee got to work, 'conditions in the labor and management fields have actually grown worse instead of better,' and improvement waited on the legislation that Eisenhower had guided into being. Women were dissatisfied with their role in bringing up the kind of super all-rounder designed to fit into and ornament society, for

Above: Fidel Castro addresses a jubilant crowd outside the Presidential Palace in Havana a few days after he seized power from President Batista on New Year's Day, 1959.
Above right: Fidel Castro, Jr aboard one of the tanks which liberated Havana and launched his father to power in Cuba.
Right: President Castro condemns the United States in an address given in Havana in November 1959.

234

Far left: President Eisenhower tees off.
Left: Another equally well-known golfer, Ben Hogan, at the US Open.

Above: President de Gaulle gives the Cross of the Liberation to his former comrade-at-arms, Winston Churchill.

233

changing diapers and hushing temper tantrums were not the fulfillment that Dr Spock had promised. It was Eisenhower who tried to bring in equal rights: what they got from the Kennedys was Robert's ruling, laid down as early as his brother's election to the Senate in 1952, 'Concentrate on the women because they do the work in a campaign – men just talk.' Everyone was frightened of the revelation by the media of the 'missile gap,' only to be told after the election that it had not existed. Above all, perhaps, they were bored with a President who was always shown playing golf. Nobody told them – certainly not the Kennedy promotional team – that Kennedy was a far better golfer than Eisenhower had ever been.

In the general activity, no one took a great deal of notice when, on the first day of 1959 an aircraft rose above Havana and headed for the Dominican Republic. President Fulgencio Batista, with his family and close adherents, was on his way to exile. His corrupt dictatorship was over. Those liberal-minded Americans whose eyes were on Cuba looked on with the same approval they had once felt for Ho Chi Minh, as the new President, Dr Manuel Arrutia, announ-

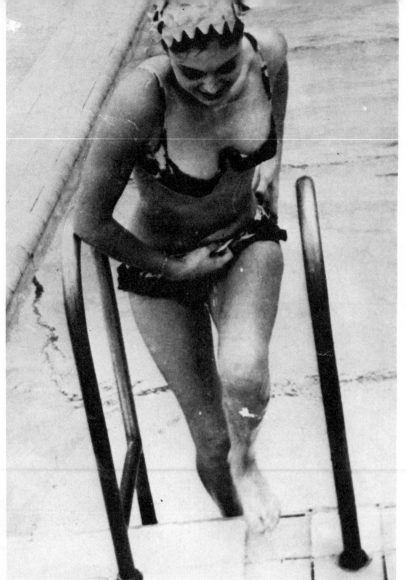

Above: Israeli actress Dahlia Lavi adjusts the bottom half of her bikini which broke at a Rio de Janeiro swimming pool.
Above center: Charley Conerly, 42-year old quarterback of the New York Giants, is grabbed by Gino Marchetti of the Baltimore Colts in an NFL football game.
Right center: Three Australian girls show off their bikinis at Sydney's Marouba Beach after the ban on wearing them was lifted.
Far right: German actress is embarrassed in South Africa after she lost the top half of her bikini.

ced his intention of creating a 'democratic, honest and worthy government.' Their eyes should rather have been on his Commander-in-Chief, the handsomely bearded Dr Fidel Castro, as he led his troops into a deliriously festive capital, rocking with the firing of guns in salute.

Castro and his brother Raoul had made their first armed attempt at overthrowing the regime in 1953, and had collected prison sentences of fifteen years apiece for their trouble. Curiously, for a dictatorship under which Castro alleged some twenty thousand had been killed and tortured, the two were released under amnesty only eleven months later. Then, after a spell in exile, Castro led a landing by eighty-two revolutionaries on 2 December 1956. Waiting government forces rapidly reduced their number to twelve, and these few survivors managed to escape into the mountain fastnesses of the Sierra Maestra in Oriente province. They mounted a guerrilla campaign, gathering new adherents as they went and arming them with weapons taken in attacks on small government garrisons.

Batista's disaffected soldiery would not risk their lives for their President, and took refuge in their concrete blockhouses, where the rebels chipped away at the fabric twenty-four hours a day with small arms. The psychological threat was enough without the need to storm the strongpoints, and the beleaguered men were then enlisted on the other side. Castro's military mastermind, Major Ernesto 'Che' Guevara,

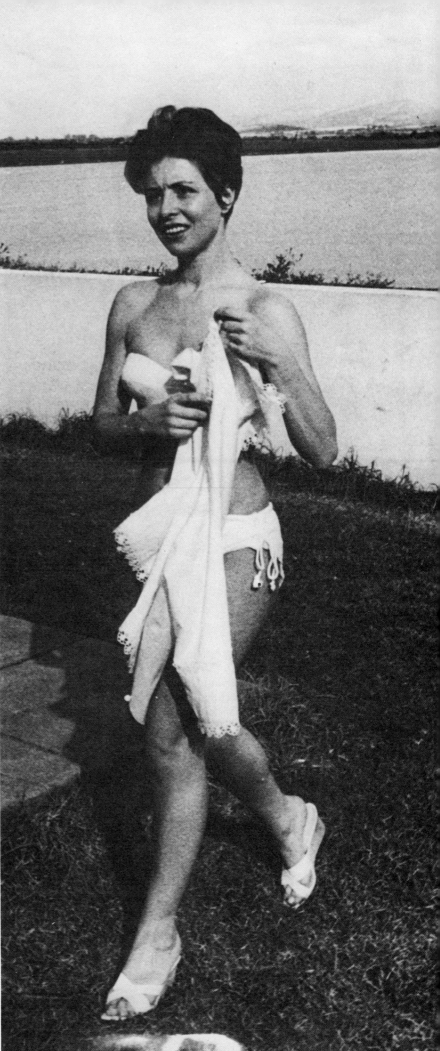

headed a force at the climax of his westward drive through the island which enabled him to knock out Batista's ramshackle force at the battle of Santa Clara.

Guevara, a cult hero of the 1960s, was an Argentinian by birth and a doctor by profession – as middle-class as the Castros. Using his theory of minimum force, he was later to move on to the Congo, and then Bolivia. In conflict for the first time with well-organized opposition, he was outwitted and died in an ambush in the wilds.

In his propaganda, Castro had proclaimed his only desire was to 'restore democracy' and, as for 'Communist sympathies,' how could anyone suspect such a thing of a man with so many good Roman Catholics among his adherents: he had no interest in power. On 16 February he was sworn in as Prime Minister, and celebrated with a visit to Central Park in New York a few weeks later, to address a mass rally of thirty thousand. By July a disillusioned President Arrutia had resigned and been replaced by a puppet. In August came the press reports of over a thousand arrests having been made. Mass trials were in full swing, with executions of counter-revolutionaries, and thirty-year prison sentences being handed out – double the sentences that Castro himself had once received from Batista and no chance of an amnesty. Abortive invasion attempts were launched on Panama, Nicaragua and the Dominican Republic, and by the end of the year Eisenhower had another frown line and invasion plans for Cuba which were passed on to Kennedy as an 'effort to be continued and accelerated.' At least it is certain that an Eisenhower invasion would have differed largely from that carried out at the Bay of Pigs.

Adding to the urge for presidential change was the Soviet Union's *Lunik* I, launched on the second day of the year. After passing the Moon within about four thousand miles, it entered on an elliptical orbit round the Sun, passing between the Earth and Mars, as the solar system's first artificial planet. The Russian habit of being first was beginning to irk America. On 12 January the National Aeronautics and Space Agency rushed out the announcement of an order just placed with the McDonnell Aircraft Corporation of St Louis. Cone-shaped, twelve to fifteen feet long, six feet wide, and weighing two to three thousand pounds, the first United States 'space capsule' designed for a human being was being 'put on the stocks.' On 27 January NASA's administrator, Dr T Keith Glennan, listed what he required of potential passengers. Candidates must have a degree in the physical sciences or engineering, military test-pilot experience of at least fifteen thousand flying hours, an age under forty, height no greater than five feet eleven inches, and superb psychological and physical condition. The wonder was that he had found as many as one hundred and ten candidates.

However it was not until America's Pioneer IV became the second artificial planet on 1 March 1959 that people began to take note and believe that the announcement of Project Saturn in September 1958 had not been a mere romantic dream. Perhaps that giant booster with eight liquid-fuelled engines generating a thrust of one million, five hundred thousand pounds – twice that of anything the Russians had so far used – might yet in spite of all misgivings, be the means of taking an American not merely up, but up and out as far as the Moon.

On 19 April the names of the handful of 'finalists' chosen from the one hundred and ten candidates were announced: Alan Shepard, Walter Schirra, Virgil Grissom, John H Glenn Jr, Scott Arpenter, Gordon Cooper, Donald Slayton . . . but it was not till 1961 that Alan Shepard was to exclaim, 'Oh what a wonderful view!' from a height of one hundred and fifteen miles.

The Russian plunge into the space race and its military implications logically aroused uneasiness in America. Paradoxically, the uneasiness on the other side of the Iron Curtain was even greater. The American response around the world had been fundamentally defensive, but as the Russians looked at the million Americans distributed in military and other capacities in nearly fifty countries in the most vital strategic positions around their borders, and at the amount of military hardware being distributed, they became increasingly insecure.

They became short of temper on issues which, on a world scale, were trivial. Topmost on their list of irritants was Berlin, a center for Western espionage situated behind the very frontiers of the countries of the Warsaw Pact alliance, created in 1955 by the Soviet Union as an answer to the North Atlantic Treaty Organ-

Dam. The technical requirements of modern man were leaving no room for his past, and a reminder came that he might not have a future when the cold statistics recorded that thirty-eight more victims of Hiroshima had died during 1959.

Woman, as distinct from man in the abstract, did not do so well in the 1950s. There was Eva Peron, whose legend survived her death in 1952, and whose embalmed body went into exile with her husband in 1955 and returned with him in 1973. By 1978 Santa Evita of the 'shirtless ones' had received her canonization in a musical, if not from the Pope, even though her charity funds had provided more silks for herself than shirts for her votaries. Nonetheless, to be a power in politics in one's own right was a very slender chance for any woman, not only in Persia, where the Shah's insistence on an heir was uninterrupted by reminders that he already had a daughter by his first marriage, but even in the upper reaches of government in the United States, Britain and the Soviet Union. Indeed in Switzerland a vote of two to one rejected the very idea of giving the franchise to women in 1959.

One place where women held a bigger audience than most of the men was Wimbledon, where Althea Gibson did more for the black image in 1957 by winning the championship than Ralph Bunche had done by being the first black Nobel Prizewinner with his Peace Award in 1950. She did not, however, get the spectacular recognition awarded to Maria Bueno, the little Brazilian who carried off the trophy in 1959 and 1960, and who sported a dress embroidered with three hundred golden gems – one for every match she had won. For her they erected in São Paulo a statue sixty feet high. A more controversial monument of the year was New York's Guggenheim Museum, begun in 1945 and opened just after the death of the architect, Frank Lloyd Wright: unique in its spiral construction, it was said by some to look more like a washtub.

In film entertainment the Biblical epic continued to hold sway, *Ben Hur* won an Oscar for the best film of 1959 and Charlton Heston was awarded one for being the best actor. Britain made her first break-through into the profitable popular market in America with *Room at the Top,* a version of John Braine's novel that featured Simone Signoret, Lawrence Harvey and Heather Sears. The feat was probably aided by the reaction of the Legion of Decency which stigmatized it as morally dubious. It was a landmark in Britain, too, since it was the first major film to have a present-day, working class hero. *Look Back in Anger* also got onto film this year, with Richard Burton in the role of Jimmy Porter, and Peter Sellers starred in *I'm All Right Jack,* which took a swipe at the convention of the heroic trade unionist, and showed shop steward and boss tarred with the same brush. Other major films of the year were *Some like it Hot,* with Marilyn Monroe in competition with Tony Curtis and Jack Lemmon in drag, and Alan Resnais' *Hiroshima, Mon Amour,* which reversed the usual sex roles and had a French girl fall in love with a Japanese man.

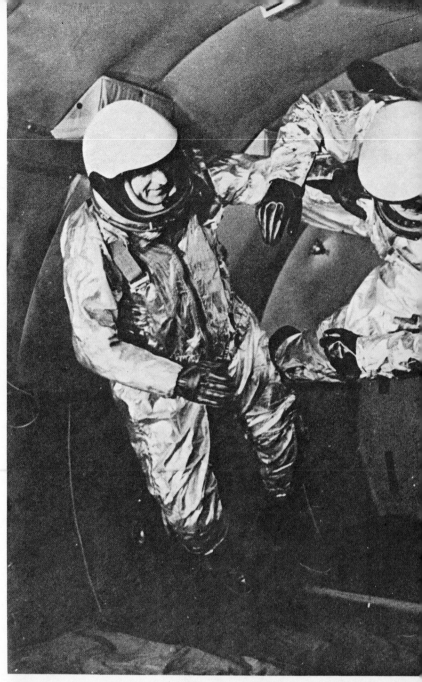

at money and can be harnessed, whereas the Communist aims at power, which feeds on itself and puts the harness on the simple souls who give it to him.

Most decades seem to those looking backwards as both starting points and finish lines, arbitrary lines of demarcation between one world and another. For those living in those times, the lines never have seemed clear-cut. The turn of the nineteenth century was a memorable landmark, but the subtle change from the late Victorianism of the 1890s to the gaudy and frivolous Edwardian Age took years to achieve, and elements of the former period continued to influence the later one. But in the light of history the two periods are worlds apart in style and in substance. Looking backward at the 1950s the same subtle but permanent changes occurred. After all, 1950, the year of Korea, could be said to have been the last of the postwar years. The reaction of the public to the invasion of South Korea was similar in many ways to the atmosphere of 1945. Combining to repel the dictators was as true of 1950 as it was in 1942. Even the uniforms worn were virtually identical to those worn by British and American soldiers in 1945, led by a hero of World War II, Douglas MacArthur. But Korea was not the same as World War II. The public reaction differed in the end; the aims were different; and the war's end was far less conclusive. But to an observer in 1950 the swing bands of Basie, Goodman, Dorsey and James rang out with a similar beat to that of 1945. The changes that took place were far more fundamental, far less superficial, and the progress of the decade indicated that.

Similarly, the year 1959, from the viewpoint of the 1960s and 1970s, is familiar territory. One can perceive the start of the protest movements which rocked the world in the 1960s. From Kerouac to Mort Sahl, from Lenny Bruce to Bob Dylan, it seems familiar. The Rock music, the rising politicians like Wilson and Kennedy and the rise of the Afro-Asian states all are redolent of the 1960s. But the world had come a long way between the landmarks of the decade. The 1950s, seemingly tranquil and even a bit boring on the surface, were anything but that. The 1950s were an age of turmoil and fundamental change, under the shadow of which we all live. It marked the midpassage of our civilization and our times.

INDEX

Page references in italic type indicate illustration captions.

Abel, Rudolph, 34–8, 190
Abu Simbel, 246
Acheson, Dean, 21
action painting, 66
Adams, Sherman, 213–16
Adenauer, Konrad, *200*
Africa, 207–8
African Queen, The, 35, 56
air travel, 222–3
Alabama, University of, 184
Aldermaston, 25, 220
Algeria, 99, 151, 208–10
Amis, Kingsley, 138
Anastasia, Albert, 18
Anderson, Robert, 80
Andrea Doria, 174
Andrew, Prince, 244
Anne, Princess, *22,* 25
Annigoni, Pietro, *113, 147*
Antarctica, *141, 142,* 220–2
Arbenz, Jacobo, 127
archaeology, 57, 174–5
Archers, The, 129, 145
architecture, 56, 65, 248
Arden, Elizabeth, 8, 111
Armstrong-Jones, Antony, 244
Arrutia, Dr Manuel, 235, 237
art, 65–6, 115–17
artificial insemination, 196
Astaire, Fred, *219*
Aswan Dam, 155–7, 166, 246–8
athletics, 110 169
Atlantic Ocean, 70
atom bomb
  British, 63
  French, 213
  Fuchs and, 30
  Russian, 21
atomic power station, 152
atomic weapons, warfare, tests, 174.
    179–82
  Dulles and, 102–3
  and Korea, 48, 50–1
  see also Campaign for Nuclear
    Disarmament; hydrogen bomb
Attlee, Clement, *39,* 48, *51,* 123, 124
automation, 137
automobiles, *see* cars

Bacall, Lauren, *95*
Balcon, Sir Michael, 13
Ball, Lucille, *27*
ballet, 169
Bandstand, 64–5
bank robberies, 15
Bannister, Roger, *103, 105,* 110
Bao Dai, 99, 127–9
Bardeen, John, 174
Bardot, Brigitte, *155*
Barry, Gerald, 53
Barry, Michael, 80
baseball, *122, 200, 231*
Batista, President, 235
Battersea Power Station, 85
beatniks, 190
Beaton, Cecil, 29
Beck, Dave, 203
Beckett, Samuel, 196–7
Bergman, Ingrid, *174, 219*
Beria, Lavrenti P, *88,* 88–92, 148–9
Berle, Milton, *73*
Berlin, 238–9
Bevan, Aneurin, 13, *130, 167*
Bevin, Ernest, 13, 124
bicycling, 66
Bidault, Georges, 102, 103
bikinis, *236*
Blackboard Jungle, 113–14
blacks, *see* racial problems
Blair House, 74
Blake, George, 143
Bloom, Claire, *157*
Blue Lamp, The, 13–14
Bluebird, 129, 138, 144
Bogart, Humphrey, *35,* 58, *95,* 196
Bohlen, Charles 'Chip,' 95
Bond, James, 77
books, literature, 26, 56, 77, 170, 190,
    227
  in Russia, 182
boutiques, 224

boxing, *29, 31,* 65, *74, 75, 129,* 144–5,
    200, 228
Boy Friend, The, 105, 106, 110, 111
Bradley, General Omar, 50
brainwashing, 92
Brando, Marlon, *55,* 115
Bricker Amendment, 95
Brink's Inc, 15
Britten, Benjamin, 56
Brown, George, 153
Brynner, Yul, 174, *223,* 231
Bueno, Maria, 248
Bulganin, Nikolai, 122, *123,* 133, *151,*
    151–2, *162,* 201
Burgess, Guy, and Maclean, Donald,
    142–3, 148
Butler, Richard Austen (Lord Butler),
    55, 70, 97, 123, 124, *169,* 178, 179

Calder Hall, 152
Callas, Maria, *252*
Campaign for Nuclear Disarmament,
    218–20
Campbell, Donald, *129, 138,* 144
Canaveral, Cape, 188
cancer, and smoking, 196
Canterbury, Archbishop of, *83,* 141–2
Cao Dai, 130
capital punishment, *125,* 145
Carne, Lieutenant-Colonel J P, 51, 92
cars, automobiles, 110, *167, 195, 210,*
    215, 217, 219, 223, 231, *243;*
    see also motor racing
Castries, General de, 104–5, *108*
Castro, Fidel, *234,* 236–7
Cat on a Hot Tin Roof, 231
Central African Federation, 207
Central Intelligence Agency, 92–4
Chandler, Raymond, 77
Chaplin, Charlie, 78
Charles, Ezzard, *29*
Chartwell, 122
Checker, Chubby, *204,* 250
Chiang Kai-shek, 19, 132
China, 19–20, 183
  and Korea, 22, 42
  and offshore islands, 132
  and Tibet, 43
  and Vietnam, 102
China, Osman, 75
Chou En-lai, 42, 102
Christie, Agatha, 77
Churchill, Sir Winston, *53,* 79, *81, 85,*
    233
  and EDC, 96
  and Eisenhower, 96–7
  election victory of, 55
  and Iran, 54–5
  and Korea, 26
  portrait of, by Sutherland, 115–17,
    144
  retirement of, 97, 122–3
  his successor, 178
  and Suez, 160
cinema, *see* films
Clark, Dick, 65
Clark, Petula, 146
clothes, *see* fashion
Cockcroft, Sir John, 63
Cockell, Don, 144
coelacanth, 70, 70–1
coffee bar, *105*
Cohn, Roy, *98,* 119–20
Colditz Story, The, 146
Collins, Canon, 220
colonies
  British, *see* Commonwealth
  French, 151, 208; *see also* Algeria;
    Indo-China
colored people, *see* racial problems
Comet, DeHavilland, *56,* 63, 222
Common Market, EEC, 192, 213
Commonwealth, 205–8
Communism
  in China, 19–20
  conflict with, *see* Korea; Malaya;
    Philippine Islands; Vietnam
Communist agents, *see* Burgess and
    Maclean; Fuchs, Klaus; Goldfus,
    Emil; Rosenberg, Julius and Ethel
Communists, measures against, in
    USA, 58–60, 95–6; *see also*
    McCarthy
Como, Perry, *185,* 232
computers, 137
Confidential Clerk, The, 78
Connolly, Maureen, 88
Conservative Party, 55, 56, 123, 138,
    178, 245
contraception, 136–7
Cooke, Alistair, 120

Coronation Stone, 26
cosmetics, make-up, 8
Costello, Frank, 16, 16–18, *31, 33*
Cousteau, Jacques, 70
Coventry Cathedral, 56
Crabb, Commander Lionel, 152–3
Crawford, Joan, 232
Creep, the, 112
Crete, 175
crime, 15–18; *see also* capital
    punishment
Cripps, Sir Stafford, 13, *25,* 98
Cruel Sea, The, 77
Cuba, 235–8
Cyprus, 151, *151,* 244

Dacron (Terylene), 25
Daily Mirror, 54–5
Daily Worker, 190
Dalai Lama, *35,* 43–5
Dali, Salvador, *93,* 115
Dam Busters, The, 146
dance, dancing, *20,* 78, *110,* 112–14,
    137, 250; see also rock music
Davis, Bette, 29
Day Doris, *42, 114, 181, 219*
Dean, James, *157,* 174
DeMille, Cecil B, 231
Democratic Party, 17
Dien Bien Phu, 100–5, *106,* 109–10
Dior, Christian, *20,* 78, 111, *120, 144,*
    146, 170
disc jockeys, 114–15
Dixon of Dock Green, 14
Docker, Sir Bernard and Lady, *91,*
    161, 172
Doctor Zhivago, 182
'domino theory,' 99
Donegan, Lonnie, 177, *188*
Donovan, James B, 190
Dors, Diana, 173
drip-dry shirts, 170
drugs
  CIA and, 94
  Kerouac and, 190
Dudintsev, Vladimir, 182
Dulles, Allen, 20
Dulles, John Foster, *79,* 105–6, *165*
  and atomic warfare, 102–3
  and China, 132
  death of, 239
  and Egypt, 157, 157–8, 159, 179
  and Guatemala, 127
  and Khrushchev, 133–4
  and Korea, 22, 58
  and McCarthy, 95
  and massive retaliation, 99
  and SEATO, 124
  and Vietnam, 124, 127
  mentioned, 96, 96–7, 160, 217

Ealing Studios, 13
East Berlin, 160
Eden, Sir Anthony, *53,* 105–6, *199*
  becomes Prime Minister, 123
  illness of, 97
  marriage of, 141
  resignation of, 178
  and Suez, 98, 154, 157–60, 178
  mentioned, 152
Edinburgh, Duke of, 11, *22*
education, *see* universities
Egypt, 96–7, 98; *see also* Suez Canal
Einstein, Albert, 137
Eisenhower, Dwight D, *65, 66,* 133–5,
    177, 233, 244, 251, 252
  and Adams, 216
  and China, 132
  and Churchill, 96
  and Civil Rights, 234
  and communications, 110
  and 'domino theory,' 99
  elected president, 58, 60, 168
  Europe, his visit to, 240–2
  illness of, 135
  and Indochina, 109–10
  and Khrushchev, 36, 133, 239
  and Korea, 60, 85
  and Lebanon, 212
  and McCarthy, 118, 120
  and Nixon, 58, 60
  and racial problems, 184, 185
  and Rosenbergs, 33–4
  and space programme, 188
  and United Nations, 95
  and Vietnam, 124

Eisenhower Doctrine, 178
Eliot, T S, 78
Elizabeth, Queen, the Queen Mother,
    22, 51, 140
Elizabeth II, Queen (Princess
    Elizabeth), *22,* 62, 81–5, *83, 85, 86,*
    200, 239, *251*
Ellis, Ruth, 145
Emery, W B, 154
Entertainer, The, 196
European Defence Community, 96
European Economic Community, 192,
    213
European unity, 57
Evans, Sir Arthur, 175
Evans, Edith, 56
Everest, Mount, 81, *81*
Everleigh, Corporal, 47–8

fabrics, synthetic, 25, 111
Faisal, King, 210, *228*
Farouk, King, 96
Faubus, Governor, 184, 185
Festival of Britain, *39, 47, 51,* 53
Fields, Gracie, 54
films, cinema, 13–14, 29, 56, 58, 77–8,
    113–14, 115, 145–6, 173–4, 196,
    231–2, 248
Fisher, Dr Geoffrey, 68
Flanders, Senator Ralph E, 119
Fleming, Alexander, *127, 137*
Fleming, Ian, 77
floods, *76,* 76–7, *79*
flying saucers, 34
Fonteyn, Margot, 169
food rationing, 12, 13, 55–6
Foxhunter, 65
France, *see* Algeria; Gaulle, General
    de; Indo-China
Fraser, Dawn, 169
Freed, Alan, 114–15
frisbee, 251
Fuchs, Klaus Emil Julius, 30–2, *41*
Fuchs, Vivian, *141,* 222
Fullmer, Gene, *200*

Gable, Clark, *116*
Gaitskell, Hugh, 13, 123–4, 139, 153
    161, 212, 244–5
Gardner, Ava, *66*
Garland, Judy, 60, 73, 113, 181, 183
Gaulle, General de, *207,* 208–10, 213,
    233,252
Gaynor, Mitzi, *186*
Genevieve, 77
Genovese, Vito, 18, 38, *239*
George VI, King, *22,* 48, *51,* 53, 54,
    62, *69,* 138–9
Germany, 13, 63
Ghana, 207
Gibson, Althea, 248
Gide, André, 26
Gigante, Vincent, 17–18
Ginsberg, Allen, 190
Glubb, General Sir John (Glubb
    Pasha), *125, 134,* 151
Gold, Harry, 33
Goldfus, Emil *see* Abel, Rudolph
golf, *134, 233*
Gomulka, Wladyslaw, 163
Graham, Billy, 68, *70, 101, 103,* 234
Graziano, Rocky, 75
Greenglass, David, 33
Gromyko, Andrei, *53*
Guatemala, 127
Guevara, Ernesto 'Che,' 236–7
Guggenheim Museum, 248
Guinness, Alec, 14, *53,* 56, 196
guitar, 30

Hailsham, Lord, 193
Haley, Bill, 113, *186*
Hancock, Tony, 250
Harding, Gilbert, *96,* 145
Harriman, Averell, 168
Harwell, 30
Hayhanen, Reino, 34–6
Hayward, Susan, *252*
Heath, Edward, 57, *199*

Helms, Richard, 54, 127
Hepburn, Katherine, *35*
Hillary, Sir Edmund, 81, *81, 141*, 222
Hiller, Wendy, 56
Hiss, Alger, 60
Hitchcock, Alfred, 58, 115
Ho Chi Minh, 98–9
Hoffa, Jimmy, 203
Hogan, Ben, *233*
Holliday, Judy, 29
Holly, Buddy, *202*
'Hollywood Ten,' 33
Home, Lord, *199*
Home, William Douglas, 176
homosexuality, 228
housing, 56, 63
hovercraft, 240, *246*
hula hoop, 251
Humphrey, Senator Hubert, 96, 203
Hungary, 163–4, 164–6, *172, 175*
Hunt, Captain Eric, 70
Hunt, Colonel John, 81, *81*
Hussein, King, *76, 93*, 210, 212, 213
hydrogen bomb, 110–11, 133, 218

identity cards, 55
Imjin River, 51
immigrants, colored, *see* racial
    problems
Indo-China, French, 99–109, *106, 108*;
    see also Vietnam
inflation, 193, 204
International Geophysical Year, 220
Iran, 54–5; Shah of, *125, 130*
Iraq, 210, 211–12
Israel, 158–9, 178

Jackson, Jack, 115
Jacobs, David, 115
jeans, 227
Jecelin, Sergeant William, 28
Jenner, Senator William, 50
jitterbugging, *20, 110*
Jodrell Bank, *178*, 187
John XXIII, Pope, *212*, 228–31
Johnson, Dr Hewlett, 32
Johnson, Lyndon B, 106, 188

Kefauver, Estes, Kefauver Committee,
    15–18, *16, 62*
Kelly, Gene, *73*
Kelly, Grace, *170*, 172, *178, 186*, 243
Kennedy, John F, 131, 202, 203–4,
    234–5
Kennedy, Robert F, 118, 202–3, 234,
    235
Kenya, *185*, 208
Kenyatta, Jomo, *185*, 208
Kerouac, Jack, 30, 190–2, 227, 246
Khama, Seretse, *28*, 73
Khrushchev, Nikita, *123, 240*
    and agricultural troubles, 122,
    198–200
    America, his visit to, 239, 240,
    242–3, *244, 246*
    Britain, his visit to, *151*, 151–3, *162*
    and Burgess and Maclean, 148
    and China, 109, 129
    and Dulles, 133
    and Egypt, 160
    and Eisenhower, 36, 133
    and Indo-China, 102, 106
    and Nixon, 240
    political maneuvers of, in Russia,
    89–90, 148–50, 200–1
    and Stalin, 148–50
Kim Il Sung, 21
King, Martin Luther, 147
King and I, The, 11, *223*
'Kisses Sweeter than Wine,' 30
Kluckhorn, Florence R, 67
Kneale, Nigel, 80
Knowland, Senator, 124
Korea, Korean War, *9, 12*, 15, *16*, 18,
    21–4, 26–9, 41–52, *47*, 58, 60, 85,
    92, 94, 118, 252, 253
Kroger, Peter and Helen, 38

Labour Party, Labour government,
    13, 26, 123–4
Lady Chatterley's Lover, 227
Laine, Frankie, 64, *113*
Lansdale, Colonel Ed, 74, 127
Lavender Hill Mob, The, 56
Le Corbusier, 65
Leakey, Mrs Louis B, 246
Lebanon, 212
Lee, Irene, 75
Leigh, Vivien, *55*, 56, 58
Liberace, *177*
Liberal Party, 245
Lie, Trygve, 22
Limelight, 78
linear B, 175
Lipton, Colonel Marcus, 143
literature, *see* books
Little Rock, 185, *195, 196*
Llewellyn, Lieutenant-Colonel Harry,
    65
Lloyd, Selwyn, *79*, 179
Lolita, 246
Lollobrigida, Gina, 146, *217*
Lonsdale, Gordon, 35, 38
Look Back in Anger, 152, 176, 248
Louis, Joe, *31*
Lovett, Robert, 58
Luciano, Lucky, 15
Lucy, Autherine, 184
Lynn, Vera, *55*, 63, *152*

MacArthur, General Douglas, 22, 23,
    37, 39, 41, 45, 47, 50–1
McCarran-Nixon Internal Security
    Act, 58
McCarthy, Senator Joseph, *20*, 32–3,
    50, 95, *98, 101*, 118–20, *119*
McClellan, John L, 203
MacDonald, Malcolm, 28
McKee, Alexander, 77
McKenna, Virginia, 173
McLeod, Iain, 179
Macmillan, Harold, *169, 251*
    becomes Foreign Secretary, 123
    becomes Prime Minister, 178–9
    Commonwealth, his tour of, 205–7
    election victory of, 244–5
    and housing, 56, 63
    and Jordan, 212–13
    'never had it so good,' 192–3, 245
    and Philby, 143
    and premium bonds, 151
    Russia, his visit to, 239
Macmillan, Maurice, *133*, 135
Mafia, 15–18
Makarios, Archbishop, *125*, 151, *151*,
    244
make-up, cosmetics, 8
Malaya, *39*, 45, 74–5
Malenkov Georgi, 89–92, 122, *141*,
    152, 200
Malik, Jacob, *25*, 52
Mallowan, Professor, 57
Man in a White Suit, 56
Mao Tse-tung, 19, 20, 22, 50, 183
Marciano, Rocky, *31*, 65, 144
Margaret, Princess, *127*, 138–42, 143,
    244
Marianas Trench, 70
Marshall, General George, *18*, 19, *93*
Martin, Dean, *215*; and Jerry Lewis,
    85, 88
Martin, Joseph W, 50
Martino, Al, 64
Marty, 145–6
Mary, Queen, *22*, 51, *79*
Mary, the Virgin, *26*
Mau-Mau, 208
Meany, George, 137
medicine, 13, 135, 136, 195–6
Men's Fashion Council, 8–11
Menzies, Robert, 50
Middle East, 151, 178, 210–13; *see
    also* Egypt
Miller, Arthur, *157*, 172, *217*
Molotov Vlachislav, 200
Monroe, Marilyn, 29, *35*, 78, *114, 116,
    119*, 146, *157*, 172, *217*, 248
Monsarrat, Nicholas, 77
Moon, the, 238, 242
Moore, Mrs Ellen, 174
Moran, 'Gorgeous Gussie,' 26
Morocco, 151
Morrison, Herbert, 13, 54, *56*, 124
Mosley, Sir Oswald, 218
Moss, Stirling, *138*, 144
Mossadeq, Mohammed, *48*
motor racing, 144
Mousetrap, The, 77
Mundt, Senator Karl, *20*

Murray, Pete, 115
Murray, Ruby, *134*, 146
Murrow, Ed, *101*, 119
music, *see* opera; popular music;
    records; songs

Nabokov, Vladimir, 246
Nagy, Imre, 164, 164–6
napalm, 28
Nasser, Colonel Gamal, 154–60, *162,
    169*, 210
National Health Service, 13
National Service, *22*, 28
Nautilus, 181
neutron bomb, 220
Ngo Dinh Diem, *108*, 129–30
Ngo Dinh Nhu, 129–30
Nimrud, 57
1984, 80–1
Nixon, Richard, 58–60, *65*, 106, 168,
    216–17, *224*, 240, *240*
Nkrumah, Kwame, 207
Norstad, General, 187
Novak, Kim, *183*
Novello, Ivor, 66
nuclear weapons, *see* atomic weapons
Nuri as Said, 157
Nutting, Anthony, 118

oceans, oceanography, 70
offshore islands, the, 132
Oklahoma, University of, 30
Olduvai Gorge, 246
Olivier, Sir Laurence, 56, 146, *157*,
    172, 196
Olson, Dr Frank, 94
Olympic Games, 65, 169
opera, 56
Oppenheimer, J. Robert, 95
Orwell, George, 80–1
Osborne, John, *152*, 176, 196

Pasternak, Boris, 182–3
Patti, Archimedes, 120
Peck, Gregory, 173
P'eng Te-huai, General, 49
Peress, Irving, 119
Peron, Eva, 248
Petrov, Vladimir, 143
Philby, Kim, 142–4
Philippine Islands, 74
pill, the, 136–7
Pinter, Harold, 196
Pius XII, Pope, *212*, 228
Pleven, René, 102–3, *108*
Poland, 163
polio, 136
Pollock, Jackson, 65–6
Ponomareva, Nina, 169
popular music, 11–12, 30, 63–5,
    112–15, 176; *see also* songs
pornography, 227–8
postwar credits, 14
Powers, Gary, 38
premium bonds, 151
Presley, Elvis, 64, 176, *177, 193*, 198,
    227, 232
Price, Dennis, 14
Puerto Rico, 74
Pyongyang, 41

Quant, Mary, 224
Quatermass Experiment, The, 80
Quemoy, 132
quizzes, 145

racial problems, blacks, colored
    people, immigrants
    in America, 30, 73, 147, 184–5, *195,
    196*
    in Britain, *58*, 73, *151*, 217–18
'Rackets Committee,' 202–3
radio, 198

radio-carbon dating, 246
Rainier, Prince, *170*, 172, 243
Rattigan, Terence, 56, 232
Ray, Johnny, *11*, 11–12, *97, 129*, 188
Rebel Without a Cause, 174
records, gramophone, 11, 115, *120*
Redgrave, Michael, 56, 146
religion, 68, 228–31, 245–6
Rhee, Synghman, 22, *41*, 45, 92, 95
Rhodesia, 207
Richardson, Sir Ralph, *156*
Ridgway, Lieutenant General
    Matthew, 48
Riesman, David, 68
roads, 110, 223
Robeson, Paul, *29*, 33
Robinson, Sugar Ray, 74, *200, 228*
rock music, 112–15, *134, 167, 190*
rocket, intercontinental, 187
roller derby, 7, *27, 28*
Room at the Top, 248
Roosevelt, Eleanor, 80
Rosenberg, Harold, 66
Rosenberg, Julius and Ethel, 33–4, *35*
Rovere, Richard, 135
royalty, 138, 224; *see also* Elizabeth II;
    Margaret, Princess
Russell, Bertrand, *142*, 220

Sagan, Françoise, *133*, 170
St Lawrence Seaway, 110, 239
Salisbury, Lord, 178
Salk, Jonas E, 136
satellites, artificial, 185–90, 238
Saud, Ibn, 210
Savile Row, 8–11
Schine, G David, *119*, 119–20
Schumann, Maurice, 102, 103
science fiction, 78
Secombe, Harry, *152*
Seoul, 22, *41*, 47, 48
Separate Tables, 232
sex, 136–7, 227–8
sexes, equality of, 8
Shaw, George Bernard, 26, 198
Shivers, Governor Allan, 96
Shute, Nevil, 26
Silverman, Sidney, 145
Sinatra, Frank, 78, *96, 97, 159, 183,
    186*
Skardon, William, 143
skiffle, 176–7
Smith, Professor J B L, 70–1
smog, *85, 105*
smoking, and cancer, 196
Snow, C P, 56
songs, singers, 11, 30, 63–5, 78, 146,
    176, *177*, 198, *205*, 232
Soraya, Queen, *125, 130*, 243
South-East Asia Treaty Organization,
    124
Spaak, Paul-Henri, 57
space flights, 238, 242, *249*
Speakman, Private, 58
speed records, 144
Spence, Basil, 56
Spock, Dr, 7
sport, *see* athletics; boxing; motor
    racing; Olympic Games; speed
    records; tennis
sputniks, *181*, 185–8
Stalin, Joseph, 22, 42, 49, 87–9, *88*
    148–50
Stalin, Svetlana, 87
Stassen, Harold, *79*, 179–81
steel industry, US, 58
Steele, Tommy, *193*
Stevenson, Adlai, 60, *62*, 65, 135, *148*,
    168, *177*, 202
Storrier, David, 75
Strachey, John, 30–2
Strand Magazine, 26
Strangers on a Train, 58
Stravinsky, Igor, 116
Streetcar Named Desire, A, *55*, 58
Streeter, Reginald, 28
submarine, nuclear, 181
Suez Canal, *37*, 48, 154–60, 164, *165*,
    166, *167, 169*, 179
Summerskill, Dr Edith, 13, *31*
'summit' meetings, 96, 133
sunglasses, 194
Sutherland, Graham, 115–17, *144*
Sutton Coldfield, 25

Tachen islands, 132
Taiwan, 19, 132
Tammany Hall, 17
Tati, Jacques, 78
Taylor, Elizabeth, *98*, 231
Tea and Sympathy, 80
Teddy Boys, 11, *20*, 27, *134*, *137*
teenagers, 7; *see also* youth
television, TV, 7, 14, 25, *25*, 55, 68–70,
  80–1, *91*, *134*, 145, 198, 250
Templar, Sir Gerald, *56*, 75
Ten Commandments, The, 231
tennis, 26, *88*, 248
Tensing, Sherpa, 81, *81*
Terylene (Dacron), 25
theater, 56, 78–80, 111, 172, 176,
  196–7
Third Man, The, 25, 29
Third World, 124
Thomas, Dylan, *81*, 117–18
Thorndike, Sybil, 56
Thorneycroft, Peter, 204
Threepenny Opera, The, 159
Tibet, 43–5, *56*
Tito, President, *55, 93,* 163, 164–6
Townsend, Group Captain Peter, *127,*
  138–42, 143
trade unions, 137, 202–3, 234
transistors, 174
Truman, Harry S, *60, 65*
  and communist subversion, 32,
    58–60
  and Eisenhower, 58
  and hydrogen bomb, 110–11
  and Korea, 22, 23, 41, 45, 52
  and Puerto Rico, 74
  and Russian atom bomb, 21
  and steel industry, 58
  and Stevenson, 60, 168
Tunisia, 151
Turner, Admiral Stansfield, 94
Twist, the, *204*, 250

Under Milk Wood, 117
unidentified flying objects, 30
United Nations
  Eisenhower and, 95
  and Korea, 22–3, 24, 41, 49
  and Suez, 159, 164
  and Tibet, 43
universities, 137–8

Valachi, Joseph, 38
Van Allen, Dr James, 188–90
Van Doren, Charles, 145
Vanguard, Project, 188
Ventris, Michael, 175
Vietnam, 98, 109, 124–31, 252; *see*
  also Indo-China
Vishinsky, Andrei, *25*
Voroshilov, Marshal Kliment, 90

Waldman, Ronnie, 80
Walton, Ernest, 63
Warner, Jack, 14
Warsaw Pact, 238
Wayne, John, 120
Welfare State, 12–13
Welles, Orson, *25*
West Indies, 208
West Point, 245
Williams, Tennessee, 58, 231
Wilson, Harold, 13, *25*, 151
Wimbledon, 26, *88*, 248
Winchell, Walter, 119
Windscale reactor, 181–2
winter sports, 170
Wolfenden Report, 228
women, 66–8, 234–5, 248
World War II, 13

Yalu River, 41, 42–3, 45
youth, the young, 7–8, 111–12, 246
Yugoslavia, 163, 164–6

Zambia, 207

Picture Credits